BOOK ONE: THE CANADIANS

DYNAMIC
ENTREPRENEURS
OF THE 21ST CENTURY

THE COMPELLING STORIES OF 20 CANADIAN COMPANIES WHOSE EXPLOSIVE GROWTH HAS LAUNCHED THEM ONTO THE WORLD STAGE

BY MICHAEL CALDWELL

Creative Classics Inc.
Kelowna, B.C.
Canada

ISBN: 978 – 0 – 9784620 – 4 – 8

Caldwell, Michael H.
Dynamic Entrepreneurs of the 21st Century
Editor: Alan Ferguson
Graphic Artist: Donna Szelest
Introduction by: Toby Jon Osborne
Research: Toby Osborne, Tony Wanless, Bonnie Bowman,
Alan Ferguson

PRINTED IN HONG KONG BY REGAL PRINTING

TABLE OF CONTENTS

Introduction

What makes a successful entrepreneur? If we knew the answer to that question there would be no mystery about it.

This book tells the personal stories of some remarkable Canadians who have reached for the top. They are stories about men and women who dreamed big dreams and possessed the courage and perseverance to make them come true. But there the similarity between them ends.

For no two individuals in these stories are the same. Comparing them is like comparing different thumbprints. From a distance they look identical. But, up close, each is distinguished by a genuinely unique style that marks them out as leaders of the pack. It is one of the enduring fascinations of successful entrepreneurship that it cannot be learned entirely from a textbook.

In these pages you will meet some hugely successful people who did not go to college, or who never attained a master's degree in business administration. They are the first to admit today that a higher education would have smoothed their path to the top. But even those who were fortunate enough to attend university, and who achieved academic excellence, will tell you a degree is not enough in itself to guarantee success in the business world.

The rich cast of characters you will encounter in these chapters illustrates the huge diversity of entrepreneurship. Without doubt there is a special mystique to the art of building a profitable enterprise.

All entrepreneurs are in some ways gamblers. Statistics show that 50 per cent of all business start-ups fail in their first five years. It's a tough world out there.

And it's not all about money.

It's about the inspiration required to create a new business model and the daring needed to implement it.

It's about putting your personal reputation on the line, not to mention your personal finances.

It's about the lifelong friendships you make along the way; the folk who give you a leg up at a crucial moment, or who advance a loan on the shake of a hand.

It's about spontaneous acts of generosity, as evidenced in stories of entrepreneurs prepared to share their wisdom with others eager to win success.

It's about lessons in human nature, such as seeing the partners you recruited to share your dream turn into jealous schemers determined to steal it from you.

It's about knowing yourself and who you want to be.

It's about having the intestinal fortitude to quit a comfortable, well-paid job with some corporate giant in order to let your creative spirit soar.

It's about being humble enough to know that inevitably you will make mistakes. And wise enough to recognize when you need help to build a functional organization.

Most of all, however, it's about believing wholeheartedly in your brilliant ideas and being prepared to devote your waking life to their realization.

And that is the common thread that invisibly unites the glittering gallery of dynamic entrepreneurs you are about to meet in this book.

Stacey Cerniuk, Founder,
President and CEO of
Annex Consulting Group Inc.

Annex Head Office Team

Annex Project Team

Annex Consulting Group Inc.

Each year in Canada, thousands of people, who possess some special skill or expertise in a specific industry or business sector, launch new businesses. Very few, however, have a proper understanding of how to organize that business. As a result, most new ventures begin as derivatives of other concepts — versions of existing businesses within their specific sector. It is, in fact, quite rare for an entrepreneur to be also a successful strategist who can address the myriad of details involved in organizational development.

This dichotomy of entrepreneurial roles is evidenced by most business plans submitted to bankers, venture capitalists, contests, private investors and others involved in financing new enterprises. Routinely, they are heavy on product or service description and finances, but extremely light on market knowledge, risk management, general management, and especially organizational development. Because entrepreneurs tend to be loners, organizational development is for most an afterthought. As a result it can be the downfall of — or at the very least an extremely negative influence on — most entrepreneurial ventures.

Too often, organizational development simply happens, usually with people bolted on to fulfill specific tasks, as per traditional corporate structures. Most small businesses simply follow the large business model in miniature, organizing into important departments and hiring people to manage them. At best, some entrepreneurs have learned to outsource some tasks, but too often the desire to oversee a company — to have visible evidence that one is the boss — rules.

However, if the entrepreneur is creative and innovative enough to step outside accepted practices and truly understand what is involved in building an organization, a new model may emerge that can produce breathtaking growth. Such an entrepreneur is Stacey

Cerniuk, whose company, Annex Consulting Group, moved from a traditional solo entrepreneur setting in 1998 to an information technology consulting and recruiting organization that within ten years became one of the largest in Canada.

An entrepreneur who has worked steadily to improve himself as a business operator, Cerniuk, at just 41 years old, is often an inspiration for other soloists, independents, or skilled people who strike out on their own and like to dream big dreams. Through a combination of astute opportunity spotting, an understanding of the value of long-term relationships, some luck, and much focus, he has formed an innovative business model that will likely be a template for many enterprises in the future.

A product of a broken family that had little money, Cerniuk is also a motivating personality who pulled himself up by his bootstraps and now freely gives lessons to other entrepreneurs, including the many independent consultants who work through Annex. He often dispenses solid, homespun advice involving the maintenance of work-life balance, personal integrity, the need for business and personal values, goal setting in business and life, and the value of harmonious relationships, both in business and within the larger community.

All this advice, says Cerniuk, is the outcome of personal beliefs that have contributed to Annex's success. The company currently has some 4,200 independent IT and business consultants on its roster, has completed 1,000 projects for 250 different clients and sports an industry leading 97 per cent customer satisfaction rating. (According to the Standish Group, 66 per cent of IT projects are considered failures.) Annex also produces $12.6 million in annual revenues while keeping costs extremely low. The company has been listed by Profit magazine for three consecutive years as one of the fastest growing in Canada, is one of the Branham 300 largest IT companies in Canada, one of the 100 largest IT solution providers in Canada, and has been on the list of the Business in Vancouver fastest growing companies in British Columbia for five years running. This astonishing growth, pegged at about 50 per cent a year, goes against the flow of most IT consulting practices. It takes place in a small region, within the confines of B.C., a relatively sparsely populated province in which the majority of people live in three cities — Metro Vancouver, Victoria and Kelowna.

Annex's growth is due largely to a unique business model combining the disciplines of IT and management consulting with recruiting. At its heart is a referral system that also includes some of the better aspects of multi-level marketing in that it harnesses the power of many to work in a single direction. In many ways, it is a model for how to conduct a 21st Century collaborative organization.

The Annex business model is that of a virtual organization with only a handful of employee/contractors to manage corporate development, sales, finance and administration. However, Annex is able to cast a wide net for projects because its sales and implementation "staff" is drawn from its pool of more than 4,000 independent IT and business consultants. This means that the company does not have to worry about many core corporate tasks such as human resources management, training, taxation administration, marketing, and other chores. As a result, the company has very low overhead. Its general and administration expenses are only two to three per cent of revenues.

The basis for this organization is a referral system involving the Annex Alliance of independent consultants, a growing force in Canada where, according to Statistics Canada, 98 per cent of businesses are small businesses, many of them micro businesses that are in reality a form of freelancing of specific skills. The Annex Alliance takes advantage of this trend by harnessing these independents into a workforce that can be deployed on dozens of projects at the same time in a system similar to the Internet itself. The large roster of skilled individuals also acts as an employment resource for organizations that require full time staff, so Annex is also a recruitment company that fills open IT positions in companies.

Underneath the corporate banner, Annex is a web of connections that disperses many traditional corporate functions such as marketing, business development and human resources among the membership. In one sense it is a leader in the trend toward the "flat" organization in which responsibility for all business functions is held not by an executive class, but is self-managed by being spread among everyone in the organization. Although it predated by several years today's popular social networking models such as Linked In and Facebook, the Annex Alliance is a continually growing network very similar to them.

Members of the Alliance are classified by skill type in a searchable database. Also, Alliance members are identified by a system that puts them into nine "bands" of competency, ranging on a descending scale from very competent and experienced to newer and inexperienced. Competency measurement is also continually dynamic, ensuring that skills are up to date and classified. Each project is rigorously analysed after completion for consultant performance. If someone does well on a project, they move up the ladder of competency; if they do poorly, they drop down.

The Alliance — and the business overall — grows because members are encouraged to recruit new members by a unique payment model. When a member refers a new consultant to the Alliance, they are compensated each time Annex uses that person on a project — for life. If Annex uses a referred consultant, the person who referred that individual receives $1 per hour from the Annex mark-up on that consultant every time Annex uses that individual on a project. In the year 2008, the average project duration was 12 months, or about 2,000 hours, which means a consultant referral generates $2,000 on average per project. This works especially well for consultants who are strong "nodal points" in networks: Several Annex consultants who are extremely well connected earn a tidy sum yearly from their referrals and so can pick and choose which projects they wish to be involved with. The highest referral earner has generated more than $100,000 in passive income.

"Think about if you were building a new house and you needed a great drywall contractor," explains Cerniuk, reaching back to a business he knew well as a youth — the home construction industry. "Imagine having a list of all the drywall contractors in your area sorted from best to worst. Would you call someone from the top or the bottom of the list? Obviously, the top. We have the same list, but in the IT industry. Need a programmer? No problem — we have well over one thousand of them. Need a project manager? We have hundreds. We start at the top competency level to secure the very best people for our projects. If we have to go down to lower levels where there is less experience, we put a more senior project manager in place to help them. "

This staff of IT and business professionals is supplemented and aided by the Annex Learning Centre, a recent innovation that offers training in project management. In fact, it is the only training organization in B.C. that focuses entirely on project management. The Centre offers a variety of workshops in project management, led by certified project managers with strong industry experience. The program also provides mentoring and coaching to students after the workshop to ensure they are applying what they learn.

The Alliance also acts as a low-cost sales force for Annex because of another referral program. Annex generates more contract opportunities in IT than any other firm in the province because as well as compensating members for growing the Alliance, it also pays them for referring projects to keep members busy. Not only is a member rewarded by a payment to recruit other members, he or she is doubly motivated to bring projects to the Alliance. If an Alliance member refers a project to Annex, he or she receives $2 per hour from the Annex mark-up on every person on that project. Since the average project duration in 2008 was 2,000 hours, the average project referral pays $4,000 — more if it is a multi-person engagement.

Many consultants simply want to complete tasks, and are uninterested in performing business development. But enough do so that the Annex referral system shows an average corporate growth rate of 50 per cent a year. In 2008, Annex completed 244 projects and paid out $125,000 in referral fees. Also, each time it sends out a referral cheque, it includes a lifetime referrals spreadsheet showing the total referrals paid to that individual across all projects and consultants they have referred.

For Annex, this is a low-cost marketing tool that allows it to avoid all the usual expenses involved in marketing. Alliance members have visible evidence each time they receive a cheque that there is an incentive to keep the referrals coming. This allows Annex to employ only a website and a brochure for marketing. At the same time, it has no cash flow issues because it pays members when clients pay it. The company is completely self funded and has never had debt, or required investment — quite an anomaly in the technology sector. It does not even have a line of credit and so is immune to the gyrations of the interest rate system, or current investment thinking. In fact, during the investment market crash in late 2008, it was relatively untouched: 2008 was Annex's strongest year ever, and the fourth quarter of 2008 was the company's best up to that point.

Lastly, this referral program extends to filling open IT employment positions in other companies. There is a shortage of experienced IT personnel in most of North America, and Annex meets this problem by transferring some of its own consultants to these open positions. Again, Alliance members have an incentive to perform this chore. If a member refers an open position, and Annex fills it, the referrer receives $500. If Annex successfully fills a position with a referred employee, the original referrer gets $500. This way, all Alliance members are in a sense front-line staffing recruiters for the industry.

This rapidly growing company began humbly when Cerniuk left a job with a large IT consulting company that was safe, secure and featured unlimited advancement potential. He wanted to strike out on his own as an independent IT consultant. All entrepreneurial endeavours are risky, but Cerniuk's was particularly adventurous. He was leaving a great job with a terrific boss. He was "up to his eyeballs" in debt and had only limited work lined up. His wife was eight months pregnant. Their first child was less than a year old. She was therefore unlikely to work to support the new venture. The couple had just purchased a house and were carrying a large mortgage. They had also just bought a new utility vehicle to transport the growing family around. In the middle of summer, a traditionally slow time in the consulting industry, Cerniuk took the plunge. He had only a three-week verbal commitment from a client with no signed contract or subsequent prospects. It occurred to him that he couldn't have picked a less propitious time to start his new venture. "My brain was telling me how stupid I was, but my heart was telling me it was the right decision to go out on my own," he says. "The entrepreneurial fire was burning so intensely that I just had to start my own business. It is never easy walking the plank and taking that final step, especially given the circumstances in my life at that time. But I did it. And it is one of the best things I ever did."

Little in Cerniuk's early life indicated that he would be this venturesome. His father had operated independent businesses in the often-brutal home construction sector. Cerniuk himself logged some time after high school digging trenches and hauling rocks to cover drain tile for his father's drainage installation business. "Maybe my dad wanted to help me by giving me work to earn some money for college," he says. "Or maybe he was smart enough to work me hard as encouragement to go to college. Either way, after a long summer, I came to the conclusion that it was never going to be 'Cerniuk & Son' in the construction business."

Instead, Cerniuk followed his major passion — computers. He

got his first videogame system at the age of 12. He began to think about how he could build his own games. As a teenager, he saved money from birthdays and Christmas to buy some of the first home computers and he learned programming from books and magazines. His school had an old computer that required punch cards and while playing with it Cerniuk understood instinctively that he craved a career in computers. At home, he was combining an artistic flair with computer graphics to create new images. He once contemplated creating a book would feature computer graphics and music.

After high school and that long, hot summer hauling rocks and digging trenches, he attended Kwantlen University College, completing a two-year diploma program. As the top computer science student in the program, his second year was paid for with a scholarship. After receiving his diploma, he transferred to Simon Fraser University where he obtained a degree in Computing Science. It was while studying at SFU that he gained experience working on technology projects for large Canadian companies via the university co-operative education program.

After a stint as a subcontractor for a small firm, Cerniuk joined SHL Systemhouse (now EDS), a multinational IT consulting company. He worked for the company for six years, advancing rapidly. "It was a great job and I loved it," he says. "SHL taught me how to be a good consultant and how a professional services organization should operate. I started off as a programmer/analyst on a large project and soon wanted more responsibility. Even though I would be one of the youngest people leading a team they gave me a lead role on the project. Then I was promoted as overall project manager of a multi-year, multi-million-dollar engagement. Overall, at SHL, my roles and responsibilities included HR Manager for the Vancouver office, senior project manager and PeopleSoft practice leader for B.C. and Asia. My boss told me I was on the managing director track."

Cerniuk was also learning how to manage other aspects of the consulting business. For example, he moved into selling and resourcing projects. He would be placed as a senior project manager on a client site, and, while there, would quickly identify other opportunities. Then he would write proposals and build a team of people to help with the project, manage the people and also the client account. But the traditional organizational structure of a large consulting operation rankled. "I was selling a lot of business but not being compensated for it," he says. "I would write a proposal, the sales person would sign on the dotted line, and we would be awarded the work. I felt I was doing all the work and then the sales person was collecting the commission."

Cerniuk was having doubts about a career with a large consulting firm and the seeds of the idea that he could do it independently began to germinate while he took on ever more responsibility within the company. He saw some of the traditional consulting practices and began to wonder whether they were truly effective. The company's head office, like most large consulting operations, insisted that the Vancouver office go after big, lucrative projects and ignore the small and medium-sized businesses that made up the majority of the province's economic landscape.

"It was feast or famine, depending on whether we could land a 'big fish'," he says, summing up the large consultancy model. "I saw lost opportunity on the small and medium-size engagements. No one wanted to serve them because the contracts were too small. But they had the most need."

Some colleagues were also talking about leaving, and, since he was analytical by nature, Cerniuk put together a 36-page plan to put the thoughts swirling in his mind into a logical structure. Once he did that, he could think of nothing else but going out on his own, performing the same tasks, but for himself instead of a big firm with a distant head office and a rigid template for how business should be conducted.

The journey from large professional services operation to independence is by no means unique. Many professionals make it after learning the ropes in large firms. Tiring of the inflexible structures of the traditional professional services model, and the long hours involved in climbing the professional services career ladder, they seek a better balance to their lives — usually taking a large financial hit to do so. While some succeed at building a small services operation and achieving that desired balance, others never completely shake off the big company mantle. They continue chasing the same markets with the same organizational models, only writ smaller. Unable to match the marketing power of larger firms, they often become adjuncts or outsourcers for those larger firms — independent, but not in the sense that they are truly entrepreneurial.

This growing army of independents was Annex's target and would provide Cerniuk with the innovative organizational development model that has turned the world of professional services upside down. But he didn't know it at the time. He was a one-person company, a soloist trying to make a living doing IT business analysis and project management consulting. And he was going through all the struggles new entrepreneurs suffer while learning about business operation.

Like many other soloists, he worked at first primarily at client sites and at home, using a dining room table as his "office." He endured the indignities that working at home with a young family can sometimes present. There was the time when an important client telephoned him at home while he was minding his two young children and his wife was running an errand. At a key moment during the call his daughter yelled, 'Daddy, can you wipe my bum?' Burning with embarrassment, Cerniuk tried to explain, tiptoeing around the fact that he was working at home. Luckily, the client saw the humour and got a good laugh out of it.

Cerniuk also worked hard to maintain contacts in the outside world so he wouldn't become isolated. Always a strong networker, he met regularly with three friends who were also freelance IT consultants. They would exchange ideas and information on various aspects of business operation such as corporate structure, business banking, workers' compensation, service offerings, sales, marketing, charge-out rates and expenses. They considered going into business together, but abandoned the plan when they realized they couldn't organize it — they all wanted to be chiefs, a partner model that has hampered many another professional services firm.

But the plan did give Cerniuk the germ of an idea. He created a spreadsheet listing all the independent IT and business consultants he knew. There were 10 of them, and they eventually grew into the 4,000-strong Annex Alliance. Cerniuk went to each one and said, 'If you find me work, I'll pay you a referral fee' — a small component of his hourly rate. They agreed to do the same. Thus, the Annex Referral Program, which is largely responsible for Annex's phenomenal growth, was born.

As he had learned in his first job, Cerniuk was a good opportunity spotter and business developer, Soon, he was able to refer work to quite a few of these consultants. Eventually, in the classic networking form, they began suggesting to other colleagues that they also contact him. The 10 became 20, then 40. When it reached 80, Cerniuk realized he had an organization that was much more than a group of friends gathered around a table. "The Annex Alliance was a living, breathing entity growing on its own thanks to the Annex Referral Program," he says.

Cerniuk's next big leap came after he moved into an office with a friend who was a software developer — he could no longer manage the network from his home office. Like many entrepreneurs who sell their time he faced the problem of capacity and downtime. There were only so many hours in a day that he could work. His income was limited. If he went on vacation, or became ill, he had to forego any income at all. While discussing this — entrepreneurs always discuss this issue among themselves, it is probably one of the independent's most vexing problems — his office partner challenged him to stop consulting and try to get 20 other people working at the same time. In other words, organize others so that the income is always flowing.

Cerniuk did just that, working under the John D. Rockefeller axiom that 'I'd rather earn one percent from one hundred men's efforts than one hundred percent from my own efforts.' And so began the classic organizational development transition: A soloist plying his trade became an entrepreneur building an organization and operating a company. Cerniuk knew this was a different kind of role for him, so he hired a one-on-one mentor to teach him the fundamentals of business operation. He also joined a masterminding group of company CEOs, to which he still belongs, to learn leadership skills and how to maintain life balance. For four years, he grew the organization to its current state as one of the largest IT consulting companies in the nation.

Now, Cerniuk is making the next big leap up the organizational pyramid because market conditions demand it. Every business today needs IT to operate, but there is a shortage of skilled workers within the industry. The Information and Communications Technology Council predicted that Canadian employers would need to recruit up to 180,000 IT workers between 2008 and 2015. In B.C. alone, 10,000 more high tech workers were required in 2008. The numbers are even larger, in the United States. Also, this shortage scenario is for the traditional corporate staffing model, which is being shattered. So, the timing is perfect for Cerniuk's growing and focused army of independents.

To meet this growth challenge, Cerniuk last year hired a Chief Operating Officer, who has two primary responsibilities. The COO will take over operations to free up Cerniuk to focus on strategic initiatives and help prepare the company for expansion. This involves strengthening the foundation of the company and installing the right processes that can govern a larger organization. And Annex plans to be a much larger company. It expects to triple in size over the next five years by expanding south into the U.S. and east across

Canada. It also plans to apply the Annex model in other industries besides IT consulting.

Always a believer in work-life balance, Cerniuk, who works only 45 hours a week in order to spend quality time with his family, coach sports teams, and volunteer in the community, is preparing for a personal future as well. He will carry on as Annex CEO while planning his own personal exit strategy. This could mean the standard entrepreneurial route of selling his firm, or it could mean grooming a new president and reducing his time with the business.

"I plan to have more 'Stacey' time in the future," he says. "Because I like to work, I'll very likely start a new business. I also want to create a foundation to help people in my community because I believe in philanthropy and want to make a difference."

Cerniuk will also work on his own personal "bucket list" of all the things he wants to achieve in life. The list, he says, is very long. "I absolutely thrive on being responsible for my own success or failure and want to reward that behaviour in others," he says. "I want to be hands-on and get involved in serving and helping others. That's where to find fulfillment."

Many adventures still lie ahead for this man with an independent streak who mobilized thousands of other independents and organized them into a powerful business association. It's a good bet that whichever projects he pursues, there will be at his side an army of like-minded people who admire and share his attitude.

*George Affleck, President and CEO of
Curve Communications*

Team Curve

Curve Communications Corp.

I f you could write a foolproof guide to guaranteed success in the business world, it wouldn't really matter what kind of person you were, as long as you read the right textbooks.

But life isn't like that, as George Affleck found out early in his career. Personality does matter. And your particular outlook on life is likely to determine, to a considerable extent, the outcome and direction of your business endeavours.

This should be no surprise when you think of the hugely successful businessmen and women whose career paths could never be considered orthodox. The Warren Buffets and George Soros' of the world are genuine mavericks, whose refusal to follow the herd, while relying on their own instincts for survival, has served them well.

Affleck, the 44-year-old owner of Vancouver's Curve Communications, a top 10 PR company for the past several years and one of the fastest growing companies in British Columbia, is a good example of the breed. An innovator and freethinker, he abhors the kind of rigid bureaucratic structures that can stifle growth and progress in traditional companies.

In his early career, he admits, his inclination to speak out independently in support of new ideas got him into trouble with superiors whose mediocrity appalled him. "My big mouth got me into trouble," Affleck says, relaxing jacketless in his office in Vancouver's trendy Yaletown district.

Born in the outer suburbs of Vancouver, Affleck grew up in a family with three sisters, a mother, and a garrulous father whose business was in real estate. There was always plenty of lively talk around the dinner table, although, in retrospect, Affleck saw that his childhood was spent in a conservative, somewhat provincial atmosphere.

His hunger for a wider experience of the world led him, at the age of 17, to take a year's student exchange in Denmark, his first exposure to the sophistication of European life. At his school in Allerod, a town north of the capital Copenhagen, the young Canadian was astonished at the progressive attitude of his fellow students.

When his classmates launched a campaign to persuade school authorities to remove from the premises carpets containing formaldehyde, which they considered an environmental hazard, he was inspired. For many months, students had been demanding the removal of the carpet, but frustrated by the lack of action they raided the school and ripped it out themselves. It was clearly an act of vandalism, Affleck concedes today, but the news stories that followed took the students' side and criticized the inaction of the school authorities. It taught Affleck about grounds for protest, about the power of news and the strength of the individual to make change.

Looking back, he says "those crazy Danes" and the carpet caper "changed my life," and "awakened my unsuspected rebellious instincts."

The discovery within himself of an irrepressible streak of anti-authoritarianism, and a gut reaction against the heavy hand of mindless conformity, was to shape his attitude in the years ahead.

There was another hint of this when Affleck returned to Canada and, at the age of 18, enrolled in business studies at Simon Fraser University. "I really hated it," he says with feeling. "They were training me to be an accountant and I wanted to be an entrepreneur."

Not one to hang about where he didn't feel comfortable, Affleck abandoned university for a full-time job as a tourism host at Vancouver's Expo'86. When that gig wound up, wanderlust sent him back to Europe where he enriched his life with stints as varied as working on a co-op in Israel's Negev desert to bartending in a pub and taking bets at a bookmaker's shop in England. In Greece he met the woman who would become his wife for the next 17 years and with whom he would have two children, a boy and a girl now aged 13 and eight.

Still searching for a career that would hold his interest, Affleck returned to Simon Fraser University, this time to study English Literature. And while the education was fascinating, he knew he was not particularly employable with a BA that focused on everything from Hemingway to Hamlet.

On the advice of a friend, he enrolled in a journalism course at Vancouver's Langara College and subsequently landed a full-time job with the Canadian Broadcasting Corporation.

At 27 years old, and with new responsibilities as a married man, Affleck threw himself into his first real job with enthusiasm, learning the tricks of the trade as a producer and on-air host. He found he had a flair for words, and his casual, easy style seemed well suited to a successful journalism career. And so it might have been, had he been content to muddle along as his bosses dictated. But that's not Affleck's style. He found the large corporation claustrophobic. Even less acceptable, his superiors didn't seem interested in his "big ideas." When he went to one senior manager to promote a grand plan to sell off some valuable CBC-owned land, she "looked at me as if I was some kind of freak." When he tried to persuade her that the proceeds from such a sale could fund CBC programs for a decade, he was reminded that he was a radio producer and that perhaps such matters should be left to those who knew better.

Affleck can joke today about his experience that shooting off at the mouth can be dangerous to your corporate health, particularly within such a large, hierarchal organization as the CBC. But he learned a valuable lesson: that once you have been saddled with a reputation for talking out of turn it has a tendency to cling to you. He knew he had compromised his position at the corporation and, in the summer of 1998, he quit his full-time job, though he continued to accept freelance assignments.

For the first time in his career, Affleck was on his own, beholden to no bureaucracy, but confident he could prosper on his own account. His earnings had taken a tumble, he was now a father, and he was heading out into the unknown. He didn't know it then, but Curve Communications was about to be born.

A stepping stone in the creation of the company came with an assignment from the BC and Yukon Community Newspapers Association to assemble an historical anthology of its member newspapers. Newspapers, and journalism, had always seized Affleck's imagination. Writers he had met during his time at CBC (as opposed to their bosses) had led him to consider them as unaffected, with few illusions of grandeur and no hang-ups about the transient nature of their work.

Affleck figured he could work well with the down-to-earth publishers of the province's community newspapers, while remaining mindful of their concerns for the bottom line. And so it transpired. The anthology, published in 1999, was a success. The Association confessed that its original vision for the book was "somewhat fuzzy," but Affleck was quick to develop that vision into something more focused.

The book led to an invitation, which Affleck gladly accepted, to take over the day-to-day operations of the Association.

At almost the same time, he had begun serious discussions with two colleagues, Laura Ballance and Duane Lennie, about possibly pooling their varied expertise, and contacts, into a new company. When it was finally launched in 2000, everything had come together so naturally "the hardest thing was coming up with a name," Affleck notes. At that time, Curve Communications consisted of just three partners, sharing a small, one-room office.

With its encouragement, Affleck took the newspaper association with him as an early Curve client. Other prominent clients included the Pacific National Exhibition and the Cloverdale Rodeo. Business expanded quickly over the next several years, though Lennie dropped out early, leaving Affleck and Ballance as sole partners. As their reputation grew, so did their client list. Affleck attributes the early growth to "taking a different approach" from the competition.

He expanded on Curve's philosophy in an interview with a local magazine: "One of the first things Curve did right was . . . really to look at the holistic approach, saying, 'We're not just a PR company, we're not just a media buying or media promotions company.' Yes, we offer all of these services, but the lines between each of them are becoming more and more blurred.

"If you can get a DJ to chat about your product or your service or your event, the listeners will assume it's editorial, but quite often it's paid for. It's part of a promotion. You can't just send a press release out and hope the DJ talks about it."

As one example of such a successful campaign, Affleck cites a "hilarious" promotion Curve did for the Cloverdale Rodeo. A media kit distributed to TV and radio stations, the "I Want to be a Cowboy Starter Kit," included a chocolate treat in the shape of a pile of cow dung. The impact was immediate. On-air personalities had a field day with the kit, pulling out the "manure" with expressions of fake disgust, and then eating it.

"It was perfect," says Affleck, "because it was visual. It got the kind of coverage you'd want for a client for very little cost."

In 2005, Curve was presented with a very different problem when a rogue bull seriously injured a police officer working as a volunteer at the rodeo. So-called "crisis communications" isn't as simple as it sounds. With the media all over a story, too often the reaction is to clam up and throw obstacles in the way of inquiring reporters.

But Affleck knows his business: "Curve was immediately able to implement an onsite crisis plan, which included situation assessment, press release and conference coordination and spokesperson work for local, national and international media."

Crisis defused.

Affleck likes to say that before he started the "communications" company he knew next to nothing about public relations. But his background in journalism taught him that you simply don't send out news releases and expect results. Most reporters and assignment editors will simply hit the kill button. They may, however, respond to a personal phone call pitching a genuine story idea.

"For most effective results, we combine press kits with customized telephone and e-mail pitches in support of the objective," Affleck says.

"First of all, you need a good story; then you need a good person to tell that story and then you need a natural sales ability to convince the journalist it's good enough to write about. It's all about the sale. If you get a journalist on the line you have literally 10 or 15 seconds to ensure they get excited about your pitch. If you blow it, you're done."

Clients can also call on Curve for lessons in how to react to media inquiries, a tricky procedure that can be a pitfall for the unwary. Plentiful are the stories of company executives who have spoken informally to journalists only to recoil in disbelief and shock at what they hear themselves saying, or how they were misquoted on TV or in the newspapers. Curve offers everything from three-hour media training seminars to daylong workshops and one-on-one sessions to "help clients develop the tools necessary to handle the toughest news interview."

By adding to its growing staff of talented writers, savvy media buyers, event planners, designers, media relations specialists and business strategists, Curve positioned itself as a one-stop shop, full-service marketing communications agency that proved increasingly attractive to an ever wider spectrum of clients.

The company scored an early success with the PNE, Vancouver's much-loved annual exhibition, with such inspired promotions as "media night" — an evening where the fairground is thrown open exclusively to journalists and their families to enjoy free rides, popcorn and hot dogs. If the media reps are sufficiently impressed to write positively about the PNE, everyone ends up a winner.

Curve has also shown a sure touch in gauging the intellectual level of popular tastes. To promote the West Coast Women's

Show, Affleck dispatched a masseuse to the homes of on-air radio personalities, who were later falling over themselves in the rush to broadcast the "groans, moans and sounds of pleasure" that the visits predictably triggered.

The company was also deeply involved in activities related to the 2010 Vancouver Winter Olympics, helping to develop and implement a province-wide initiative called Spirit of BC Week. The project involved working in close co-operation with no fewer than 92 B.C. communities, helping them to organize special events and providing media relations' expertise to win them exposure. The Dalai Lama's extraordinarily successful visit to Vancouver demanded especially sensitive handling and Curve provided a vital liaison between His Holiness, the media and the University of British Columbia organizing committee.

An outside observer of the company at this point in its history might have seen nothing to disturb a picture of sustained growth at around 25 percent a year, and a blossoming list of prestigious clients. But there was a developing drama at the core of the enterprise that would significantly change its future. Cracks were appearing in the partnership of Affleck and Ballance. There was a growing difference in philosophy over how the company should expand. It eventually became clear to Affleck that there was no alternative but the dissolution of the partnership, regardless of the inevitable disruption to the company's business that would follow.

"We had different visions and a different approach." he explains. "It was not a positive environment." Ironically, the break-up took effect Sept. 1, 2008, the very day Affleck learned that Curve had been ranked the 63rd fastest growing company in B.C. Affleck bought out Ballance, who took with her as part of the deal a sizeable portfolio of the company's longtime clients.

"I looked at the year ahead and said, 'Oh, my god,'" recalls Affleck, now left in sole charge as President and Chief Executive Officer. "It was like starting from scratch. It was more scary in some ways than the first time — the day the original company was launched."

As he retells the story, one senses, however, that Affleck quickly came to welcome the separation with a feeling of relief and newfound freedom. He consoled himself that "things were back in focus, similar to the early days." And so it has turned out.

By summer 2009, the "new Curve," as Affleck thinks of it, was back to its size before the restructuring, business was ahead of budget and he had grown accustomed to his new role as the public face of the company.

"I'd always been hidden in the background," he says. "I wasn't interested in being the face of the company. Now I'm faced with a situation where I have to be. And it's important to raise the profile of the company so that we can continue to succeed."

For someone who, in his early life, was so forward with his opinions, this publicity-shy aspect of Affleck's personality might seem uncharacteristic. But it has always been the quality of the ideas and the excitement of the game that have energized him, not a hankering for personal fame or recognition.

There's a similar streak of self-restraint in the way he views his business philosophy, which helps further explain why he feels more comfortable as the sole proprietor of Curve. His outlook is uncommon among many entrepreneurs of the past decade, for whom money and ever-larger profits have often been the sole reason for existence. But 2008's financial collapse in Wall Street, and the exposure of the ugly excesses of capitalism, may turn out to be the harbinger of a less greedy, less aggressive business ethic. If so, Affleck will be ahead of the curve.

"For me, I don't run a business the way some people run a business," he says. "The bottom line has never been anything in my life. I've never been driven by money, ever. For me, it's about the quality of life, about being a better person. It's about doing interesting work, diverse work. That's what drives me. I believe the money comes if you do what you want and do it right. It really does."

This is no idle claim on Affleck's part. In business, he actively seeks out clients who have a keen environmental consciousness. And, in private, "I've made choices about being green. I didn't drive a car for 20 years, not because I couldn't afford it, but because I didn't want to."

Recently, after becoming a father again, necessity has forced him to get behind the wheel. But he lives with his new partner and three children just five minutes from the office in a "fairly small" downtown Vancouver home. Colleagues are surprised he hasn't moved to a larger house. "People look at it and say, 'Are you crazy?' and I say, 'No. I like having my kids close by. That's just a personal thing."

Having good people around him, and knowing how to select them, has been one of Affleck's strengths since Curve began. He knows that the very nature of his business makes the individual commitment of each member of the company's staff its key asset.

"The way it works here is that I empower my staff a lot," he says.

"Certainly, I have clients that I carry the lead on. But I can't see every single client. It's impossible. My style of management is collegial. I sit down with my staff individually and we go through different processes and they pick my brain for ideas. What we do is not complex but it does take a lot of tenacity and work to get the right people in roles where they can succeed."

The average age of his handpicked team is remarkably young, around 27 years. Affleck claims to have discovered the secret to satisfying the career goals of young, talented people: Make sure they are given a variety of projects or challenges. Provide the proper training for employees and managers. Give them adequate direction and create a culture that nurtures their aspirations. And, lastly but perhaps most importantly, maintain the lines of communication between employees and managers.

"My approach to managing my team in today's volatile and competitive market is to create a collegial workplace that offers diverse work coupled with high demands for success. Salary is not a priority, but I don't cheap out either. The question I have always asked myself is one I ask my staff: Are you happy in what you are doing?"

The newly reorganized team, with Affleck alone at the helm, faced its first major challenge when one of Vancouver's cultural icons, Ballet BC, turned to the company for help as it confronted the prospect of bankruptcy proceedings. Supporters of the arts were astonished to learn in November, 2008 that Ballet BC's board of directors had been forced to terminate its 38 staff and dancers in the face of mounting debts, flagging subscriptions and desultory ticket sales. The ballet company had scheduled performances of the Nutcracker by the famous Moscow Classical Ballet for the holiday season, and a good box office promised to rescue the company from its dire financial straits, possibly allowing it to re-engage its talented dancers. But ticket sales were slow, and time was running short.

Enter Affleck and his team.

With a severely limited advertising budget (a traditional media buy had to be cancelled for lack of funds) Curve devised a unique grassroots campaign to save the day. It involved mobilizing the resources of such "new" media as online blogs, Facebook groups and YouTube videos. A campaign to persuade people to buy Nutcracker tickets as Christmas presents quickly caught the attention of the media. It produced an anonymous well wisher who donated $42,000 to buy 1,000 tickets for underprivileged kids. In a smart interlacing of themes, Curve's campaign succeeded in imprinting on the public's mind that while the ballet was in mortal danger, selling enough Nutcracker tickets could save it. Dancers from Ballet BC were recruited to the campaign, making public appearances at retail hotspots to read holiday classics to kids and hand out flyers at the Santa Claus parade. A sense of mounting excitement was maintained by issuing daily bulletins on ticket sales.

The effect was electrifying.

Within days, Graeme Barrit, chairman and president of Ballet BC board of directors, was able to state in a Curve press release: "Since Dec. 1, ticket sales have almost doubled. The ballet's progress has been amazing." Ultimately, some 14,000 tickets were sold, surpassing the initial goal by 156 per cent and increasing the previous year's revenue by $100,000.

The story of the ballet's struggle to at the very least finish its season might not in less capable hands have made it beyond the arts pages of the local dailies. In fact, the story was picked up not only across Canada, but also in dance trade publications in England and the U.S., as well as in major newspapers such as The New York Times. And there was another aspect to this saga that became a point of pride for Affleck's team. The company's work with Ballet BC highlighted the importance for arts funding in Canada on several government levels, and prompted healthy discussions within the media about the increasingly fragile state of arts and culture across the nation.

Affleck believes his company's strength lies in its ability to position, create, and place effective messages in the media, developing campaigns that cut through marketplace clutter and take advantage of media opportunities that less adventurous firms might overlook.

"We carved a niche in the ballet world," he says with undisguised satisfaction. And his success did not go unnoticed in the wider world. Other cultural organizations have since beaten a path to Curve's door and one immediate result saw Curve sign a coveted contract with Canada's prestigious National Ballet.

"To be a successful entrepreneur you always have to be intrigued by all sorts of things," Affleck says. "As an entrepreneur you always have to pay attention to what's going on and I think we're doing things differently and doing them better than anyone else."

As far as the future is concerned, Affleck is keenly aware of how quickly the media sands are shifting and how rapidly the traditional outlets for marketing and publicity are taking new forms. There are so many different ways now to get a message out that it can be confusing for clients accustomed to the old way of doing things, and some are reluctant to change.

"Most of our clients still set their sights on receiving coverage in traditional media and it is part of our challenge to educate them," he says. But as the ballet campaign emphasized, the mainstream daily newspapers, with the notable exception of a vital and prosperous community newspaper market, are struggling to maintain their former power and influence. And, particularly among the young, the Internet is an integral part of the communications mix that any contemporary marketing agency ignores at its peril.

Affleck cites Curve's client, the United Nations' Children's Fund (UNICEF), as the "perfect example" of any agency taking full advantage of today's new media.

"UNICEF uses Facebook and other social marketing sites for accessing the youth market they need. And that's the thing. If you have a client that attracts a young demographic, under 25 say, then being online is key. Everything's done online and they really get how to utilize the online resources."

As a leader in integrated marketing for several years, Affleck believes Curve's expansion into Web 2.0 is a natural development, from which many of its clients, and Curve itself, are already benefiting. "Most of our new business calls come from our website, and the launch of our Blog, Facebook and Twitter accounts have enhanced our optimization on the Web."

About future projects, he says: "There are lots of other areas in communications that we could be working in, including video production." He mentions that his current domestic partner, the mother of his new baby, works as a television producer. "There would be some synergy there," he says thoughtfully.

But whatever new directions the company may take, one philosophy will remain central to its role: "We love the arts but we also love working on start-ups and entrepreneurial clients," says Affleck.

"When I take one of these clients on, I take it on personally. I take on a kind of ownership of their work. Failure is not an option to me, and my staff agrees. We must treat customers and all the people we work with — media, sales reps, promotions people — with respect. It was always drilled into me that the customer comes first. Basic 'Sales 101' techniques, you might say. But, heck, it works."

As the global economy took a sharp dive in 2008, and the immediate outlook for the future was not promising, Affleck remained upbeat. Curve was still in an expansionist mood. "Quite often," he said, "businesses worry about what their competitors are doing, or if they are losing business to them. For me, it has never been about that. It has been about doing good work, about creating a product, a service that is simply the best. Second best does not cut it at Curve."

It's a winning formula that has set Curve on a path of continual growth, fuelled by word of mouth that has always been extremely positive. And that growth shows no sign of slowing down.

CLOCKWISE:

Steve Spencer accessing the multilayer biometric security at Network Operation Centre

Steve and wife Rebecca at a London TechAlliance award function

Steve in the Disaster Recovery Lab

Paul Campbell, Director of Business Development, with Steve in the Network Operations Centre, One London Place

Digital Fortress Corporation

L istening to Steve Spencer telling the story of his career it's hard not to be spellbound by the apparent ease with which the 48-year-old entrepreneur rose to eminence in the business world. At the age of 12, he was earning more than his grade school teacher. In the era before desktop computers, he built his own. And, without the benefit of a university education, he is today a corporate CEO, highly regarded IT expert and sought-after lecturer at centres of advanced learning.

Spencer was born with a multiplicity of skills that he himself did not fully recognize right away. He once thought all people were similarly blessed. It came as a surprise to him to realize that they were not. Only now that he is confident of his position in the world can he deliver with disarming honesty a self-appraisal that in others might be taken for hubris: "I'd always self-described as being a jack of all trades, master of none, until I realized that I really was a master of most trades and a jack of nearly none." He had an unusually high IQ, but could never have been described as "nerdy." Everything he tried he excelled at, and he didn't know that wasn't normal — he just expected it. Business, finance, sports, music, technology, trades, leadership, social skills — doing well in all these things came naturally. In retrospect, he sees that his main weakness lay in observing and measuring himself against others: "I was completely naïve about my potential. I attribute some of this to my strong Christian upbringing that stressed that all men were created equal and that pride and boastfulness was immoral. The meek were to inherit the earth, so even though I was repeatedly told I was smart, I was discouraged from considering myself better than anyone else."

Spencer's ascendancy during the early years of the computer revolution, and his arrival at the pinnacle of success as a master of complex computer networking in the past decades, amply support his self-assessment. And as founder, president and chief technical officer of London, Ont.-based Digital Fortress Corporation, he presides today at the cutting edge of developments in information technology, leading — as we shall see — a personal crusade against the "monolithic, monopolistic" giants of the Canadian telecommunications and computing industries.

As kind as the fates were, however, in bestowing upon Spencer such ample talents, his early childhood experiences might easily have derailed, or at least delayed, his ambitions. Spencer tells the story without emotion: His birth in 1961 in Saskatoon and subsequent move to Vancouver, where his father, an electrical technologist, found work with B.C. Hydro. He lived first in an impoverished section of the big city, growing up with a new baby sister and a housebound mother, and attending a large grade school. Then, still only 10 years old, he was "whisked away" to a small, poor farm village near Courtenay on Vancouver Island. There he went to a one-room, single teacher Christian school. Being top student there made him the bully target of other kids. At the same time, his parents' marriage was failing. His father was working away from home much of the time and they were eventually divorced. Spencer recalls with anguish the day he accompanied his mother to the hospital bedside where his father lay in intensive care after an operation to remove a brain tumour. There and then, his mother served his father with the divorce papers. The emotional scars went deep. While his father recovered from the operation, his son felt that he was never the same man. To compound matters, his mother became seriously depressed and her son had to quickly learn to take care of himself and his little sister. Essentially, he became the man of the house. "I grew up fast," he says. Both parents eventually remarried into extended families.

Thus the young Spencer experienced most of his youth in changing circumstances and in different places. There were times, he admits, when "I had to go through hell" to make the best of his talents while dealing with major personal challenges. In hindsight, he can perceive a wider truth: "The turbulence of my youth honed my survival skills," he says today. "It redirected my intelligence and eliminated my fears. Losses made me tough, made me angry enough to do things my way." He recalls with satisfaction and pride the summer he spent as a 12-year-old working part-time for his mother and new stepfather, who held the franchise in Campbell River for one of the early home electronics stores.

"It was, literally, the first time you could buy records, eight-tracks, cassettes and stereo systems in one store," says Spencer. "It was a very good business." He worked evenings and weekends at the family store selling quadraphonic stereo systems. "I was outselling every salesperson we had and I was doing it only part time," he says. "I made more commissions on my income tax return than my teacher was making in the private local Christian elementary school."

Spencer remembers being excited at realizing he possessed both a rare knack for salesmanship and an uncanny ability to explain to others the complex technicalities of innovative products. But his first brush with entrepreneurship ended when he was sent at the age of 14 to a boarding academy in the United States for secondary school. The choice of Auburn Academy, a "private, strict, co-educational Christian high school" in Auburn, Washington, was perhaps intended to provide him with some faith-based stability for his continuing Christian schooling not available in the rural environment. Commissions he earned during summers at home covered his school fees.

The problem was that, academically, U.S. educational standards were "at least a couple of years behind the Canadian system." Spencer found his studies a "cakewalk" — not surprisingly, since he was going over old ground. "I had a fine old time because I got straight As with hardly any work," he laughs. That left lots of time for the extracurricular activities that he found "fantastic." Aside from a full gamut of excellent sports training, lettering in several, he took advantage of extracurricular programs, learning scuba diving, skiing, weight training, martial arts and advanced music opportunities. He toured and performed extensively as the first chair French horn in the school orchestra. In addition, he earned a nursing diploma with advanced training in the local hospital in post-operative care and pathology. "I was eager to take in as much as I could since there was nothing like this available at home," he says. As a dormitory resident he was taking care of himself, but to help alleviate the cost of his private education, he had to perform four hours of work five days a week. He did his work duty in the school cafeteria, gaining culinary skills that were useful when he later went to live with his father, who had relocated from Vancouver Island to the newly booming Fort McMurray, and to complete high school in Alberta.

Spencer's relationship with his mother and stepfather in B.C. had deteriorated to a point where he had to change "families." That also ended the source of tuition fees to fund his private education. Finding a part time job with a restaurant in Alberta was the easy part. It was when he enrolled to complete high school that his pleasant sojourn at Auburn "came back to bite me." He discovered that Alberta then had one of the highest educational standards in North America. "I was literally almost two years behind and had to just about kill myself with full class periods a day, five days a week, just to catch up and get enough credits for my Grade 12 matriculation diploma. It was like missing school for three years and then going back and having to finish. It was very, very tough. I excelled in the sciences but ended up with about a 70-per-cent grade average, down from an honors 4.0GPA at Auburn. I just barely made it through." It was a sobering experience from several perspectives. No more fun and games — and even his music had to be put aside. There were few programs in an austere public school and he certainly had no spare time. "I still had to work part time to pay my share of the household expenses. Most significantly, it put university right out of the picture. There were no scholarships or loans, and certainly no money on that side of the family."

Looking back today, Spencer acknowledges: "Not going on to University was a turning point. They were just starting to put computers in the classrooms and I missed it. I missed the PC revolution from an educational standpoint, but I was certainly as well prepared as anyone else from a professional standpoint. I had an affinity for sales and performing in public, as well as technology, and my greatest talent — one that has probably carried me through my career — was my ability to explain complex technology, and the benefits of it, to non-technical people and to customize that understanding on the fly. And that's really what I'm still doing today."

As a teenager in Fort McMurray, however, all this was in the future. For one of the rare times in his life, Spencer was obliged upon graduation to do "what everybody else did" — get a job. Any job. He took one as an apprentice electrician with Syncrude, then the major player in the Fort McMurray oil sands development. At that time, of the 30,000 people in town just 5,000 were true locals — "everyone else was a transplant. We were all there for work from all over Canada and the bars were just as busy as the plants. It was definitely the 'wild west.' By this time I was no longer a practicing Christian and with my new freedom I did my share of losing my paycheque, and many brain cells, on the weekends like everyone else."

For Spencer, this period of his life also had its defining moments. He fell in love with his high school sweetheart, beginning a happy and successful relationship that has prospered through more than 25 years of marriage. For another, his childhood delight in computers as a hobby brought him closer to his father. Spencer cannot recall ever seeing a computer at school, even in Grade 12: "There was no computer class to be taken." But as young as 13, with the help of his father, he had built his first computer using a do-it-yourself kit.

"It was the only way you could get anything close to a personal computer, though it was mostly an electronic calculator, when people were still using adding machines. It was kind of 'gee-whiz wow' thing for the most part. I was fascinated with the technology then and have been ever since. When personal computers first became commercially available, I was first in line to get one and promptly tore it apart to see how it ticked."

It would be a couple more years, however, before Spencer's love of computers translated into meaningful employment. In the early 1980s, Canada was in a period of recession. Jobs became scarce, and he and his fiancée spent time once again on Vancouver Island. But the economy on the Island also turned bad and he couldn't keep steady work.

"We left our first house behind and trudged back to Fort McMurray for work, still unclear about our future in an uncertain environment. We were basically chasing jobs," Spencer says. The couple eventually decided to relocate to his fiancée's hometown in London, Ont. Her father, who owned a business interior design company, offered Spencer a job selling a new line of desk and table furniture specifically designed for the computers just then beginning to invade the office environment. The computer connection was tantalizingly close to the business Spencer yearned to be a part of — but not quite close enough. "I'd been an electronics hobbyist since I was a child and decided I didn't want to continue to sell furniture. The first chance I got I took a job with an emerging small computer company — one of the very first in town. Basically, they were selling fancy word processors, because there were no real business PCs yet."

Spencer toiled during the day selling the first PC networks while attending computer science classes at Fanshawe College. It took him four years of studying at nights to gain his advanced diploma. He was now 25 and looking for his first big break. It arrived in the form of an offer from Commodore Computers to become the London-based regional sales manager for southwestern Ontario. Commodore at that time was the "king of desktop computers" and had become the standard for home use. It was also the computer of choice for schools in the region. A major part of Spencer's new responsibilities was to manage the business relationships with area school boards.

"It was quite a jump from working in a family store, to a restaurant, to working in a remote oil sands plant, to working in a small retail sales environment, to all of a sudden becoming a regional sales manager with a territory and four employees in a 'big' city. But I loved it — this was the big time for a small town western boy," he says.

Spencer stayed with Commodore for some six years between 1985 and 1991, a period during which the now-defunct company would become indelibly associated with the early history of the computer phenomenon. It was also a period during which Spencer built the basis of his reputation. Commodore had begun as an office supply company, building filing cabinets along with its adding machines. The Commodore PET (personal electronic transactor), first produced in 1977, quickly became a top seller in the Canadian, U.S. and U.K. educational markets.

Schools were introducing the first computer-equipped classrooms, offering courses first as an elective, later as mandatory. Colleges and universities were soon populated with computers and computer science "really took off," Spencer remembers. "There was quite a revolution through that period and I sort of rode through it with Commodore at a high level and did very well. A lot of people 'adored their 64'."

One reason for his success was his ability to perform equally well as both salesman and technician. In other regions, Commodore was forced to hire different people for each function — except in London. "In my region, they never had to send technicians, because I was just as good as any of them. They really got two for one. They got someone who could manage the business relationship, make the sales numbers work, and if the network failed at the school I could go and fix it. At the time you were usually either a salesman or a technician. I was both."

After Commodore went bust in 1991, Spencer's talents were much in demand. He looks back at the company's demise as a classic case of a firm with a good product but no notion of how to sell it. "They really didn't understand marketing," he says. "Everything they had ever produced, they sold. They had a mindset that, if they made it, people would buy it." But, when competition arrived in the form of IBM and Apple products "they pretty much lost their dominance in the classrooms, didn't have the credibility for the office environment and then they started losing home users." A similar lack of marketing expertise doomed Commodore's attempt to re-capture the home computer market with its introduction in 1985 of the Amiga model.

"Amiga was probably the most amazing personal computer ever designed," says Spencer. "It was at least 10 years ahead of its time but they had no idea how to market it. Commodore was unprepared to compete in that market and by 1991 they were left completely behind and the company closed. Even though I had personally sold $30 million of PCs, we were all let go."

Spencer and his wife, who continues to hold a secure job at the city library, were determined to remain living in London. The comparatively featureless landscape around the city had come as an initial shock to Spencer, who was used to "forests, seas and mountains. Everything around here is flat and farmland and the Great Lakes just aren't the same as the ocean. I still sometimes feel like a dog on the tundra looking for a tree, and most of my vacations are back to the Pacific."

However, London was becoming a hotbed of technological innovation and when GE Capital Technology Services, a leading provider of office technology across Canada, offered him a job based in the city he was quick to accept. Spencer's ostensible responsibility at GE was in sales, but when his new employer discovered he was also a gifted network technician he became, as he says, "a sort of guru attached to GE's regional sales teams."

It was a role he engaged in subsequently over the next decade or more on behalf of an array of blue chip corporations. He designed private and Internet-based network solutions with providers such as Wang, Husky, IBM, Fonorola, and Unitel-AT&T-Allstream and Radiant using technologies from NetFrame, Novell, Microsoft, Cisco, Sun, 3Com, Checkpoint, Symantec, Juniper, Adtran and Astrocom.

Notable private sector clients included Power Financial Corp., where Spencer led a team that effectively created the world's largest Internet-based virtual private network serving more than 10,000 employees. He's also managed major accounts like General Motors, General Dynamics, 3M, Ford, Volvo, London Life, Heinz and the Canadian Medical Association. Public sector clients have included government departments and ministries in Ottawa, Ontario, Quebec, New Brunswick, Alberta and British Columbia. "I was consistently flown into the high security accounts like DND, RCMP and CSIS as I had early on earned a high security clearance and background with the police and military colleges and selling ruggedized military hardware applications with Commodore and Husky Computers."

From 1996 onwards, Spencer worked almost exclusively with Canada's major telecommunications companies. They were preoccupied with the surging "tech bubble" demand for data centres and local area networks that needed to be securely connected over a wider region. Spencer found the telecoms eager to meet the demand, but sorely lacking the necessary expertise. It was a discovery that eventually prompted him to start his own company and begin what became a crusade for excellence in the industry. The problem as he describes it was that the telecoms had not fully evolved from their origins as providers of traditional telephone services.

"Their sales and sales support people were all telephone support teams who were now selling data networks and yet they had no idea what they were talking about in front of the customer," he says. "They started to hire people from the computer networking world who would at least know the environment and the different acronyms and concepts. It was a natural for me. I spent nearly 10 years in the telecommunications industry as basically the major account anchor for secure network technology, wide area networks and the integration of the Internet into all of these applications. They called me a network architect, but I was really in a 'go-to-guy' sales support role for the complex deals."

What Spencer really became was a one-man phenomenon. The telecoms were used to putting a salesperson in front of a customer, who then called upon technical support staff to answer technical questions. "In my case those people (technicians) rarely came along," he says. "My team was very tight, because there were few technical questions I couldn't answer." Spencer's skill at sales and business, his talent for understanding the complex technology — and being able to explain it — meant that he "ended up doing a great many of these deals myself. So they would just wind me up and put me in front of a customer white board and let me go. And at the end of the day we usually ended up with a sale and a happy customer with a well-designed network and I got well paid for that."

Indeed he was. When the average person in sales was making maybe $40,000 to $60,000 a year, Spencer, wearing the twin hats of sales whiz and technical expert, was consistently making six figures. "I did extremely well for not being in one of the major centres, consistently winning national awards and bonuses." It helped that he was adamant about remaining in London and refusing to be drawn into the "vortex" of Toronto or local management. "I had the opportunity to do what I did (in the SWO regional office) because there was usually one manager who was responsible for all the business lines and they let me work them all. Anyone in a larger centre would have been quickly pigeonholed to a specific role or promoted out of the field, something I did not want."

Spencer saw his days as a maverick were numbered while working for Allstream, formerly AT&T, one of Canada's leading providers of communications and networking products. New head office management eventually assigned more technical support people to Spencer's fiefdom in London, convinced that there was revenue that they were missing. Inevitably, there was friction.

"They were supposed to come along with me on sales calls, but it would just end up being my show because there was no need for anyone else. At that point I had reached what I thought was a pinnacle because, without moving to Toronto, there was no place I was going to go that would pay me that amount of money and allow me to be the tech expert as well as the sales and business expert. Plus, constant waves of new management were always looking to find ways to claw back my income — it stood out. I knew that the time had come for me to go out on my own." He left Allstream in 2004 when they were looking to trim enough to be sold to MTS. "I had spent six years with them, and they handed me a very large package," he says.

After a stint as GM for a local system integrator, Spencer spent the next year building what he calls the "ultimate, state-of-the-art data centre" in the No.1 office tower in downtown London as the centrepiece of his newly formed enterprise, Digital Fortress Corporation. The early years were tough sledding. It took two years to get to break-even point. A major expansion occurred in 2008 with the opening of a second facility, an event that garnered much publicity and prompted a tribute from Peter White, president of the London Economic Development Corp.: "Digital Fortress brings business to London," he said. "The company provides IT services that are essential to continue to attract industries to the area that have mission critical data security and availability requirements." An extensive report in the local daily paper focused on the elaborate security arrangements at Digital Fortress, comparing the physical security measures to scenes from the vintage TV series Get Smart.

The premises do indeed employ a seven-layer, custom security system using infrared beams, motion sensors, fingerprint scanners and other classified devices, making use of Spencer's knowledge of government systems. A back-up generator on one floor guarantees an uninterrupted power supply that could light up a whole city block. "We're like a high-tech, ultra-secure hotel for IT infrastructures," Spencer told the newspaper. "Our clients bring their own networks and servers, we provide security, advanced cooling systems and, most importantly, make sure the power is always on and the Internet is fast and never goes down."

Companies, including web hosters, IT firms and other small to medium-sized businesses, pay up to $5,000 a month to keep their systems safe. Digital Fortress guarantees its hardware stays on 99.99 percent of the time or it is liable for stiff penalties. "Once people figure out what we do, they're amazed at the level of service we can provide compared to the large telecoms," Spencer says.

Clients unfamiliar with Digital's hallmark technology sometimes need to be convinced: "There's not any sales process we go through that doesn't end up with me in the boardroom at some point with the tech people from the customer side wanting to understand the differentiation between us and our competitors. That's where we draw pictures on the white board and explain how we've got everyone else beat. For the same price as going to Primus or Bell I can give you a better product. The service we can provide is unmatched in the industry and we are now partnering with other specialized IT firms to be able to make Digital Fortress a globally recognized brand in the foreseeable future." The new group of entrepreneurial companies that create the symbiotic relationship required to go global was conceived and named The Fortress IT Group by Spencer.

From the outset, Spencer was set upon the principle that it must be the quality of the service offered by Digital that mattered, not the ambience in which it was provided. Despite the gushing newspaper reports about advanced technology, Spencer says that he built his data centres on a budget. "You'd be surprised how much you can build when you buy off-lease," he says. "I don't have rows and rows of spiffy, perfectly matched racks. My goal is not to look pretty, not to be the perfect data centre from an appearance standpoint. My goal is to provide the perfect product to companies who need it. When customers understand that, we can steal them from the fancy telecom data centres that can't keep their Internet up or provide 24/7 convenient access to the facility. Only an independent operator can do things like offer to house a client's own data cabinets or support their existing contracted network connections, and many independents won't even offer this level of freedom; it might cost them a dollar or two of extra revenue."

Spencer's obsession with the failings of the big telecoms for which he worked has taken on the nature of a personal crusade. "I would never have seen myself as an entrepreneur without having to prove a point," he says. His point, expressed with typical bluntness, is that the Internet and other network solutions as well as the data centre packages that customers are "shoehorned" into by the telecoms are, in his considered opinion, "lousy." Spencer's denouncement of the telecoms is long and detailed. It boils down to his view that every customer is a custom solution and not a problem looking for a canned solution from a menu. He says that in protecting their proprietary brands and refusing to admit that there might be any useful or credible value in partnering with the "competition", the major telecoms are depriving their customers of a reliable service, particularly since the Internet has become the ubiquitous network of choice.

With the telecoms, says Spencer, it was always "verboten" even to consider recommending to a client that to guarantee reliability they should take an Internet connection from more than one supplier. "If you even mentioned that the customer should be talking to the competition you would be fired on the spot," he says.

What the telecoms fail to acknowledge, he says, is that "the Internet is a public network designed initially by the U.S. military to only work continuously well when it is shared between multiple peers. The only way to get the Internet to be bulletproof is to bond multiple, diverse Internet feeds together. To do that you have to go to different providers right at the data centre level, not just upstream somewhere."

At Digital Fortress, Spencer did just that. "As an independent, I spend my days managing multiple Tier 1 upstream providers, bonding them together and selling customers networks with Internet that doesn't fail — ever. We've not had a customer impacting outage longer than five minutes, and that's based on proper Internet design using multiple, diverse peers as suppliers and us becoming a supplier to the client, delivering what other people can't or won't. You won't find many people who can say they had an Internet connection that never went down — yet that's what we do at Digital Fortress. We have a 100 percent customer retention rate. Why? Because we do it the way it's supposed to be done, not the way the telecoms do it."

Spencer rails at the "monopolistic, monolithic" environment at the major telecoms. "They have a chokehold, in conjunction with the cable companies, on primary distribution of the Internet. Most places in Canada, if you want primary Internet connection, you've got one or two choices, possibly three. In much of the U.S., you can get 12 different quotes from 12 different telephone companies. Here, there is collusion in the marketplace and, with tariff access pricing set by the CRTC, it all combines to make a monopoly, and people end up getting a single source network feed to service their company. And that's not the way the Internet was designed to work. There's no way these companies can give a solid connection to the customer, yet that's what they promise. For them, the story is that, because the Internet is a public network, it can't always be up. And that's the big lie. The Internet can always be up if you design it with multiple peers. The telecoms don't want people to know that, because then they'll expect an Internet that's always on."

Spencer allows that he has become a thorn in the side of the competition — "my face is up on a few of their dart boards, I'm absolutely positive." And it frustrates him that some telecom customers remain complacent about the levels of service they are receiving. "People will take outages and say, 'Oh darn, that's the Internet down.' That's not normal, not acceptable. I've proven that." But he's also confident the tide is turning in his favour.

With the increasing "webification" (his word) of the business world, and the growing dependency on the Internet in business to consumer relationships, he sees demand for his company's services continuing to grow. He is busy consolidating processing power which customers will rent from multiple data centres such as Digital Fortress, rather than own it themselves. He says his company will avoid the major centres and concentrate on serving mid-sized centres, like London, which are under-supplied with reliable Internet connections. "The world is webifying — everyone wants everything through the Internet, and especially IT professionals. They need it where they live and work, which is everywhere now — the workplace and IT centres of excellence are no longer clustered in the big cities, They are now virtual to accommodate where the talent is and their quality of life demands.

"Consumers want it through their browser which is now on the mobile device that's on their hip. Internet reliability becomes mission critical. When the Internet is not running, their company is not running. Webification is a wave that is cresting now and will continue to do so for a number of years." Whatever happens, says Spencer, "the key for me is beating the telecoms at the Internet delivery game. It really is a crusade and our expansion is going to mean more of the same — if we can find like-minded partners and backers who will help us take the message to the masses."

A final blueprint for the future of Digital Fortress is still percolating in Spencer's head.

"Future possibilities are endless, but the operation doesn't lend itself to the franchise model. It's not the easiest thing to try to maintain a corporate structure without the right people and the right technical skills. We've been able to do all the wonderful things we've done with a very tight staff, in essence with my hand on much of what's going on. The challenge is to step back and find a way to operate in other centres without me being there. I've got a great team, but we're going to have to hire several people at each location and teach them to do what I do in London, because how everything works is fairly unique. Of course, we feel that the way we do things is really setting the standard and other independents at least will start to follow, which is great — it proves my point."

Spencer says he's looking forward to the future, "but first we have to get past this downturn. While recessions generally generate more outsourcing, which has been good for us, the next jump is going to be a big one and it's going to require a lot of capital." For the present, however: "We're trying to keep our heads down. We're a very tasty takeover target. I'd like to see how the story ends with my hand still at the helm."

For the time being, Spencer is content to enjoy the stability and prestige of his position within the community of London, where his Digital Fortress Corporation was recently selected for the London City Feature Company Award for adding value to the business community. Digital Fortress also made the Branham 300 top 25 fastest growing tech companies in Canada. Spencer himself sits on the Entrepreneur Peer Group board with the Tech Alliance — and he still does network consulting for major enterprises. Locally, he is a volunteer Medical First Responder and trainer for the St. John Ambulance, devoting more than 2,000 hours to the brigade over the past five years. And he was recently recruited as a new Professor of Information Security Management at London's Fanshawe College, where a new graduate program is to start classes in the fall of 2009 – all delivered on the Web, of course. Not bad for a guy whose tumultuous upbringing once denied him the chance to go to university.

ExitCertified founding partners Hees Ham and Tim Mabey receiving Mid Market Business of the Year award at the 2007 Greater Ottawa Chamber of Commerce awards gala.

ExitCertified Corporation

Businesses, just like families, are driven by different dynamics — some a force for good, others a recipe for disaster. What decides between success and failure? No two situations will be identical, but as a rule the enterprise that prospers will be one that sets long-term, realistic expectations and nourishes a culture that values honesty and good ethics.

It is not too fanciful to take the family metaphor further by studying how a successful business evolves over generations, carving out its special niche, cultivating its identity and imprinting its managers and employees with its unique DNA.

As in families, the "offspring" of these model businesses will sometimes branch out on their own. Former executives may establish themselves on their own account, fortified with the knowledge and nurture they received at "home." Two young Ottawa entrepreneurs, Hees Ham and Tim Mabey, had the good fortune in their early careers to be exposed to a premium "parenting" experience. Both worked for companies that excelled at what they did and that instilled in employees the skills and instincts that would enable them to survive and prosper if they were ever to leave the "nest" to venture out on their own.

Mabey spent seven years in the early nineties working his way up to become manager of operations for Harris Computer Systems, reporting directly to the president. The Ottawa-based company, which specialized in software application development for municipalities and utilities, consistently qualified among the Best 50 Managed Companies in Canada.

Ham's first job after graduating with an honours degree from Queen's University in 1995 was as district sales manager in Toronto for Automatic Data Processing Inc., one of the world's largest providers of business outsourcing solutions. When it comes to companies with a distinguished family pedigree, ADP is a prime example. Founded in 1949 in an office over an ice cream shop in New Jersey, ADP today employs more than 42,000 associates worldwide serving more than 585,000 companies. It has annual revenues in the region of $9 billion US.

For both Ham and Mabey, now joint partners in ExitCertified, Canada's fastest growing IT training organization, their early experiences in such quality working environments were to prove invaluable. And when the two men later became close colleagues, working together in Ottawa for a company called Learnix, they found they shared much in common when it came to the philosophy of running a good business.

At the time they joined the firm, Learnix was an IT education company specializing in instructor-led training with offices in Ottawa, Montreal, Toronto, Calgary, Vancouver, Sacramento, San Francisco, Seattle and Portland. It had more than 100 employees and 40 classrooms offering technical training on behalf of such major corporations as Oracle, Microsoft, HP, Veritas and Sun Microsystems. Prospects were looking favourable. The economy was in great shape, IT education was a booming industry and Learnix was ahead of the curve. But then occurred an event that changed everything. In 1999, the company founder, Nigel Harris, sold Learnix to Quebec-based TMI — just as earlier he had sold his previously successful venture, Harris Computer Systems. At first, not much changed at Learnix. Harris agreed to stay running the firm on contract for two years. But when he eventually left, Learnix was immediately folded in to the larger organization.

Mabey and Ham were "leaned on" to stay on as vice presidents of operations and sales respectively. Together they helped steer the company through a period of further extensive growth, taking it from around $10 million in revenues in 1999 to over $18 million in 2001. But almost from the beginning, the two men had an uneasy feeling about the direction TMI was taking Learnix. It appeared to them that the company's priority was to acquire as many businesses in the e-learning field as they could before taking the company public.

Ham and Mabey had grown to appreciate what had made Learnix a "very successful and special organization" and it upset them to see it starting to go into decline. "Some of the other organizations that were acquired weren't as profitable as Learnix and were operating in areas outside of what we enjoyed doing," says Ham. "We also noticed that they seemed to be going in a direction that we did not believe to be sustainable long term."

Their instincts were right. TMI was soon in deep trouble. The company "family" was staring at a catastrophic break-up. In the spring of 2001, Ham and Mabey started to question the leadership and viability of the company and began to think they should get out. "Hees and I didn't necessarily want to start our own business," says Mabey, "but we felt these guys were going to drive the thing into the ground."

Both men realized they had a good opportunity to start up their own organization. Sun Microsystems had been a major part of the business of Learnix and the pair had developed strong relationships with Sun personnel, and with other vendors.

"We decided we could make a go of it," says Ham. "And basically what that meant was we were going to leverage some relationships that we had made while at Learnix, and the main one was with Sun Microsystems."

As soon as they had severed their connections with TMI, Ham and Mabey renewed their old contacts with Sun, suggesting they would be interested in presenting a business plan. "They accepted, and we went to Broomfield, Colorado, and pitched our idea about how we were interested in starting up our own training business centred around being a Sun-authorized training partner," says Ham. "They listened to our presentation and liked what they heard. They obviously had some concerns with Learnix because, all of a sudden, senior managers were leaving and that was a sign maybe something was not right. Sun agreed to give us the authorized partnership in Ottawa and at that point we had 90 days to find a location, hire people and be up and running. And that was how it all started."

The timing of their move to independence seemed propitious. Leading up to the summer of 2001, information technology was booming and companies offering vendor-authorized learning courses were a hot ticket. As Mabey recalls, tech firms had enjoyed a long stretch of fat years; organizations had big budgets and were purchasing "lots and lots of hardware and software. The experience was new to most of them, so it was a great time to be in the training industry. We were kind of riding the wave with them."

The first challenge the new company faced was to secure appropriate premises within the 90 days Sun had stipulated. It wasn't a simple task. The start-up firm had no history, no record of success. Any potential landlord likely would need assurances of its viability. The partners were fortunate in that they managed to find existing training space and were able to convince the landlord that further investments would not be necessary.

"Obviously they were a little concerned," says Ham. "The reason that landlords are often a little bit leery about training organizations is that it's not conventional space. They're concerned about the longevity of the organization. If they have to put money into the building, and then something happens, they're exposed to being out their investment. We really had to put a hard sell on why we felt we would be reliable tenants, and why we had a viable business plan."

Finally, the paperwork was done and ExitCertified had secured a five-year sublease on around 6,000 square feet of space in downtown Ottawa. "That was the first investment that Tim and I made out of our own pockets," says Ham. "We had to write a cheque for just under $40,000 to do that." Some of the money came from savings, some from family members — and some from wherever it could be scraped up.

"The concept of saving for me at that time was a little elusive," jokes Mabey. "You know, you receive those credit cards in the mail that say 'Sign up for this low percentage,' and that's what I was using at the time."

The lease for the office premises was signed Sept. 9, 2001. Two days later, terrorists attacked the U.S. and the twin towers of the World Trade Centre in New York crumbled to the ground, killing almost 3,000 people. "It was an interesting time for the whole world," says Ham, "but certainly for Tim and I. We had just made this big plunge to go out on our own, and made that commitment for five years. We all know what happened. 9/11 really changed the world, and that was what accelerated the tech meltdown, so to speak."

Their timing, once looking so good, now threatened to be plain awful. They counted their blessings. Chief among them was their newly minted partnership with Sun, a company big enough to weather the post-9/11 world. Sun had shown their confidence in the two men, having worked in harmony with them for several years. Sun was prepared to give them an opportunity to open up a learning centre in Ottawa, even though they would be competing initially against their former employer, Learnix. That was unusual. Historically, Sun would authorize just one partner in each geographical region. But Sun weren't sure what was going to happen with Learnix in the long term. Nor were Mabey and Ham. But they had a gut feeling about it.

"We were thinking that there was an opportunity to build this business, and at the same time we weren't sure what the future of Learnix was going to be," says Ham. "We thought that if Learnix went away there would be a really good opportunity for us to benefit very quickly. It was speculation. We weren't sure. But the thought was certainly out there."

In the second week of November, ExitCertified ran its first training course in Ottawa on behalf of Sun and for the next three months competed directly with Learnix. But the rot within Learnix/ TMI had gone deep. Key personnel had been lost. Its formerly strong relationships with vendors had gone sour. In February 2002, Learnix/ TMI went bankrupt. Its collapse came as no surprise to Tim Mabey.

"One of the reasons ours is a successful business is that it's a relationship business with the vendors. When we were at Learnix our job was maintaining that relationship with the vendors so that everybody wins. But the reality is that what killed Learnix was the new ownership. It was a combination of arrogance and ignorance of what they were doing. They basically went to the vendors and said, 'Hey, we're really in the driver's seat, because we have exclusivity. So what are you going to do for us?' And that's when things really started to go downhill. You just don't walk up to a vendor like Sun or Oracle and say, 'What are you going to do for me?' That's when we started to see that Learnix was going to go away, whether we did our thing or not."

With Learnix out of the picture, ExitCertified was presented with a huge opportunity after only three months' existence. Among other things, Learnix had been Sun's cross-Canada provider of IT training. Within days, Sun approached Mabey and Ham with a proposal. "They came to us and said, 'We'd like you guys to open up in Montreal and in Sacramento, California.' It was our first expansion."

In the training industry, most large hardware and software vendors either provide training directly to their customers or outsource it to partners such as ExitCertified. Sun, for example, has for many years operated a hybrid model where in major cities such as New York, Boston, Los Angeles and Chicago, they run their own training centres. But in smaller cities, they outsource to partners to deliver training. The authorized partner shares its revenue with the vendor and benefits from vendor marketing and web presence. Customers who register for courses through the vendor typically end up taking them at the partner's facility.

The key to being a successful partner is, crucially, to nurture your relationship with the vendor, while also offering the highest quality of instruction. In the case of ExitCertified, neither Ham nor

Mabey had a training background. But when they put together a business plan in the summer of 2001 they had a clear idea of what the organization was going to look like.

"Once we had a good appreciation of what was needed, we determined who we thought would be the best fit," says Mabey. In fact, of the six positions they quickly filled — two instructors, two sales people, a marketing person and a receptionist — all ended up coming from Learnix.

Learnix was still operating at that time, even though its future was uncertain. So it required a big leap of faith for employees who were considering jumping ship to join the new start-up. "We really had to rely on these folks joining us based on a belief and a trust that we knew what we were doing, and could really grow this vision that we had," says Ham. "The other decision they consciously made was that they weren't giving up a good living. We didn't want them to take a step backwards. We believed 100 percent that we could make this thing go. So we were willing to make that upfront commitment to them. Everybody essentially came on board for the same remuneration they were making at Learnix. That made the decision a lot easier for them."

It was a much riskier proposition for Ham and Mabey, who had to start paying staff salaries even before the company had any revenue coming in through the door. "We were paying their salaries out of our pockets and making nothing ourselves at the start."

Having Sun as an anchor for their fledgling company gave the partners a measure of confidence, but they were well aware that to depend on a single vendor was a risky proposition. "From the get-go, it was our strategy to bring in new vendors," says Ham. "That task was made easier because of the confidence and trust we had established in the relationships with other vendors at Learnix."

As long as Learnix remained in business, however, the partners met a mixed reaction whenever they made new contacts. They were the new kids on the block and their reputation had still to be established. As soon, however, as Learnix did declare bankruptcy, many IT companies suddenly found themselves without a Canadian partner. "It left a lot of vendors exposed," says Ham.

Almost immediately, they signed a major deal with Veritas Software, since acquired by Symantec Corporation, and other vendors soon followed. As their client list grew, so did the complexity of the job, both from a sales and operational standpoint. Each new vendor had its own way of doing things, meaning ExitCertified's growing team had to master a different range of processes. Ham and Mabey quickly came to realize they had underestimated the challenge of managing multiple vendor businesses in an ever-changing environment.

"It's been a challenge," Ham says. "But I think one of the strengths that Tim and I have — one that has allowed us to grow so quickly — is that we had a good appreciation of the training business and a really good understanding of what our partners expected of us. We were able to convey those expectations to our staff, who were themselves experienced in the sales and operations side. They have been a tremendous help in allowing us to manage growth."

For the next five years, Ham and Mabey had a "really exciting" time as they pursued new vendor relationships. IBM and Oracle signed them up, so did Red Hat, MySQL, Apple and others. As word spread, other vendors began seeking them out. "We started to develop good brand awareness within the training industry, and we've had several situations where vendors have approached us first," Ham says.

Winning a premier reputation didn't come without effort. In the tightly knit world of training, vendors keep an eagle eye on their training partners, closely monitoring the quality of their teaching and their ability to meet revenue targets. Every student who attends an ExitCertified course completes an evaluation form. "We will train 7,000 to 8,000 students this year, and we go through every single one of their evaluations," says Ham. "If there are issues and concerns we have to go back to the vendors with an action plan as to how we are not only going to resolve the situation, but to ensure that such situations are minimized in the future. When there's a partner that isn't performing, changes are made."

It is a tribute to ExitCertified that the only major adjustment it has been obliged to make is to continue to expand its presence in Canada as demand for its services have grown. The relationship with Sun, in particular, has proved mutually beneficial to the point that it has reached a level unique in the training industry. The partnership was cemented three years ago when Sun signed up ExitCertified to serve the Toronto market, making the company the single provider of Sun training for the whole of Canada.

At that point, says Ham, "They outsourced all of the sales and delivery of their training to us. We are now effectively Sun Learning Services in Canada. We work with three key individuals from Sun SLS Canada that manage the overall relationship internally, but we are the field organization from a sales and delivery standpoint."

Ham and Mabey have been careful when choosing vendors to avoid competitive conflicts. They decided not to partner with Microsoft because of a possible conflict of interest with Sun. They are confident their unique relationship with Sun would not have been possible had they done otherwise.

"In the training we provide there's not a lot of overlap or competition for the vendors," says Ham. "And that's why we're attractive to them. We're non-threatening to our vendors. We made a conscious decision from the get-go — and continue to make today — to be a pure training provider. There have been opportunities where even the vendor has approached us and said, 'Look, do you want to be selling our hardware or software as well, because you've got great relations with your customers?' But we made the decision not to pursue those other opportunities because we wanted to be able to maintain our neutrality. We didn't want to be in a position where we could influence a customer's technology purchasing decision."

In just over seven years, ExitCertified has built a national training infrastructure in six major cities across Canada and serves smaller cities through on-site training. If a customer needs training in the Maritimes, Saskatchewan or Manitoba, the company can ship in equipment and an instructor. In fact, in terms of geographical expansion in Canada, the company has reached close to its optimal strength. It still sees opportunities within Canada for organic growth at its existing permanent centres by bringing on new partners. Apple, for example, was a recent client acquisition in 2008.

ExitCertified already has three locations in California and one in Phoenix, Arizona. Until the onset of the recession in late 2008, the lion's share of new opportunities for the company appeared to lie south of the border. Suddenly, however, no one could be sure what the immediate future would bring. Unwelcome as the economic slowdown was, it did however give the company a chance to catch its breath.

"Tim and I have been going through these discussions for a couple of years," says Ham. "We really haven't had a whole lot of time to relax, we have been expanding so quickly. In 2008 we made a conscious decision that it was in the best interests of the company to focus internally and to make sure that the company is built on a really strong foundation. It's fair to say that for the first five years we were playing catch-up. We were making the transition from a small to a medium-sized company. To keep that growth going we needed to make sure the infrastructure was in place. We've really focused on doing that, and with the slowdown in the market that ended up being a good decision. There were other opportunities for some pretty large markets and we purposely chose not to pursue those opportunities."

Because of the nature of the training industry, and its many different modalities, it is difficult to measure precisely what share of the market ExitCertified has corralled. But Ham believes with "a fair amount of confidence" that it is the second largest independent IT training company based in Canada, where it earns some two-thirds of its revenue. In 2008, total revenues amounted to $16 million, one-third coming from its U.S. centres.

"For the first five or six years we were doubling every two years," says Ham. The company has twice made PROFIT magazine's list of Canada's fastest growing companies. It placed 32nd overall on the Hot 50 list for companies with the fastest two-year growth for 2004/05. And, in 2008, it ranked 122nd on PROFIT 100's list measuring five-year growth. The company workforce has grown exponentially, with 65 full-time sales, administration and instructor personnel, plus part-timers and a large number of contractors.

In a business where technical skills are highly prized, retaining employees is an ever-present challenge that ExitCertified works hard to meet. With staff spread across two countries, conference calls are a monthly fixture. Regional managers talk every week.

"We really try to get everybody to understand that it's all about how their individual effort contributes to the greater good and that's a challenge certainly, given all the offices we have and the geography," says Mabey. "We constantly ask for feedback and we try to empower our regional managers who are responsible for the overall management of morale in their regions. We have an HR person, and an HR consultant, and we push this whole thing of honesty."

Being honest with staff means giving them the bad news along with the good. "Like everyone else on the planet" ExitCertified was recording softer numbers during the recession. Says Mabey: "We're telling everybody where we're at, and that it's not like the last six years of 'yee-ha, look at the growth!' We tell them that everything they do makes a difference. We ask for feedback and what we get is very positive. It confirms that our culture is one of teamwork."

Ham and Mabey say they are "big fans of one-off recognition," especially for administrative and non-commissioned employees among whom it is sometimes harder to assess achievement. Rewards might be in the form of dinners out, gift certificates, or company wide recognition through e-mails or monthly conference calls during the "Beyond the Call" portion. This is in addition to commissions for the sales team and bonuses to the instructor group for extensive travel.

"We've been fortunate that our retention rate is high," says Mabey. "I think it's the individual recognition that helps, and the honesty, telling people where we're at. We tell them what we can do and what we can't. The result is everybody is willing to step up when asked. Our main function is to make sure they're happy doing what they do, because we can't do it all ourselves."

Ham and Mabey also believe that if people take pride in the organization, and feel that they have contributed to its success, it will help with retention and overall commitment. Along with the PROFIT magazine lists, the company has garnered a number of awards from vendor partners such as Oracle, winning Partner of the Year, sales achievement and overall instructor quality awards over the past couple of years.

"One of the awards we are particularly proud of is the bronze award for the 2007 Ottawa Chamber of Commerce Mid-Market Business of the Year," says Mabey. "It is very rewarding to be recognized by the members of your own business community."

Every three months or so, Ham and Mabey get together away from the office and the "day-to-day stuff" to think outside the box. "The first question we ask ourselves is 'Are we still happy doing what we're doing?'" says Ham. "Second, 'What do we want the business to look like in the future?' From my standpoint, I love the learning aspect of the business and the opportunity of being your own boss."

Both partners, perhaps surprisingly, saw the economic recession as less of a threat, more as an opportunity. "The most exciting thing we're going through right now is actually the downturn in the market," says Ham. "It's something new for us, not something we've had a whole lot of exposure to. We need to put our thinking caps on and figure out, not only how to get through the softness, but how to differentiate ourselves from some of the competition. Now is the time we should be making strategic decisions for when the market starts to pick up, so we're in a good position to benefit from that. So, despite the challenges, we're looking at making some significant investments in technology to help the business and trying to anticipate where we think the future of learning is going."

Mabey shares his partner's enthusiasm: "What do we do when this recession finally turns around? That's the message we're giving to everybody in the organization. Personally, for me, it's very exciting. We're confident we're going to get through it, even though there are some painful things that we might have to do. Who knows? Are we looking at a year before this thing turns around? To be able to control our future so that it fits in to the world when things get going again — that's fun for me, that's exciting."

ExitCertified has been blessed by the fact that its two founding partners possess different but complementary skill sets. Ham, with his extensive formal education, has guided growth on the sales side and monitored the financial picture. Mabey, at 42 the elder of the partners by five years, has extensive managerial experience in the U.S., the Caribbean and South Africa. He looks after operations and human resources. The two men combine their talents on the marketing side. Because of this, and unlike many fast-growing new companies, ExitCertified has had little need to recruit organizational advice from the outside.

"At Learnix, we worked for an individual where it was trial by fire," says Mabey. "If you were capable, the opportunity to learn was massive. When we started this company we knew the risks involved. We knew what cash flow was all about. We knew how important that was."

Despite the differences between the two partners, "We seem to just click," says Mabey. "We've always been honest and able to talk to each other. One of the main concerns people had when we started this business was, 'What about you guys? How are you protecting yourselves? You might start fighting and it all goes.' Fortunately, that's never happened, and we've been together a long time."

Both partners agree: "We have always wanted to run an ethical and moral organization. That's what drove us to start our own organization, because of what we were seeing on the other side."

FOODSERVICE AND HOSPITALITY

CANADA'S HOSPITALITY BUSINESS MAGAZINE

PLUS: SENSATIONAL SOUS-VIDE · HOLDING SERVE · TIP

PLUS THE 2009 FRANCHISE REPORT

MUCHO GUSTO

The three amigos behind Mucho Burrito put an extreme spin on Mexican QSR chains

FEBRUARY 2009 · $20

The 3 Amigos behind Extreme Brandz – Parent Company of Extreme Pita and Mucho Burrito

Co-founders of Extreme Pita – Alex and Mark Rechichi

Extreme Brandz

Back in 1996, brothers Alex and Mark Rechichi were having a day much like any other. Alex was in his car at an airport parking lot waiting for Mark to return from a business trip to Cuba. Both men, although only in their 20s, had already enjoyed relative success in the business world. Mark, a chartered accountant and chartered financial analyst, was working with Price Waterhouse. Alex was in sales and marketing for an industrial supply company. An objective observer might have seen two good looking, university educated Italian boys on their way to a bright and secure future. The observer might not have guessed — and the Rechichi brothers themselves did not know — that this day would change everything.

As Alex was idly flipping through a copy of Entrepreneur magazine, he was perhaps recalling their carefree high school days when he and Mark had run a couple small businesses. One such venture, cleaning and sealing interlocking brick driveways, had helped put them both through Queen's University. Or perhaps Alex was feeling the pull of his family's entrepreneurial genes and hearing his family's advice about working for yourself: "You could make just as much money as you make now, if not more. It might take you a little bit longer but at least you'll enjoy what you're doing for yourself."

Whatever was in Alex's mind, in front of his eyes in this particular issue of Entrepreneur was an article on the subject of sandwiches — specifically, submarine sandwiches. Food had always drawn Alex's attention and, being a good businessman, the enormous potential of the sub chains caught his entrepreneurial fancy. One brand that stood out was Blimpy's. Chuckling over what he considered an amusing name, he read further into the article. He discovered that Blimpy's had 2,000 locations — no laughing matter at all — and as he put down

the magazine he experienced what he calls his "lightbulb moment —
it made me realize how big the category was. I had no idea." When
Mark jumped into his brother's car, the copy of Entrepreneur was
tossed into his lap as Alex drove down the highway like a man on a
mission, exclaiming: "Take a drive with me! I want to take you out
to a couple places."

One year later the brothers were celebrating the opening of their
first sandwich shop, Extreme Pita. No one who knew them well was
surprised. After all, they had smarts, they had drive and creativity
and they'd already proven they could work well together. What few
could have predicted, including the brothers themselves, was that
12 years later they would be running a supremely successful, multi-
branded platform with close to 300 franchise locations operating
in Canada and the United States. Today, they have expectations of
crossing the 500-store mark by the end of 2010 with expansion into
overseas markets.

Opening one small sandwich shop with no restaurant experience
is one thing. Creating an internationally established franchise
operation with combined revenues of over $80 million is quite
another. Alex, the younger of the two brothers by 15 months, tells
the story of how it happened while sitting at his desk at Extreme
Brandz' head office in Mississauga, west of Toronto. Situated in an
industrial type park on a quiet side street, the one-storey building
is as unassuming in appearance as the President of Extreme Brandz
himself. Despite their success, there is nothing pretentious about the
offices, no ostentatious furnishings or lavishly appointed lobby. But
there is a sense of playfulness. It is reflected in the bright, primary
blues, reds and yellows — the brand colours of Extreme Pita. A
tray of fresh pita sandwiches sits on the reception counter. Product
development and sandwich experimentation takes place in a fully
equipped training kitchen. The business of sandwiches seems like a
lot of fun.

The casual atmosphere belies the serious business behind the scenes — much like Alex's ready laugh, relaxed disposition and casual openness overlie a shrewd business sense. Asked if the ever-expanding sandwich empire truly started from his "lightbulb moment" in the parking lot, Alex grins, "Pretty much."

And therein lies a key difference. Many budding entrepreneurs may experience their own "lightbulb moment," but most take it no further. The bulb dims and burns out. The Rechichi brothers, like all successful entrepreneurs, understand there's no reward without risk, no satisfaction without sacrifice. And when you're opening a restaurant with zero restaurant experience, sometimes, the brothers say, it's not a bad thing to suffer from a little ignorance.

"When we first started, our lawyer said: 'I'm not sure whether entrepreneurs are the smartest people or the dumbest people,'" Mark recalls, speaking on the phone from his Montreal office. "You start off doing something you love but you're not making any money doing it. Once you do, you've gotta stay focused, make a decision and go for it and stick to your guns."

The brothers didn't take long to make their initial decision. What they lacked in restaurant experience they made up for in a belief in hard work and a passion for food that sprang from, as Alex says, "growing up in an Italian family."

While growing up, Alex and Mark remember good food as being a big part of the way they enjoyed family. They recall huge Christmas dinners at their grandparents' house in Montreal where sometimes 70 people would all gather in the spirit of feasting and family, with his grandmother making fresh pasta and his grandfather roasting fresh lamb. From a very early age, they were exposed to fresh, quality foods. They continue the tradition of healthy eating in their restaurants that boast fresh, quality ingredients with no additives and feature nutritional information in every location. Their parents would approve. "It's the way we were raised," Alex says. "Both my father and my mother love to cook and that just gets passed down to you when you're exposed to that."

Perhaps in retrospect, it's no surprise that the Rechichi brothers would prosper in the food business. But pitas and burritos? It goes back to the lightbulb moment, when Alex first recognized the possibilities in a simple sandwich. That, combined with his personal leanings to fresh, quality ingredients and healthful living, led him initially to pitas. At the time, pita sandwiches weren't nearly as omnipresent as the sub chains. They were still considered "ethnic." But what pitas did offer was a healthier alternative to the bread-heavy submarine sandwiches that had initially piqued Alex's interest.

"I liked the fact that there was a healthy connotation to pita bread and there really wasn't a chain out there focusing on pita bread. So Mark and I looked at that and we said: 'Well, is there a way to bring this into the mainstream?'"

Armed with the glimmer of an idea, the brothers toured a couple of restaurant operations that offered various sandwiches, including pitas. At the time, few if any locations were devoted exclusively to the pita sandwich, which, combined with the trend towards a healthy lifestyle, seemed fortuitous.

"People in the mid-90s were really starting to focus on not just working out or being athletic, but also balancing that with the right eating," Alex says. "A lot of those things started to permeate the industry and you started to see the largest sub chain in the world focusing their efforts on 'Eat fresh' or 'We're healthy, we're healthy, we're healthy.'" The trend, combined with the relative obscurity of the pita sandwich, seemed a perfect fit with the interests of the two entrepreneurial siblings.

"We talked about it," says Alex. "I stated my position about really focusing on the health benefits with pita bread and we both saw the opportunity that that's where the market was going." Adds Mark: "Today, people of all ages, nationalities and gender are much more educated about the nutritional benefits of what they eat."

It didn't take much to convince the brothers that backing pitas was a wise move. Next step — open a restaurant. But first — money!

After checking their respective bank accounts, Alex and Mark came up with $5,000 each to invest in the enterprise. They realized a need for partners: "We didn't want to borrow from our parents, in case something went drastically wrong. After all, we did not know anything about the business we were getting into other than what people told us. Most new restaurants fail, and the industry is highly competitive." Some calls were made to a few close friends and old high school buddies who were persuaded to take a chance on the enterprise. "Our friends trusted us," says Alex. "They knew that we were hardworking, no bullshit type of guys who always said things the way they were. I'm sure they saw the passion we had about the venture," says Alex.

Mark recalls hanging out at their parents' place with their new partners trying to decide on the first restaurant location. A simple solution presented itself. "We said, 'What do we know best?'" Alex said. "Well, we had just graduated from university … let's start in a university market.'" Prophetic words, as it turned out. They didn't know it then, but their first location choice would end up being part of a blueprint they followed for successive locations, an integral part of their future success.

One of their partners, a former football captain at Wilfred Laurier University in Waterloo, suggested opening a restaurant near his alma mater, an hour's drive from the Rechichis' home in Mississauga. They took a drive to Waterloo and found a location. Although it was in an alley, with no visibility from the main street, it was directly across from the university. The consensus was, according to Mark, "Okay, why don't we do this? We didn't know anything about the location selection other than the rent was good and they didn't want a personal guarantee."

And so the work began, literally from the ground up. Still working fulltime at their 'day' jobs, the brothers spent every spare minute at the restaurant, sleeping in a back room, renovating the premises and working on recipes in their mother's kitchen. They pulled every favour they could, including using their father's services as a contractor to help build the restaurant.

"We didn't know anything about construction but then my dad would come in and save the day. He'd say to us, 'Okay, what the hell are you guys doing?' We must have had, like, $3,000 worth of 2 x 4s in the front counter alone. I don't know how it held. I don't know how they passed permits when I look back today. I think they just felt sorry for us and it wasn't worth the headache," Mark says with a chuckle. A year later, the first Extreme Pita opened on Feb. 7, 1997, coincidentally Alex's birthday. "We moved fast," he says.

Between word of mouth and a good marketing push, Extreme Pita took off and, in Alex's words, became "wildly successful." Although their decision to open a second restaurant seemed obvious, there were differences of opinion between the Rechichis and their three partners as to the vision and direction they were taking. The brothers were always on the same page — "blood is thicker than water" — sharing the perspective that whatever money they made should go directly back into the business. "We weren't doing this to make an extra $25,000 or $30,000 a year," Mark says. "We were doing this to build something."

Little differences with the partners turned into big differences, according to Alex, and they hit a crossroads. At one point, as they were driving to a meeting, Alex said to Mark: "It's just not worth it. Let's just get out and let these guys run with it and we'll go do something else." They pulled into a parking lot and sat for several minutes. "I looked over at Mark and said, 'You know what? I don't know if I want to let this thing go so easily.'"

They didn't. With financial help from their parents, they bought out the partners and went at it "full tilt." While still working at their full-time jobs, they opened a second restaurant and worked nights and weekends between both locations, with a plan to continue expanding the business. Then they heard from someone interested in obtaining a franchise. It came from an unlikely source — Alex's boss at his day job, Steve Travers. "Believe it or not, he was out on the town one night and ended up dropping into our pita shop. He saw me working behind the counter late on a Saturday night," says Alex. Intrigued, Travers expressed interest in Alex's double life and soon became the first franchisee.

Committed to growing the business, but in need of additional capital, the brothers brought in an uncle as a silent investor. Then a second franchisee, Sean Black, joined the team and opened the first Ottawa franchise. Black later became responsible for developing the Ottawa market. He was young, too, but he had some restaurant experience. At the age of 18, he had opened an independent coffee shop. It became a thriving, high-volume enterprise. "He kind of took a stab in the dark and said, 'I'd like to become a partner,'" Alex says.

Although they felt a bond with Black, the brothers weren't keen on adding partners because of their previous experience. Neither was willing to give up shares. Instead, they suggested to Black that if he could reach an agreement with their uncle to buy out his shares, they'd be willing to work it out, as long as Black understood where they were coming from.

Alex recalls: "I said to him, 'As long as you understand that I'm not pulling a salary and neither is Mark and there's a lot of sweat equity going into this. If you're willing to make that commitment with us up front, then I'm comfortable with you working out an arrangement to buy the silent partner out.'"

Today, Black not only remains as a "not so silent" partner, but he is currently Vice President of Development.

Before Black's arrival, a similar situation had developed with Travers. He didn't have the money to buy out the silent partner, but what he lacked in finances he made up for in enthusiasm and an interest in broadening the scope of the concept. Travers approached the brothers to express both an interest in greater involvement and a desire to move to Western Canada.

"We said, 'Okay, if you want to be the guy to take this concept to a market and start it from scratch out there, let's see if we can work out a joint venture,'" Alex says.

A tour of British Columbia and Alberta ensued, with the result that Calgary was chosen as a base, partly because "it felt a lot like home" in a city offering many of the same large brands found in Ontario. There was a sense of familiarity about it, Alex said. Under a joint venture with Travers to develop Alberta, the brothers took 51 per cent of the new company. Currently, Travers is Area Developer for a territory that now also encompasses British Columbia. He has 70 restaurants under his direction.

In the early years, before Black came on board in 1999, Alex and Mark were still working nine-to-five jobs during the day. They were still living with their parents, working in the basement until midnight on their restaurants. Despite the huge workload, they had managed to build the business into four or five restaurants.

"At the time I was thinking it's just ridiculous the hours we were working," says Alex. "Obviously it impacted all the personal relationships in our lives. We were consumed by full-time jobs and the company we were trying to build, so when Sean (Black) decided he was coming on board, I decided it was time for me to move on."

The deciding moment came when he answered the phone one day saying 'Extreme Pita." Only problem was that the phone he answered was at his day job. "It was really a moment of, 'Oh damn, there's a clue. It's time for me to move on.'"

And move on they did. With Black and Mark both on board with Alex, they pushed ahead, opening a handful of scattered restaurants in what Alex dubbed a "shotgun approach" to development. The three of them settled into their respective roles with Mark looking after finance and accounting, Alex focusing on development and Black, with his previous restaurant experience, taking on operations. Black had also brought along with him one of his restaurant managers to take on the role of helping to open new restaurants and train new franchisees. Events moved quickly. In a few years, the trio had gone from opening five to 10 stores a year to opening almost 50 restaurants all across Canada in 2004 alone.

With their Canadian operation growing successfully, the brothers' next goal was to infiltrate the U.S. market. Since the shotgun approach had worked so well in Canada, they adopted a similar stance in the States. Alex and Black would keep an eye on discount flights and then randomly pick a university town to visit. "We thought about starting the same way we started here and trying to duplicate that model," he says.

Extensive travel ensued, by air and automobile, with Alex and Black visiting almost every campus on the Eastern Seaboard in an effort to assess the market. They found an area developer for Atlantic Canada while they continued to help Travers grow his Western Canada division. Their plan was to plant key people geographically throughout North America to be responsible for developing the brand in the local market. This model, based on exponential growth, was simply just good math, according to Alex. "You can do 100 to 150 restaurants a year quite conceivably within a decentralized development approach," he said. To this point, the operation was still a mobile, high energy, high-spirited business. Decisions were still made in a vigorous entrepreneurial style. As Alex puts it, "Whatever felt right in the gut, that was the decision."

But as the business grew larger, it was apparent that it was time for a formal decision-making structure and a long-term strategy. Although intuition would continue to serve, as it always had, this was no longer a two- or three-person operation. Roles between the brothers and Black became more specifically defined and tailored to their strengths. They began hiring seasoned executives and managers who could run their own departments and develop their own people. Currently, there are 27 people working at Extreme Brandz' head office in Mississauga, with others working in Western Canada, Montreal and in a satellite office in Arizona. In all, counting the franchisees, with 10 people per store minimum and various regional overseers, there are currently close to 3,000 people working within the Extreme Brandz family.

Extreme Brandz is now firmly established in the U.S., with about 35 restaurants opened and 50 more expected in 2010. Its first American restaurant opened in the unlikely town of Blacksburg, Virginia, at Virginia Tech University. "Don't ask me how we started there," Alex laughs. How it happened was fittingly random for the early days. A Canadian franchisee decided to move to Blacksburg and opened a restaurant. It did well, but when problems arose they tired of the enterprise, sold their assets and returned to Canada.

The lesson the brothers learned was that, when operating in America, go with Americans. As it happened, some Americans ran across the brand while travelling in Canada and their interest led to the real beginning of U.S. development. Starting off in Arizona, development has since spread widely with area developers now located in central, southern and northern California, Texas, all of New England, Washington State and Las Vegas.

With Extreme Pita's seemingly limitless potential, the brothers might be forgiven for resting on their laurels. But that would go against their entrepreneurial natures. Having spent a good deal of time in the U.S. building the brand, they found themselves eating a lot of gourmet Mexican food. Much as they did with pitas, the partners recognized that Mexican food was highly underrepresented in Canada. They saw that a burrito could have the same potential as a pita sandwich — the wrap was light and the fillings could be made from quality, fresh ingredients with an emphasis on healthy eating. Intrigued, they began to imagine how best to capture the brand. They elected to personify it in a character named Johnny Mucho.

Says Alex: "We said we wanted the music to be cool, we want it to be a bit rugged, we don't want it to be Juan Valdez-ish Mexican, we want it to be hip and current and we thought, 'Y'know, Mucho is a cool name . . . how about Johnny Mucho?" Adds Mark: "Everyone likes a Johnny. He's always a good guy."

Johnny Mucho isn't a visible presence in the restaurants. He appears only in cartoon form on the wall of Alex's office, complete with a back story that includes his guitar playing abilities and a hot senorita girlfriend named Maria. "We've kept him in the background because we haven't figured out exactly how he's going to represent the brand. We don't want to do it in a tacky way," Alex says. "For now, it's our internal spoof of Johnny. It's kind of fun." Although Johnny Mucho is an imaginary character for the moment, Alex says he'd like to see the "King of Burritos, Purveyor of Food and Music and Love" come to life one day. "I like to believe he is a real person somewhere out there and probably does exist. You never know, he might actually come to visit us one day."

The Mucho Burrito brand was introduced in 2007, the same year that the company became Extreme Brandz. Two years later, Mucho Burrito had 21 locations in Canada and 25 more in development. Initially, Alex says, they were going to focus solely on Canada, but because of the interest in the U.S., it was likely the Mucho Burrito brand would soon follow Extreme Pita into the American market.

The burritos offered in the new restaurants are packed full of healthy, fresh ingredients in varying flavour combinations and dressed up with a Mexican flair. Quality as usual is key, and skimping is not an option. "We said we didn't want to sell a 99-cent burrito. We wanted to sell quality, we wanted to sell freshness and we wanted to sell it in an environment that people are going to enjoy. And Mucho Burrito has been very successful for us," Alex says. "We're one of the fortunate multi-branded platforms where we've got two very, very successful growing brands and there's a lot of interest in both of them."

A big part of Extreme Brandz' ongoing success is due not only to concepts that focus on fresh, customized foods, but also to the diligence of its creators in staying ahead of industry curves in terms of flavour profiles and trends. The product development kitchen is a busy, innovative place that has created a pita lineup including Thai, Rustic Italian, Fiesta Mexicana, Mandarin Asian and Philly Cheesesteak, among others. The marketplace trending to healthier lifestyles in the early days not only helped shape their mission statement, it earned them a growing, loyal customer base that was craving a "quality, quick service restaurant."

"Our core customer is someone who lives life to the fullest, is active, always on the go, and they don't want to sacrifice choices in the food decisions they make. There are flavour profiles, there's depth, there's selection, there's customization — all the things you wouldn't expect in a typical fast food environment. "We don't pretend to say, 'Just eat pitas or burritos and you're going to be super healthier.' It's about a lifestyle."

In accordance with that healthy lifestyle, much attention is paid not only to the freshness of the vegetables and fruits but also to the types of ingredients. Again, ahead of the curve, Alex states that Extreme Brandz uses only non-processed and non-genetically modified foods.

"The first movement was healthy eating and the next movement is, 'What kind of food are you really eating?' Are there dyes in my food? Are they processed? Are there antibiotics or hormones, what is the origin of the raw material, how was this animal fed and cared for?'"

Since the first day of operation, Extreme Pita was one of the first chains to post nutritional information at the point of ordering. According to Alex, 50 per cent of their customers order off the information, which also includes pocket guides and nutritional calculators on the website. It would be safe to say that Alex subscribes to a term he recently heard: "Healthy is the new wealthy."

Putting their money where their mouth is, so to speak, the Rechichis also parlay some of their wealth into health by their involvement with numerous charitable endeavours. In 2006, they were the national supporter of the Easter Seals Drop Zone to help children with physical disabilities. They recently supported the 24-Hour Spin at the Hershey Centre in Mississauga to raise money for the Trillium Health Centre Foundation, where they donated 4,000 pitas to participating cyclists. And over and above their ongoing support of various other local charities, they recently founded their own charity called Extreme Pita Cares. Through that foundation, they will support charities focused on children and health and advancing children through education or sport in healthy lifestyles. Both brothers are married, with three children each, and fully appreciate the role good nutrition and a healthy, active lifestyle plays in the well-being of children and families.

Whether it's for their business savvy or their charitable work, it's easy to see why the Rechichis have garnered numerous awards and recognition for their efforts. The walls of the modest waiting room at Extreme Brandz' head office boast a collection of prestigious plaques and certificates, including but not limited to the Caldwell Partners' Canada's Top 40 Under 40 Award in 2007 and the Foodservice and Hospitality Magazine's Pinnacle Award for Entrepreneurs of the Year in 2006.

Among the notable recognitions they've received over the years, Alex mentions that he and Mark also recently received a New Generations Award from the Italian Chamber of Commerce.

As to where the Rechichis go from here, there's no shortage of ideas or opportunities. A third brand is in the works and the international market beckons, with a focus on the Middle East, Australia and New Zealand. They've spent time investigating the Chinese marketplace and, according to what Alex has discovered, there's no market like it in the world. "China is a market that would just swallow up our two brands," he says. "I think we would do phenomenally there." Had he ever dreamt he would be discussing China as a viable future market? Alex laughs and shakes his head. "I remember sitting there with my brother when we had one restaurant, way back when, and I said to Mark, 'One day we're going to have six restaurants.' Here we are now, sitting on the verge of eclipsing 300 very shortly. Our goal is 500 in the next two years."

And after that?

"After that, we want to be one of the Canadian success stories that has well over 1,000 restaurants in operation." There's no doubt that as long as the Rechichi brothers and their partner Sean Black remain passionate about their vision, there's nothing stopping their brand evolving into a ubiquitous player on the world stage.

Scott Gilmore, Kevin Higgins, Tim Magwood and the Fusion Team

(left to right) Scott Gilmore, Partner, Tim Magwood, Founding Partner and Kevin Higgins, Managing Partner

Fusion Learning Inc.

An actor, an artist and a businessman walk into a bar and — this is no joke — they build a company that is one of the fastest growing of its kind in Canada. Tim Magwood, Kevin Higgins and Scott Gilmore, the three formidable partners behind Fusion Learning Inc., have managed to put their different skills and diverse talents together to grow an enterprise that has become a leading player in the sales learning industry.

And today when walk into a bar, which they've been known to do, there's plenty to celebrate about their company's steady success story. As founding partner Magwood says, "We've been very good at celebrating along the way."

On paper, success for Fusion can be measured easily enough by its inclusion in Profit magazine's list of Canada's 100 fastest growing companies for two years running (2007 and 2008 for results in 2006/07 respectively) and by its steadily increasing revenues. In the past few years, revenues have jumped dramatically, with 2008 showing a 33-per-cent increase over the previous year, hitting $3.5 million. According to Higgins, the initial 2007 listing reflected Fusion's growth over five years from $200,000 to $1.8 million.

"We set the base in 2002 to 2004 and then we accelerated," managing partner Higgins notes. "The acceleration was so great we made the Profit 100 in 2007 and made it again in 2008 and we will be close for 2009."

Despite the economic downturn of 2009, Magwood was predicting Fusion would still hit its predicted target of $4 million for the year. The goal, according to Magwood and Higgins, is to become a $10-million firm within five years and be recognized as the go-to sales effectiveness brand in Canada. The target is right on track and Fusion's focus is clear.

"We're not trying to grow like crazy," Higgins says, adding that they have no desire to license out their business, open other offices or buy up other companies.

What they want, he says, is strong, well-managed growth concentrating on three main areas: sales strategy, sales leadership and sales effectiveness.

"What we're interested in is to stay true to our philosophy that we deliver great results, we make a difference in the organizations we work with, we make a big difference for the people who work for us and we are truly successful."

Steadily increasing revenues tell only one side of the Fusion success story. Ultimately, it's the people who make the company. And among Fusion's personnel, you couldn't ask for a more likeable or professional cast of characters.

From the age of 21 to 24, Magwood was a professional theatre actor, taking his bows in such vaunted productions as Les Miserables and Napoleon. In between his turns on the big stage, he did television and commercial work. After "doing the actor thing," which included stints of "waiting tables around the edges," Magwood says he came to realize: "Damn, this is hard, man."

Today, as Magwood relaxes in a conference room at Fusion's Toronto office, he embodies the character of a successful businessman. But the actor is never far from the surface. It's there in his engaging manner and his infectious passion for all the parts he's played, both past and present.

A turning point in his life came when as a young actor his attention was drawn to a production he enjoyed from the other side of the footlights. This was a show called The Old Man's Band (Jon Roby) that was produced by the Blyth Festival, a respected home to Canadian theatre for 35 years.

"I loved it," Magwood recalls. "I thought: Wow, what a great show. It deserves a home in Toronto."

Magwood suddenly found himself in a new and unfamiliar role.

He determined to bring The Old Man's Band to a new audience. And what he may have lacked in business acumen, he more than made up for in boundless enthusiasm for the project.

"I loved it so much that, you know what? I incorporated a business called Magwood Productions and I got the rights to the show within the GTA (Greater Toronto Area) for a limited amount of time. I got a director, I cast it and put it on at the du Maurier Theatre."

Within six months, Magwood had accomplished the remarkable feat of putting the business together, securing the rights, marketing the production, selling it, casting it and finally holding a three-week run of the musical cabaret show. The result of this whirlwind of activity netted the fledgling producer four Dora nominations and plaudits from Geoff Chapman, a Toronto critic who praised it in December 1994 as the highlight of Toronto theatre.

For a guy who graduated from Queen's University with a degree in drama, Magwood says his experience was an intense crash course in business. Magwood Productions was, in effect, his equivalent of an MBA.

"But it was better than an MBA, because I had to do everything — the sales, the marketing, the business plan, the financials — although I didn't do so well on the financials," he says with an easy grin.

Magwood's creative flair combines with the entrepreneurial genes he says he inherited from his father. And, from his mother, he inherited a love for teaching and coaching. And in building Fusion Learning he has found an outlet for all his skills and passions. It's a role in which he can help to communicate to clients his strategies and his enthusiasm.

"I've always loved to help people grow," Magwood says. "You might say I have the heart of a teacher, the brain of an entrepreneur and the soul of an artist."

After giving up the stage, Magwood worked first for Corel Corporation as public relations manager. He spearheaded reviews and editorial coverage for Corel's consumer and Internet products and acted as the company's spokesperson on radio and television throughout North America. He followed this with a stint at Nexus Interactive as a founding partner, overseeing the branding and development of its initial web presence and acting as client liaison. Moving on, Magwood then landed at ICE (Integrated Communications & Entertainment) where, as executive producer of "the CN Tower multimedia installation," he led his teams to conceptualize, blueprint and produce a $1.5-million interactive exhibit at the base of the CN Tower, garnering the team a New Media Magazine "Invision Award" silver medal in 1998.

The following year, 1999, at Horn and Associates, Magwood found himself back in the relished role of trainer and training consultant, bringing his coaching skills to such well-known clients as Pitney Bowes and IBM. Although Magwood didn't foresee a long-term future with Horn, the sales learning field felt like a perfect fit. It fulfilled his love of coaching and offered room for artistic expression. The only thing his job at Horn wasn't fulfilling was his entrepreneurial drive. Recognizing a void, Magwood set about to correct it.

"I asked myself, 'Why isn't there a de facto leader in the sales learning business in Canada?'"

Answer: Create one.

Crediting Horn with allowing him the freedom to restructure his role and become a contractor while simultaneously starting up a competing business, Magwood seized his moment.

"My vision was to create a business that would be the sales learning leader in Canada within 10 years," Magwood recalls, adding, "We are well on track."

Today, Fusion's downtown Toronto office is a sprawling 5,200-square-foot renovated warehouse space with a calm, welcoming atmosphere. It's a far cry from Magwood's cramped basement where he began developing his vision in what he dubs his "rugged individualistic phase".

"Picture this," he says. "It's July of 2000 and I'm in the basement on a phone call with a client. I've got a six-month-old at the time, Ryan, who is crying upstairs, the dog is barking. And I'm saying to the client, 'Can you hold a minute?'"

For a year-and-a-half Magwood toiled in his basement office, largely subcontracting clients through Horn, and coming to realize that being a 'rugged individualist' was a struggle. Once again, he found himself wearing all the hats, doing the work, designing the work, doing the accounting, selling the work. And although he was skilled at, and motivated by, the sales and delivery end of things, Magwood found he was doing only a quarter of what he wanted to do.

"I kept asking myself, 'Why am I doing this? This is crazy!' And I just barely hung in there, I would say."

What he did cling to was his belief that something would come of all his hard work, a belief that has been more than realized with Fusion's success and recognition within the industry. But for all its charms, individualism has its limits and Magwood well understood the value of a supportive ensemble cast in broadening the scope of his vision.

Enter Kevin Higgins, bearing the gift of business management expertise. Or, as Higgins himself drily puts it: "I'm the token business guy."

An Honours Business Administration graduate of the Richard Ivey School of Business at the University of Western Ontario, Higgins initially chose to teach at his alma mater for two years as an instructor of Introductory Business to first-year students. With business and teaching under his belt, Higgins next changed gears to sales at Xerox Canada as senior account representative, where he stayed for two years, earning Toronto East District Sales Representative of the Year in his first year. With teaching and sales as two of his acknowledged passions, Higgins found himself gravitating to the world of sales learning, a milieu that complemented his interests and skills.

From 1992, Higgins found a home for 10 years at Forum Corporation, a global leadership and sales learning company, where he steadily moved up through the ranks from sales to consulting to eventually Executive Vice President, Midwest U.S.A. and Canada. In this role, Higgins turned the two divisions around in record time.

"I turned it around from low-morale/unprofitable to high-morale/profitable," Higgins says of the Canadian division that he grew from $1.5-million in revenue to $5.5-million in 18 months.

"From that I was asked by Forum to turn around another division, which was the Midwest U.S. division, and same thing. I turned that office around."

As part of Forum's management team, Higgins was responsible for 60 people and about $15 million in revenue of a $75-million company. But, after 10 years, he concedes he was looking for a new challenge. In a fortunate bit of timing, a decision was made to sell Forum in 2000. The sale only confirmed Higgins' decision to leave the company. After doing some contract work for Forum, and taking time off to travel, he was a free agent by the spring of 2002. Having had ample time to consider his options, Higgins says he decided that he wanted to have equity in a business, to be part and partner in either a business that was in trouble that he could turn around, or a good concept that he could help to grow.

By good fortune, he met Magwood, who had been scouting around for assistance on an early project.

Magwood recalls: "A good friend of Kevin said, 'You should talk to this great guy, Kevin Higgins, who is talented and smart and all these great things.'"

Their early discussions revolved around making Fusion a product-based business — Higgins' short-lived idea — or a sales oriented e-learning business — Magwood's idea. Both proposals were scuttled because of the huge technology investment required. Together they realized a common goal in focusing exclusively on sales learning with the aim of making Fusion a leader in the field.

As Higgins points out, the start-up for sales learning is comparatively minimal. "If you do classroom-based learning, the capital required is a pack of flip charts and markers and a computer that can print out some paper. So there is an investment there, but you can start creating that pretty easily."

Higgins was further encouraged by Magwood's willingness to take on a partner. And he also liked Magwood's choice of the company name, Fusion. Although Magwood had considered a few different names, he was always clear on one thing: "I didn't want it to be Magwood & Associates."

"I didn't want my name in it. That was a pretty conscious decision," Magwood says. "To me, Magwood & Associates was very limiting. I wanted it to be bigger than Tim Magwood. I always wanted it to be an organization that was progressive and dynamic."

"When he told me that story," says Higgins, "it was attractive to me because I know he was expecting from the beginning that there would be other partners.

"When I came full circle, from products back to learning, the thing that attracted me here was that Tim was willing to give up sole ownership in the business. Tim was saying, 'I get that you're bringing a lot to the table,' and so he was willing to sell me some of the equity in the business."

With Higgins happily on board after purchasing 50 percent of the company in 2002, he joined Magwood in a 300 sq. ft. downtown Toronto office space to help put together a business plan. The plan called for the immediate hiring of two additional people, an office administrator/desktop publisher and a salesperson. With the two new hires, things were cramped for a few months until they moved to a 1,000 sq. ft. space in the same area. Revenues admittedly didn't cover the increase in overhead initially and much of 2003 was supported through subcontracting services to former employers Horn and Forum.

"At the end of 2003, Fusion was still a part-time project, really," Magwood notes.

But the next year, Fusion Learning Inc. realized its first million in revenues and by the summer both Magwood and Higgins ended their respective relationships with Horn and Forum and began using subcontractors themselves. "It was a breakthrough," says Higgins.

By 2006, the first year Fusion made the Profit 100 list, the company was steadily gaining momentum in terms of recognition and loyalty, revenues, clients and products. Higgins and Magwood saw the need for another professional in order to unlock the company's growth potential. That was when Scott Gilmore, an expert in sales and marketing, became an integral member of the Fusion team.

"Tim and I are both good at selling and we're both good at delivering," says Higgins. "I'm good at running the business, but I was spread across all three and Tim was spread across two. So the model was that Scott would come in, then Tim would be in sales and marketing and delivery and I could start to ease out of the selling and run the business and deliver and produce."

Gilmore had been in the business for a while, says Higgins. "He had other places he could go, but he's like, 'I want to join you guys.' And he was willing to invest money into this young business."

Sealing the deal for both Fusion and Gilmore was the willingness of Magwood and Higgins to allow and encourage a third partner. For both Gilmore and Higgins it had always been an expectation and, for Magwood, a no-brainer.

"The reality is that high-calibre professional service folks need incentive to perform well and to stay around for more than two or three years," Magwood notes, adding that the model from the beginning was to have senior people able to participate in the equity.

"Part of what Scott brought to the table, because Kevin and I have been building the core offering as we went, was an expertise around vision and leadership. So Scott helped us create a new program called Strategic Sales BluePRINT, which is a strategy offering. He was instrumental in that."

Gilmore, now Vice President of Marketing, first invested in the company in January 2006. He was brought on board to head up sales and marketing and look after client acquisition and growth. Because Fusion has quadrupled in size since his arrival, he has now relinquished his sales leadership responsibilities to Brad McCamus, Fusion's current VP of Sales. This frees him up to concentrate on his Strategic Sales BluePRINT process and be on the executive team, finding and working with his own clients and heading up marketing, for which he professes a great passion.

Gilmore brought with him 16 years of experience in the training and development industry, primarily at his father's company, Gilmore & Associates, where he ultimately headed up sales and marketing. When his father, Blake, founded the company in 1980, the then 16-year-old Scott witnessed a company being built up virtually from scratch into a premier quality training and development company boasting sales of almost $10 million. Did this inspire him to follow in his dad's footsteps? Apparently not, according to the junior Gilmore.

"I wanted to be an artist," he says. This wasn't an idle dream. At 19, he enrolled in Toronto's Ontario College of Art (now the Ontario College of Art & Design) focusing on creative pursuits including painting, sculpting, photography and filmmaking. His passion for filmmaking led him to make several independent films, some of which were sold to such prestige organizations as CBC and CityTV.

His expertise behind the camera won the admiration of his father, whose company was now 10 years old. A good businessman and a proud father, he offered his son the opportunity to take charge of a prime project for Gilmore & Associates. Scott's assignment was to produce, direct and edit a major corporate video. "It was a massive video project that took an entire year of my life to complete," Gilmore says.

Blake and other key people at Gilmore & Associates were so impressed by Scott's work that they asked him if he would like to sell the project and do some consulting around it, a request that Scott concedes "scared" him at the time.

"I was young, I was green and I was naïve. And this was a total quality management system — calling on senior executives in Canadian business and selling them consulting services around strategy and leadership and continuous improvement and things like that."

"It was a bit of a tall order for a 26-year-old and it was a little daunting. But that was a major turning point for me and I decided, 'You know what? I think I can do this' and I stepped into it."

Since then, as Gilmore says: "There's been no turning back."

Gilmore & Associates was eventually sold to CDI Education, creating new opportunities for both father and son. Blake Gilmore was asked by Magwood and Higgins to serve on Fusion's board, a seat he has held for six years. Scott stayed at CDI for three years to help with the transition, before taking a sabbatical. Then he, too, approached Fusion.

"I was looking for an entrepreneurial, fast-growing, fast-moving company with like-minded people that I could really relate to and work well with and I was super fortunate to have found Fusion Learning and Tim Magwood and Kevin Higgins.

"I can say that joining Fusion and investing in this company has been the best business decision that I've made in my career. Working with creative, high-energy, like-minded partners and Fusion people — it's very exciting."

Scott Gilmore also considers himself fortunate to have worked alongside his father, who has played a large part in his son's career, including introducing him to the work Fusion was doing. Scott did his own research into the company and made his own decision to approach Fusion with a view to investing.

He doesn't do much in the way of fine art any more: "They work me too hard here to do my art," he jokes. But he does find his job at Fusion provides its own creative outlet.

"I believe that there's a very strong creative side to sales, more unconscious than conscious, and I also believe that there's certainly a creative side to the marketing equation of things. My artistic background lends itself well to that. I also think there's some creativity in how you approach business development, how you approach finding and working with clients.

"Some people say, 'Oh my God, what is it about training or this business that you love so much?' It may sound corny but this business is about helping people grow and reaching their full potential. It's also about providing them with some life skills to help them be more effective at work and in their personal life as well.

"We see that a lot. The impact of our work helps people become more successful in their careers and you say to yourself at the end of the day, 'Boy, what's not to love about that?' That's pretty gratifying stuff."

Listening to the three partners discussing Fusion's culture and strategic sales learning tools, one gets the sense that the learning and the teaching are complementary, each feeding off the other. All three share the sentiment that "we practice what we teach," meaning that the skills they share with their clients have already been tested in the Fusion laboratory. Gilmore's BluePRINT offering, for example, is about articulating a three-year sales strategy that the Fusion team tried out on themselves before offering it to clients.

"We were guinea pigs for the sales BluePRINT," Gilmore says. "We went through it and found that it was an amazingly powerful process. It's great to do that because not only does it provide you with the business strategy, it also helps us talk to clients about it because we've experienced it ourselves. So that's pretty cool."

Some of Canada's leading organizations have experienced Fusion's Strategic Sales BluePRINT, including ADP Canada, Corby

Distilleries, Grand & Toy, Baxter Corporation, Sony of Canada and Rogers.

The three, canny, 40-something businessmen thrive on providing creative, smart ideas backed up by a solid and progressive team. They are proud to discuss Fusion's early trials, steady growth, current successes and optimistic future predictions. And what really makes them excited is when they talk about the culture at Fusion and the people they work with — their nuclear Fusion family, so to speak. The family thrives in a collegial atmosphere of inclusion, professionally and otherwise. This includes not only the 12 full-time Fusion employees, but also the 10 contract facilitators, dubbed the Fusion Players.

As Higgins points out, when you work in a professional service firm "your product is your people. Our clients say, 'We bought from you because we want our salespeople to act like you,'" he says.

When it comes to praise and acknowledgement, that's about as gratifying as it can get.

The sense of inclusion at work in the Fusion offices is evident from the moment you walk through the door of the warehouse space. It was chosen and designed specifically to promote a sense of wellbeing and comfort for staff and clients alike. Juxtaposed against the old-world charm of the original warehouse, with its wooden beams, exposed industrial ceiling ducts and brick walls, the airy space includes a spotless, fully equipped kitchen and a roomy staff washroom with shower with a relaxed, spa-like ambience. The space reflects the partners' cutting edge vision and skills, while also suggesting a sense of camaraderie and such 'old-fashioned' notions as nurturing and rewarding those closest to you.

Every Fusion employee has received a bonus every quarter since the company started. And the partners also believe in nurturing the soul. In 2008, for example, they took their entire team, including spouses, to New York to celebrate the previous year's success. In 2009, they were planning a similar trip to Blue Mountain for a weekend of celebration. Whether it's a bonus or a trip, it's all about respect.

"We love to have fun," Higgins says. "We believe in promoting from within and developing from within. We've not had a single person who's ever left us who we wanted to stay on the team."

Magwood points out that, in fact, this philosophy is part of BluePRINT and something they help other companies with.

"Zero per cent voluntary turnover is important to us," he says. "It's one of our leading indicators. We want high-quality people and we want to treat them well. We want to develop them and we want to hold onto them."

Gilmore agrees: "We work hard but we also play hard and there's a real feeling of spirit and teamwork and support. People are really engaged and really love the work. We know how to celebrate and we also know how to have a good time."

Away from their professional lives, the three partners pursue their own special interests.

Gilmore indulges in photography, enjoys nature with his family and admits he's "a little addicted to running," having run several half-marathons and completed one grueling full marathon: "I won't do that again any time soon."

Higgins spends as much time as he can at his cottage, where he and his wife enjoy mountain biking, waterskiing, snowboarding, snowmobiling and other outdoor recreational activities. He also finds time to serve on the board of a charity in Toronto's Regent Park area, where they are about to create 87 affordable housing units for the homeless: "There's some great work being done there."

And where might you find Magwood when he's not in the office? Perhaps not surprisingly, you might find him back under the spotlights. In June 2009 he launched his own Slow Down CD of original soul tunes: "Think Norah Jones meets David Gray meets Ron Sexsmith meets a little bit of U2."

To cite one of Magwood's theatre analogies, the three partners

— actor, artist and businessman — are Fusion's conductor, executive producer and general manager respectively. When you add the strong cast of Fusion employees and players to the production, what you've most certainly got is a hit show.

*Amar Doman, Founder,
President and CEO of
The Futura Corporation*

The Futura Corporation

The panoramic view from the top floor corner office of an upscale Vancouver high-rise provides Amar Doman with one of the most stunning vistas that this famously scenic city has to offer. Snow-capped mountains provide a breathtaking backdrop to Burrard Inlet, where cruise liners, container ships and fishing trawlers dot the blue waters alongside sleek sailboats and luxurious motor yachts. Looking down on some of Canada's priciest shoreline real estate, this lofty vantage point is ideal for showcasing the young city's thriving prosperity.

It's a fitting setting for a man who seems to have the world literally at his feet. Tall, trim, sophisticated and good looking, Amar Doman, 38, has everything he needs if he ever chose to live a playboy lifestyle in this oceanfront, metropolitan paradise. He's one of the richest men in Canada under the age of 40, and ranks 81st on a list of the 100 wealthiest Canadians.

How wealthy? Well, good breeding and good manners preclude him from being anything other than politely vague on the subject. According to the winter 2008/2009 special edition of Canadian Business Magazine, his assets are worth around $600 million. This respected publication has for many years compiled the nation's definitive directory of who counts the most in terms of financial clout.

Yet, it's not money that keeps this captain of industry buried in his work, almost oblivious to the priceless view and the treasured sunsets that often illuminate the conclusion of his grueling 12-hour minimum workdays.

Doman's tireless work habits, which also include long hours on weekends, are in his blood. It is a testament to the life lessons that he learned from his father and uncle when he was a youngster eager to follow in their footsteps.

In particular, much of the inspiration always to be at his best in business comes from his father, Ted Doman, and his uncle, Herb Doman. The eldest of three brothers who all devoted themselves to nurturing the fledgling family business, Herb was its obvious leader, as well as its strategist and relentless driving force. He was also the ever-enterprising risk taker — the one who best personified the company's uphill struggle to outwit and outmanoeuvre the major forestry companies with which it competed so successfully.

A truly inspirational figure for any aspiring entrepreneur, Herb Doman emerged as a Vancouver Island rags-to-riches tycoon in the lumber industry, traditionally the backbone of British Columbia's economy. In this sense, he literally helped build one of North America's most successful regional economies out of wooden planks and plywood. Tens of millions of them.

For more than five decades, Herb and his brothers shrewdly developed Duncan-based Doman Industries into a renowned and well-respected family business that provided steady, well-paid jobs for thousands of hard-working blue collar British Columbians. Even during the downturns in the cyclical forestry industry he kept as many people working as possible. This did not always make the best economic sense. However, his humble beginnings and his early experiences of struggling to put food on the table during hard times gave him a strong sense of loyalty to his workers.

Born Harbanse, but later known by the easier-to-remember acronym, 'Herb', he started working at age 12 after the untimely death of his father from illness while only in his 40s. As the eldest of five children, Herb was forced to quit school and support the family, working from 6 a.m. to nightfall, seven days a week. Initially, he delivered newspapers and sold magazine subscriptions in the small logging town of Duncan where he grew up and later rose to great prominence.

Herb and his younger brothers, Ted (Amar's father), and Gordon started the Doman Lumber Company in 1953. Their impressive work ethic soon won over a growing nucleus of loyal customers — people who aspired to a better standard of living and wanted more than just the bare necessities.

After all, the 1950's represented an era of unprecedented economic growth in North America that saw the average Canadian living wage skyrocket. And that translated into a thriving marketplace for larger, better homes, which in turn precipitated a growing marketplace for wholesale building supplies. So, Herb and his brothers worked non-stop to keep busy Vancouver Island lumber yards and hardware suppliers well stocked with finished wood products.

A decade later in 1964, the company took on a more fitting name — Doman Industries — that better reflected its gradual evolution into a more all-encompassing player in Vancouver Island's thriving forestry industry. This new era saw the company enter the sawmilling and logging businesses, and later the wholesaling of hardware supplies.

Doman Industries' first major sawmill was established in 1967 in the small coastal town of Ladysmith, near Duncan. In the early days, the company thrived on processing smaller trees that nobody else wanted once the forests had been cleared of much larger stands of lumber. With a nod to environmentalism before the term had even been coined, the Domans were the first to make planks that were four inches in diameter out of 'waste' trees that would otherwise be burned by the big forestry companies.

Herb Doman and his brothers were driven to succeed by more than just a desire to break free of the shackles of poverty. They also wanted to fulfill their immigrant father's unrealized dream of building a successful forestry business.

A penniless Sikh from India, who arrived in Canada in 1905, Doman Singh was quick to embrace the rugged work life of a West Coast lumberjack. The chilly, temperate rain forests of Vancouver Island may have been a world away from the sweltering heat of his native land. But he had found an environment where he fit in. It was where a man's worth wasn't measured by the colour of his skin but by his devotion to honest hard work and also by the strong bonds of trust that were forged with co-workers, whose lives so often depended on one another in such a dangerous job.

An ambitious man, Doman had dreams of running his own logging and milling business in order to make a name in his adopted country. But fate intervened to cut his life short in 1942, leaving behind his despairing wife and five young children.

That was when his eldest son, Herb Doman, stepped up to become the family breadwinner. Though still only a child, he was as determined as his father to get ahead in life and to ensure that the new Doman family name would not fade into obscurity. (The family had decided to adopt 'Doman' for its last name out of respect for their lost patriarch, as 'Singh' is a widely used spiritual name in the Sikh tradition that is considered somewhat impersonal).

"I built the company up for my father, for his family and for the family name," he explained to the media a few years ago.

Furthermore, Herb's overriding sense of loyalty and devotion to family, community and friends were core values that sustained him throughout his life and gave it a clear sense of meaning. He was also proud of what the family had achieved and of their esteemed reputation in the West Coast forestry business and among the hard-working Duncan town folk the Domans considered work colleagues, friends and neighbours.

Above all, Herb and his two brothers had made the Doman family name a force to be reckoned with in Canada's resource-based economy. They had set the bar for the next generation. And it was Amar Doman who decided straight out of high school that it was now his turn to take the Doman brand to the next level.

At around 5.45 a.m., Amar Doman arrives at his office ready to meet whatever multiple challenges each day will bring. He typically starts his day by scanning the business sections of no less than five newspapers to assess the overall health of the economy and to seek out new opportunities. He then starts to work the phones to check up on the sales figures for his many enterprises (starting out with those that are based in the East and are already open for business).

A self-confessed fitness addict who always finds time during his arduous work weeks to jog daily and lift weights, he is continually "measuring the pulse" of his various businesses to assess ways for them to push harder, to become leaner and more competitive. An obvious 'Type A' personality, Amar is driven by a desire to continually prove himself in an increasingly high stakes business environment. It's a "survival of the fittest" mindset that he also inherited from his father and uncle.

He has been running on adrenaline since he was 18 years old when he borrowed $30,000 from his mother to start his first lumber remanufacturing business, First Class Lumber Remanufacturing. The company's nine employees took lumber from mills and resized and re-graded it for export. Determined to succeed at all costs, Amar worked up to 15 hours a day, handling all of the managerial responsibilities by himself. His industrious nature and shrewd business instincts paid off. He was able to repay his mother's loan out of profits 12 months later.

"I had to prove myself. And the next step was to build on my early success. I thrive on fear and hard work, as well as taking risks. It's all about keeping ahead of the competition," he says.

A little over a year out of high school, he bought out of bankruptcy a larger remanufacturing business with 20 employees and turned the venture around, much to the relief of its re-energized and somewhat surprised labour force.

"I had learned from my family that buying things that others couldn't make a go of is a good strategy, at least for our family," Amar says of his first big gamble.

Then at 20, he acquired a plant that pressure treated lumber for export. Next, he bought out his main competitor. He continued to add several more acquisitions to his burgeoning conglomerate and kept up a relentless pace to always stay one step ahead of the competition.

By 1999 and a little over a decade out of high school, his emerging businesses were generating $100 million a year in revenues.

He had come a long way since his early teens, when he had jumped at the chance to work in one of the family's sawmills, and spent summers piling lumber, loading trucks and sweeping up. However, it wasn't just about making pocket change. By getting his hands dirty doing menial chores, he was learning the business from the ground floor up, just as his father and both uncles had done before him.

In 1999 he consolidated his various companies under the umbrella of a new organization, the Futura Corporation, a holding company in which he remains the sole shareholder and decision maker. He adopted the name Futura in a nod to his father, who ran a company by that name in the 1970s.

Even though his well-managed enterprises were generating plenty of cash flow by now, very little of this money went to Amar's lifestyle. "I was still living in a 1,000 sq. ft. duplex and driving a Ford truck. I was just too focused on work to start living it up," he says.

Instead, a steady stream of profits was ploughed right back into the furnace of a business locomotive that was showing no signs of slowing down. And all of Doman's acquisitions were made with cold, hard cash. There were no leveraged buy-outs to fluff up his holding company's sense of grandiosity.

Indeed, Futura has kept a tight rein on its subsidiaries, which by now dot the landscape all through North America. They are all managed in much the same vein as Doman Industries during its first three decades of exponential growth. And that's with an austere, old-fashioned preoccupation with the bottom line, particularly with cost containment in mind.

During the last decade, the business world may have eschewed such an unswerving commitment to steady organic growth as being unexciting and "old school." Yet, it's also proven to be a prescient survival skill in a tough new economy in which over-reaching, over-confident and over-leveraged hotshot corporations, particularly in the financial sector, have collapsed in spectacular fashion.

Fortunately, borrowing a company's way to prosperity is not Amar Doman's style. Unlike many power players of his generation, who until recently made a lucrative living peddling worthless toxic investments, he does more than just demonstrate financial sobriety. His companies actually deal in things of real substance, products that are literally and figuratively as tangible as bricks and mortar. That's because bricks and mortar, and every other imaginable kind of building supplies, are what he distributes all over North America. They are used in the building of homes, hospitals, office towers, and many other types of building structures.

Such upstanding business practices were very much out of step with the times during the 2001-2007 housing boom that allowed Doman's budding business empire to go from strength to strength. Indeed, this was a heady, intoxicating era of prosperity. "Leveraging one's opportunities" was the cool catchphrase that much of the Western business world latched onto as a guiltless way of borrowing and spending way more money than anyone could ever pay back.

Yet, Doman was able to capitalize on the credit-fueled economic prosperity of the new millennium in a much more tangible way. In 1999, just on the cusp of the most recent housing boom, he showed some impeccable timing (a knack that sometimes eluded his uncle Herb) by acquiring his most prized asset, CanWel Building Materials Ltd.

Even though the 'one-stop-shopping' building supplier was doing over $400 million a year in revenues, it was not a profitable business at the time and its owners were looking to unload it. There were no takers at first and CanWel had actually been taken off the market. Doman felt he could cut costs and accommodate the needs of fast-emerging, home improvement big box stores that were going national, such as Home Hardware Stores Ltd., Rona Inc. and of course The Home Depot Inc.

"Now that these major retailers were establishing themselves coast to coast, they needed to be serviced by a national wholesale distributor that they could rely on from the standpoint of quality control and to ensure an uninterrupted supply chain. CanWel was ideally suited to that role," Doman says.

His much-envied corporate turnaround expertise paid off yet again. He has since more than doubled the company's sales figures and ensured that CanWel has turned a profit every year since 1999. The company's products are now sold in 30 countries and in Canada they can be found in around 1,600 hardware stores.

"We've done a very good job of expanding into hardware and specialty items over the past number of years, and certainly it's paying off. We now sell over 50,000 products, most of which can be found at any neighbourhood hardware or lumber dealer," he says. "We had our second best year ever in 2008."

It has always been integral to Doman's long-term business strategy gradually to diversify his stable of ventures away from the lumber business. That's because he is determined to avoid the same trap that eventually snared Doman Industries, brought down by an over-exposure to unexpected downturns in the lumber and pulp marketplace, along with a heavy debt load.

Even the good times are not so lucrative any more. Forestry is a business that Doman refers to a "sunset industry" in Canada, due to a number of key factors. Not the least of these is the advent of cheap competition from emerging economies. Wood products used to account for 100 per cent of Doman's business. Now, it's down to around 30 per cent.

Amar's private investment firm, Futura, now has major stakes in four public companies, along with a dozen privately held subsidiaries. All told, the building supplies sector proved very lucrative during the recent building boom, pushing Futura's revenues comfortably beyond the C$1 billion mark.

The building of any business empire is never a seamless process. Along the way there are always setbacks and false starts to test the wits and willpower of all great entrepreneurs. And Doman is no exception, having learned some hard lessons that he believes have made him a better businessman, with more finely tuned deal-making instincts.

By way of example, he recounts the time that he approached a struggling publicly traded building supplies business in 2007 (which he prefers not to name) with an unsolicited $200 million offer that he thought was a reasonable price to pay.

"We understood that we were negotiating with them on an exclusive basis. But then they came back and said there was another party that had suddenly shown an interest in buying them since we began our discussions," Doman says. "We were told to come back with a higher bid."

"They were obviously playing games with the company's valuation. So we just walked away," he adds. "Nothing came of the other apparent offer. They were left with a failing business and no exit strategy. The valuation of the company has since dropped about 90 per cent to $20 million."

The company's biggest mistake, Doman says, was to play brinkmanship when he was well aware of the fact that its board of directors had no equity in the company. Yet, they were prepared to engage in high stakes gambling with the shareholders' interests at stake.

Ironically, one of Doman's companies has since become the biggest shareholder in the under-performing building supplies manufacturer. He was able to capitalize on the board of directors' mismanagement by buying shares at a deep discount to his original offer.

"Now that I have a meaningful stake, I'm helping the board to rebuild the business and to survive the economic downturn. By being the biggest shareholder, I believe I'm serving the best interests of all of the shareholders now," he says.

"This story illustrates how it's always so important for senior management to have skin in the game as they always perform better than companies that are run by people who don't. That's why I have a personal stake in all of the companies that I control."

With so much at stake, Doman is always ready to match his hard work ethic with an equal commitment to creative problem solving and to facing the unpredictable challenges of an ever-shifting business landscape. For instance, when the home construction industry started to flounder, he began looking to the home renovations business to help keep Futura's bottom line healthy.

Many people were no longer moving into more expensive homes, but instead were settling for second best by gradually making improvements to their existing homes, he explains. When house prices eventually rebound, then the homeowners who have put the most effort into refurbishing their existing homes will reap the greatest benefits when they put them on the market.

"Home renovations will prime the economy for its eventual recovery," Doman declares. "Housing will lead us out of the recession. It's such a big economic engine that it creates all sorts of ancillary businesses that will put people back to work. Whether it's construction supplies or household appliances, or even electronics and landscaping, it all creates lots of jobs."

Another major positive development for Futura is the fact that the current economic crisis has made some of the competition in the building supply sector much weaker. This is especially the case for publicly traded acquisition targets that are now trading at fire-sale prices.

"Because of the recession, we're seeing a once- in-a-generation opportunity right now. The share prices of some of these publicly traded building material companies that we're interested in are down as much as 90 per cent," Doman says.

He has set his sights on competing in the building supplies marketplace across the whole of North America and is undaunted by the task that lies ahead. After all, Futura's revenues have now seen 20 years' of non-stop growth, in spite of other economic downturns that he has experienced. He admits that the severity of the current economic malaise may slow Futura's growth, but he believes it will not be a major impediment.

On his way to becoming a bona fide 21st century North American building supplies tycoon, Doman intends to find time to start a family. In early 2009, he had just celebrated a spring wedding with his fiancée, Natallie, at postcard-perfect Newport Beach, California.

Will life change for this self-confessed workaholic now that he has embarked upon a marital commitment that will surely tempt him away from the office? Maybe not, he says. He hopes to start a family, but even having children won't necessarily slow down this consummate serial entrepreneur. He says he will just have to be diligent about squeezing some quality "family time" into his hectic daily schedule.

Over lunch and a glass of red wine, Doman is able to relax and talk candidly about himself. But as coffee is served, he leans forward, gently taps his fingers on the table and politely mentions his need to get back to the office. This is a man who cannot be idle for long. There aren't enough hours in the day for him to fulfill all of his aspirations.

"I admit that I'm passionate about my work. I love it. Ironically, it's this passion that helps to keep me centred and to be at peace. It's a great feeling," he says. "And I feel blessed to live in Canada, which is a land of opportunity that has been a wonderful home to my family over the last century since my grandparents arrived here as poor immigrants.

"The Doman family has thrived over the years because Canada

is a meritocracy where success can be achieved by virtually anyone as a result of hard work, passion and vision," he adds.

It is this philosophical sense of gratitude to the Doman family's adopted country that brings out the budding philanthropist in Doman, who says his most cherished long- term goal is to finance charitable causes. In particular, he wants to help young people in countries where an oppressive burden of extreme poverty so often snuffs out any hope of social mobility.

"Ultimately, I would like to set up an international foundation to help people get an education with a view to getting a head start in life," he says.

"This will be my lasting legacy, rather than being merely recognized as a talented businessman. After all, it's great to be successful. But it's just as important to give back."

Anthony, enjoying the SHAMBA Foundation's patio space

global*live*

Anthony celebrating one of his passions

Business in Motion

Globalive
Communications Corp.

Anthony Lacavera's Broadway presentation of Tennessee Williams' classic play Cat on a Hot Tin Roof was so successful in New York he began immediately to plan for a performance in London's West End, anticipating a similar box office bonanza.

Closer to home, the 34-year-old Toronto entrepreneur was among a group of 25 Italian families who contributed $13-million towards the Galleria Italia at the revamped Art Gallery of Ontario, turning it into one of the foremost cultural and architectural landmarks of North America.

Any Canadian would be proud to have been involved in any one of these things. But, in Lacavera's case, they are adornments to a spectacular business career that gives him so much pleasure he doesn't regard it as hard work. "I'm having so much fun," he says, "it doesn't even feel like I'm working."

In the space of a decade, Lacavera has created from virtual scratch a telecommunications company with a global reach whose profits now enable him, among other things, to lend a helping hand to other entrepreneurs whose ideas inspire him. His success also enables him to champion charitable works — and not just those of his choosing. He has created a facility in downtown Toronto designed specifically to help other charities raise money for their causes. In fact, Lacavera enjoys a rich and varied career that is a model of inspiration to budding entrepreneurs across a glittering spectrum of opportunities.

As Founder, Chairman, and Chief Executive Officer of Globalive Communications Corp., Lacavera masterminds a mushrooming empire that has seized the opportunities presented by phone deregulation to create innovative enterprises that use virtuosity and flair to attract an ever-wider network of users in an ever-growing number of nations. Globalive businesses now connect people in more than 30 countries, using state-of-the-art communications technology. Pick up a phone in many major hospitals, hotels and universities across Canada and the chances are you are being served by a Globalive subsidiary.

To achieve his success, Lacavera has had to compete with the giants of the telecom industry. His company may still be small in comparison, but by remaining nimble and flexible, he has been able to penetrate previously untapped niche markets. Lacavera's business and residential customers have learned to appreciate the most affordable rates, along with an ever-expanding suite of reliable services and products. Meanwhile, the CEO focuses on developing a stimulating and fulfilling environment for his employees. Lacavera has made it his mission to build Globalive into a company that is equally attractive to its customers and workers.

This high-flying enterprise had its origins in 1997 when Lacavera, fresh out of college, founded Globalive. He recruited his closest classmates to help launch his new company. "I had just graduated from the University of Toronto," he recalls. But even before graduating, while still studying at the U of T engineering school, he had been helping a start-up web development business launch into new markets. He used the profits to start Globalive Communications — "my first real venture on my own."

Over the next ten years, Globalive developed into an industry leader, but the fledgling telecom company got its start by selling services to hotels. "At that time, in January 1998, the phone market in Canada was being deregulated," says Lacavera. "Our plan was to create a company to sell services such as phone teleconferencing to hotels and then to hospitals. Also, I wanted to sell services to the newly emerging competitors to the big phone companies." Competition in the home phone market was heating up. At the same time, the high-speed Internet market was starting to evolve. In the rapidly changing world of communications, Lacavera could identify plenty of opportunities.

Coincidentally, another innovative telecom company was founded in 1998 by an acquaintance of Lacavera's. It was called Yak Communications, a name now synonymous with money-saving, long distance calling in the residential market. The two entrepreneurs talked about ideas they might develop together. But, in the fall of 2006, Globalive acquired Yak in a coup that took financial markets by surprise. Against the odds, Globalive managed to seal the deal for $75 million in cash.

"It was amazing," Lacavera says. "We were successful at borrowing the money from the Canadian banks, which are known to be very conservative and often require substantial security. I'm very proud of that fact, as the banks are known for being very difficult to convince about coming in on more risky types of investments, or what are perceived as more risky investments. They could easily have said, 'You know what, this doesn't meet our risk profile' and that would have made it impossible for us, without their support. But we were successful in putting a business plan together that attracted several of the big name banks, so we could acquire Yak, for cash, and integrate it into our Globalive business and fold it into our umbrella of companies.

"The Yak acquisition was really about us wanting to get out there and expand aggressively. We've always had a business plan, always had a feeling that we wanted to get bigger and expand our business. This was really an opportunity to jump on that and do that. Obviously, we were a long shot to acquire Yak. Nobody expected that we would secure the financing, since Yak was bigger than Globalive at the time."

Since that dramatic acquisition, the Globalive group has grown to include OneConnect Services, Canopco Hospitality Telecom and Globalive Carrier Services. As a consequence, Globalive now provides services to a wide range of customers, including more than one million Canadian households under the Yak Communications brand. In addition, the Canopco brand provides local and long distance lines, and operator services, to more than 3,000 hotels, hospitals, universities and colleges in more than 30 countries.

Canopco is, in fact, the largest multilingual operator services provider and its brand extends into Internet services and in-room entertainment with clients that include Marriott hotels, Choice hotels, Comfort Inn, Fairmont, Delta, Econo Lodge, York University, McGill University, Calgary University and Vancouver General Hospital.

Globalive Carrier Services provides wholesale, billing and collection services to carriers around the world via Assemble and its InterClear product. Assemble provides audio and web conferencing services worldwide, while InterClear offers fraud detection and prevention to the originating carrier or service provider. Globalive also connects more than 5,000 small and medium businesses in North America, who are provided with applications and telecom services through Globalive's OneConnect Services brand.

These Globalive services utilize traditional phone lines as well as Internet-based VoIP. "We have a Voice over Internet Protocol service and we've developed software applications that run on Internet connections, including voice applications. We've also developed a lot of data applications," says Lacavera. "In the Yak business, we also sell home phone service using the traditional copper phone lines."

With its extraordinary versatility and reach across various markets, and through numerous branded identities, Globalive is poised to emerge as the undisputed leader in the industry. Moreover, Lacavera is confident that there are still more opportunities to develop and conquer. He has taken steps to position Globalive as a major wireless carrier in Canada's $16-billion wireless industry.

In May of 2008, the company was provisionally awarded wireless spectrum licenses in Industry Canada's Advanced Wireless Spectrum (AWS) auction. In March 2009, these were officially confirmed by Industry Canada. Having satisfied Industry Canada's review process,

Globalive Wireless is aiming to launch in 2010 with an investment of more than $442 million, creating a potential 1,000 new jobs in the marketplace.

"We are one huge step closer to improving the wireless experience for Canadians by giving them a wireless company that listens, responds and collaborates with its customers," says Lacavera. "Globalive Wireless will provide voice, text and data services across Canada on a next-generation GSM network." In the build-up to the official launch of Globalive Wireless the company launched a virtual 'wireless soapbox' to solicit thoughts and suggestions from potential wireless customers and to act as "a forum for people who believe that cellular can be done better." Lacavera himself is a regular contributor to the soapbox, adding his feedback and comments to users on the site at the new address (wirelesssoapbox.com).

The move into wireless is a bold one in a country such as Canada where only 70 per cent of the population owns a wireless device, such as a mobile phone, compared to almost 90 per cent in the U.S. and close to 100 per cent in the U.K. Can Globalive offer the service and the lower rates to penetrate a market where major players have failed to gain a foothold? Canadians currently pay an average of 60 per cent more for mobile wireless services than Americans. Globalive's goal is to bring affordability, and therefore more customers, to this sector of the telecom market.

Lacavera dismisses the prospect of slaying any giants: "I'm a big believer that there's no such thing as a real David and Goliath story. I believe if we tackle them (the major telecoms) head on we're going to get killed. We're in a market that is dominated by very high profile, very well known companies — Bell, Telus, Rogers, Shaw — very powerful, very well run companies. I have a huge amount of respect and admiration for the companies they've built."

Nevertheless, Globalive has shown it can more than hold its own alongside the big name competition in the telecom sphere. The company may not be 'slaying' any telecom giants yet, but it is giving them a run for their money and aims to grab a sizeable chunk of the market.

"We're still a relatively young company, but we've done a tremendous amount of learning," says Lacavera. "By the metrics of those companies, we're still a small company. We recognize that we have a unique opportunity to take advantage of our size and be flexible and nimble and get to market faster. Speed and innovation are key to our success. We've always been fastest to market and we develop software solutions that would take the bigger companies a lot longer to put into the market."

Globalive has received many accolades, such as ranking No.1 on Profit magazine's listing of Canada's 100 fastest growing companies in 2004, plus earning the Deloitte Technology Fast 50 and being named one of Canada's 50 Hottest Start-ups. In 2006, Lacavera was named one of Canada's Top 40 Under 40 in recognition of his outstanding leadership, achievement and vision.

Lacavera credits his company's progress to dedication and hard work. "It's definitely been a very long challenging road to get to this point," he says. "But what's made us ultimately successful and differentiated us from the other 'smaller' telecom companies is that we've looked consistently for niche markets where we can create a solution." The company deliberately seeks out markets its competitors either overlook or ignore.

With a watchful eye for what constitutes a good opportunity, Lacavera has drawn satisfaction from being able to help like-minded entrepreneurs fulfill their dreams of launching a company. "Besides being a telecom service provider, we run a small merchant bank and we make investments in other telecom start-ups. We know and understand telecom services, so it's important for us to 'stick to our knitting' if you will. We focus on that area and there are a number of small companies we have made investments in."

Nevertheless, Lacavera is involved with two up-and-coming companies that are outside his usual sphere of interest, yet managed to inspire and stoke his entrepreneurial fires. One is Lingomedia (lingomedia.com) and its subsidiary Speak2me (speak2me.com), which teach conversational English to Chinese people online. "It's a very, very large market in China. There's such a demand for conversational English. And there's a big difference between us and a product such as Rosetta Stone. We're offering practical English that travellers can use in everyday conversation."

The potential with this project is immense, Lacavera believes, and will eventually reach beyond the gigantic market of China's one-billion-plus population. "We can use the same technology to teach any language, so I'm very excited about that company, mostly because of the viral growth that we're experiencing in the user base. In China, we went from zero to one million users in six months. We haven't spent a single dollar on advertising. It's incredibly exciting because of the growth trajectory."

Another promising prospect that attracted Lacavera's interest is ECHOage, a company offering eco-friendly birthday parties for kids. "ECHOage is about environmentally sustainable parties. It's another huge market and a very novel idea, too," he says. "We have a patent pending on both of those. I'm into developing an intellectual property base, using the patent process to protect start-up assets more than I have in the past. I've become more of a believer in it."

Aside from his aspirations for these two enterprises, Lacavera takes time to become involved with other companies in start-up mode. "I'm a really big believer in supporting other entrepreneurs. I know from personal experience how hard it can be and how hard it was for me to get financing when I started out. I have a lot of respect and admiration for people who are starting a business from scratch. I have an affinity for them and we try to support people where we can."

This spirit of offering a helping hand reaches to the core of Lacavera's company culture. "We obviously want to be a positive organization and we've considered how we can integrate our company with the community. Thus, we've made philanthropic activity an important part of our company," he says.

In 2007, he founded a non-profit organization called SHAMBA, which takes advantage of Globalive's infrastructure to make a difference in the community as a charity that helps other charities raise money. "As opposed to just writing a cheque for a charity, as most companies do, we've made 'giving back' a core part of our operations," Lacavera says. "Virtually every employee now participates in the SHAMBA foundation."

The name 'shamba' derives from the Swahili word for 'farm' and the concept of an urban farm reflects the old adage that 'many hands make light work.' A 2,500 sq. ft. rooftop terrace at Globalive's headquarters designated as the 'SHAMBA Space' has been used by, among others, Habitat for Humanity Toronto, POGO (Pediatric Oncology Group of Ontario), and Transforming Faces Worldwide. "Essentially, a charity can come in and host a fundraiser at our facility at zero cost to the charity. That way 100 percent of ticket sales can go to the cause," says Lacavera.

Globalive employees volunteer their time to SHAMBA and have helped raise hundreds of thousands of dollars for numerous charities. "It's one thing to contribute dollars, and quite another for people to contribute time and effort," Lacavera says. "There is a great deal of satisfaction amongst our team, knowing that they're having a hands on impact for a charitable cause."

Globalive is proud to be recognized as one of Canadian Business magazine's Top 30 Workplaces in Canada, and, for five years in succession, as one of Canada's 50 Best Managed Companies. "Globalive is a lot smaller than many of the companies in that ranking, which is based on anonymous surveys by actual employees. Of course, I'm proud that we're building a team here, a community, who are happy to be working at Globalive. A big part of our success has been focusing on our culture and our community of people. We also take a very fiscally disciplined approach. So, it comes down to financial discipline, focusing on niche markets, building the team, and making a difference in the community."

Lacavera's philanthropic activities extend beyond those in which his company is directly engaged. As an individual citizen determined to make a difference, he has lent his entrepreneurial expertise to numerous community-focused endeavours. These are projects that are close to his heart and true to his proud Italian heritage. For his efforts on behalf of reconstruction of the Art Gallery of Ontario (AGO) in downtown Toronto, Lacavera received in 2008 the designation of Commendatore in the Order of the Star of Italian Solidarity from the government of Italy.

"That's an interesting award," he says. "It's given to Italians living abroad who are contributing back to Italian prosperity. "I was awarded the Star for my involvement with the newly revamped AGO. The whole front of the new art gallery on Dundas St. was part of an initiative by a group of 25 Italian families. We got together to create the Galleria Italia, essentially a promenade. The entire glass façade is filled with beautiful artwork.

Lacavera's family was among 25 Italian-Canadian families who contributed the $13 million that made Galleria Italia possible. "It marks the first time a group of Italian families got together, outside of Italy, and donated something of this kind, doing something for the community," he says. Designed by the world-renowned Guggenheim Museum architect, Toronto-born Frank Gehry, the stunning space has curving floor-to-ceiling wooden beams like the exposed hull of a ship. Visually, the long, sleek gallery makes a statement in itself. Spanning almost an entire city block, the large windows provide a light and airy space for sculptures from the AGO's permanent collection, as well as temporary exhibitions.

Another, quite separate, aspect of Lacavera's personality is his love of theatre. His passion has its roots in high school days when he took to the stage, playing, wholly out of real character, the miser's lead in Scrooge. And it led him in 2008 to become involved in a successful production of a Broadway play with a difference. The concept he helped to develop with a friend in New York was to take a classic play and redo it with an African-American cast. The 2008 run of Cat on a Hot Tin Roof proved to be a critical success.

"It was a really fun project," he says. "It was completely our concept, done by myself and the executive producer who was my partner in the venture. James Earl Jones played the lead character alongside Oscar-nominee Terrence Howard and Phylicia Rashad (from the Cosby Show). It was very well put together with a star-studded cast. We had a really successful run. It was a complete sell-out." In fact, the restaging of the Tennessee Williams' classic was such a success that the production was due to be taken to London's West End at the end of 2009, with James Earl Jones and Phylicia Rashad reprising their roles. Lacavera has purchased the rights to all of Williams' plays and is working on restaging at least one more of them.

The bright lights of Broadway are a world away from telecommunications, but Lacavera indulges his passions and pursues whatever his heart desires. "I've always really enjoyed Broadway and always wanted to get involved," he says. "I was waiting for the right opportunity. Obviously, many people lose a lot of money on Broadway. Fortunately, we made a bit of money, but it wasn't about that at all for me. I truly enjoyed doing it, and learning about the process. It's part of my personality that I enjoy trying my hand at different things. It gives you new opportunities to meet exciting, energetic and creative people and that's what life is about, meeting amazing people. I will definitely do it again."

Considering Lacavera's busy schedule, one might wonder where he finds the time and energy. "Am I a workaholic? I get asked that all the time. Like I said, it doesn't feel that way. I'm just having a good time, and working hard."

And he is always has one eye to the future. "My ultimate goal right now is to build the company, long term. I always focus on the long term. I'm very cognizant of the current macroeconomic environment. Obviously, we don't want to do anything that might hurt our long-term opportunities, just because we're reacting to short term turmoil. The plan is to keep running our business well and focus on the important issues: customer service, building our service offerings and establishing our wireless offerings.

"We have a great company and a great culture. We don't want to jump into a different industry at the moment. I do want to continue to expand but in the same disciplined, cost-conscious, way with the same focus on building our community within the organization and building SHAMBA links to our external community. We're still building holistically, not just focusing on revenue itself. We want to increase our impact, holistically."

One thing's for sure: Whatever future success may lie in store for Lacavera, you can guarantee he'll be enjoying himself immensely.

HOLEYS™

Joyce Groote, M.Sc., MBA
President and CEO
of Holeys

Holeys

ompany builders are gifted people with a variety of behavioural traits that they can activate at any time. They must be able to grasp the big picture and vision, while at the same time possessing the ability to focus on details. They must be individualistic, and sometimes rebellious, but also communal and collaborative. They need a lone-wolf attitude so they can run outside the familiar confines of communal thinking, but be able to join and work with the pack when required. Especially, builders must be able to react with ferocity when confronted with competition and threat, but be flexible enough to channel that ferocity to its best effect.

These competitive threats are a fact of life for most entrepreneurs, but what distinguishes those who merely apply a skill in a business from true builders of companies — the winners from the also-rans — is often how they cope with competitive friction. Joyce Groote, CEO of the Vancouver-area shoe distributor Holeys, knows all about competition, especially over business concepts. Once, she was hit in the face with a pie thrown during a press conference by someone who held a view different from her own.

The pie incident happened in Groote's pre-entrepreneurial life when she was a lobbyist working on behalf of the president of BIOTECanada, the biotechnology association that helped organize the Global Industry Coalition, a group of companies using genetics to create new agricultural and health care products. The coalition advised governments on the cross-border movement of products developed using biotechnology and was a political lightning rod for zealots and traditionalists vehemently opposed to any kind of genetics research. It was one of those fanatics who 'pied' her as she was outlining the coalition stance on an issue during a United National meeting on biotechnology.

Although shocked by the incident, Joyce Groote handled it with aplomb. She stepped aside, wiped the goop from her face and hair and marched back to her seat at the front of the room in the middle of the press conference. Facing the cameras and the crowd of reporters who were wondering how she would react, she calmly continued to advance her group's position on the issue. And, refusing to allow the attack to fluster her, she turned the pie incident to her advantage. The childish protest, she pointed out, was an example of disruptive confrontation aimed at squelching discussion of important business and ethical issues. On the other hand, she said, the coalition believed in constructive dialogue that would help business and government to reach doable solutions on how scientific advances should be integrated into its collective thinking.

That kind of cool stood her in good stead when she later took the helm of Holeys, then called Holey Soles. The young biotechnologist turned shoe merchant achieved some early successes with a new style of shoe, a foam clog that took the world by storm in 2002. Customers fell in love with their utility, comfort and funkiness. But this dramatic success led to fierce competition between Holeys and Crocs®, the world's two largest distributors of the iconic clogs, for dominance in the world casual footwear market, valued at more than $1 billion.

Holeys first sourced its products from Quebec manufacturer Finproject. So did Western Brands LLC (later to become Crocs Inc.), and several other competitors. All sold similar clogs between 2002 and 2004 under a variety of brand names. Holeys called its clog the "Holey Soles" model while Western Brands called their version "Crocs".

After Western Brands became Crocs Inc., however, this friendly arrangement ended. In early 2005, with the help of the Canada's federal government, Crocs® bought Finproject, renamed it Foam Creations and cut off Holeys, and other distributors, from its supply. Crocs then threatened legal battles over intellectual property, claiming it had the exclusive right to sell, manufacture and import the first-designed foam clog. Luckily, after ensuring that no patents existed on the shoes, Holeys had already turned to China for its shoe supply as Finproject had been running into cost and supply issues for some time. Holeys also used the opportunity to begin transforming its shoes by listening to consumers and using innovative designs.

Market observers have long suggested that the Crocs® lawsuits appeared to be a business strategy. It's a strategy that an aggressive competitor uses as a tactical manoeuvre aimed at diverting competitors' resources away from growing their business. The result can be a long, drawn-out war conducted through a series of courtroom battles where the weapons of choice are obscure patent laws and intellectual property rulings. A legal version of the First World War's trench warfare, the idea is that the competitor with the best ability to afford lawyers will drain a smaller opponent's resources until it gives in and goes away. Many companies, including other makers of the clogs, have folded when faced with the crippling legal costs involved in defending their products. Other companies with greater resources, such as RIM, the makers of the BlackBerry device, have simply ceded vast sums to the litigant in order to stop the war.

But the Crocs litigious strategy didn't faze Groote. She was prepared to dig in for a long, protracted war of attrition over intellectual property rights in order to protect her young business. As someone raised in the idea hothouse of genetics, where people held conflicting views and sometimes vociferously advanced them, she was familiar with aggression, conflict, protracted debate and vehement argument. Faced with ongoing legal challenges that threatened to disrupt her business, she would remain cool under fire.

Groote knew that, prior to the lawsuit, all the companies selling the original new-look shoes had been purchasing them from a single supplier. She expected that when the courts were provided with this information, they would rule in Holeys favour. Further, designs had changed so much by the time the lawsuits were launched that they had no bearing on the original shoe. For example, even before the lawsuit was launched, Groote had had her own clog designs created, had begun opening up new product lines and had moved manufacturing to Asia — as much because she could better control the quality of production as to avoid confrontation with Crocs®.

To entrench this argument, and so mitigate the legal broadside from her larger opponent, she used a "go slow" strategy, in essence refusing to respond to legal attacks until the last second, thereby letting the dispute drag on. While the suits bogged down in the courts, Groote continued to change her product to better meet marketing needs, which also had the benefit of removing any elements that might provide even small opportunities for suggestions of infringement. These guerrilla tactics meant that the legal jousting became just another recurring business expense, a line item in the expense column of the financial statements.

Although the first case still remains nominally open, cumulative legal decisions have all but nullified the Crocs® positions. Four legal decisions in 2007 and 2008 support Holeys' position that the facts and law are on its side. Most recently, the United States International Trade Commission (ITC) issued a judgment in favour of Holeys in July 2008. The Commission found that Holeys did not infringe Crocs® patents, and that Crocs® utility patent was invalid. Simply, the Commission recognized that the clogs could not be patented due to "obviousness." Also, in 2007, the Canadian Intellectual Property Office (CIPO) rescinded its decision to give Crocs® the equivalent of a Design Patent. Later that same year, the European Union's Office of Harmonization (OHIM) also found against Crocs® when it ruled that Crocs® Registered Community Design was not valid.

Meanwhile Groote continued to expand and grow her business in other, international markets, where her opponent had little power. First year sales for the company under its original founder were $60,000. After she took over the company, Groote increased that to $600,000 in 2004, $3.5 million in 2005 and $11.5 million in 2006. Revenues in 2007 topped $17 million. Profit magazine named Holeys first and fourth respectively in its Hot 50 companies for 2006 and 2007.

Groote was able to engage in this guerrilla war for years because she had learned how to operate in complex organizations and pursue a vision with determination and dedication. For example, while her competitor was attempting to conquer the market for clogs through aggressive sales tactics and litigation, she emphasized orderly growth built on customer service. It is a technique she used from her early days with the company when she turned down some attractive contracts and restricted growth to ensure she had the infrastructure to re-fill orders for her product in a timely manner. Even today, Groote continues to insist that orders be processed in one day and shipped within five working days.

"It lets the retail stores feel confident that when they put in an order they're going to receive it and when the customers walk into the stores looking for the shoes they'll find them," she says.

This determination and sense of management for the future came early for the CEO. Growing up in Ontario, Groote was drawn to science by one of the jobs she held as a student. Among the usual camp counselling, waitressing and other jobs, she also worked in a garden centre and developed a love of plants. Soon she was off to the University of Alberta to gain her Bachelor of Science degree. Next came a Master's degree in forestry, but with a twist. She was fascinated by the emerging world of genetics, which became the focus of her studies. She became the first person to clone a tree gene, a "housekeeping gene" known as Actin.

However, while she loved the concept of science, lab work was not so much to her taste. She joined the federal government's department of agriculture, Agriculture Canada, in the Pesticide Directorate. This regulatory body was charged with the emerging discipline of biotechnology. Groote rose to chair a group on biotechnology regulation. But she soon saw that the department did not have the capacity to deal with the many issues that were emerging. She lobbied hard for the creation of a Biotechnology Strategies and Co-ordination Office within Agriculture Canada. It was a hint of things to come for Groote, whose prime skills are strategy and organization.

"I like to create," Groote says. "I'm a true builder. I was always building things when I was a child. In fact, I still have my first Lego set."

Government departments move slowly, however, and Groote began to chafe under the limited vision and glacial pace of her work. She returned to school for her MBA, specializing in strategy and marketing. During this time, she was recruited to be president of the new Food Biotechnology and Communication Network. She then became president of the Industrial Biotech Association of Canada, which was working in the emerging, and contentious, biotechnology sector. "It was exciting, and a challenge," she says. "We were shaping a new industry."

Eventually Groote became president of BIOTECanada, founded as a result of a merger between her group and a sister biotech association. The new group was active in providing the United Nations with information to help create a global bio-safety protocol providing guidelines for biotech issues, such as the movement of genetically modified crops.

The formation of BIOTECanada also led to a more personal partnership for Groote. While negotiating the merger that created BIOTECanada, she worked closely with Rick Walter. Eventually, they married. Today, Walter is Vice President of Operations for Holeys.

"We realized we meshed, not only in regards to our work, but in our private lives," says Groote. "We both loved renovating and had worked on our own houses. I had a compound mitre saw and he had a table saw, so we just knew we were meant to be together. We've continued to do renovations ever since and have completely renovated our house in Vancouver. We've evolved to have separate, but complementary skills, however. I do dry-walling and plastering and he does plumbing and electrical."

Groote's move to BIOTECanada resulted in the pie incident. While she was able to weather that particular storm, the intensity of feeling around her scientific endeavours was troubling. Painted by extremists as the designated villain of genetics research, she was obliged to hire a bodyguard. This led her to re-examine her career and her life.

"I started to think about where I would go next," says Groote. "I went to the cottage and developed a personal business plan. I have a healthy and balanced mindset, so I tend to see everything as an opportunity. When I decide what I want to do in life, I act as if it's impossible to fail."

The plan drawn up at the cottage led Groote to British Columbia, where she and her husband proposed to buy a business. That opportunity collapsed, and Groote instead became a consultant on the organization and support of the region's emerging biotech companies. Among other things, she created and led a biotech venture capital operation that invested in 10 companies. It became one of the most successful venture capital companies in North America.

So how did the scientist, the geneticist, the organizer of associations that operated on a world scale, become a shoe seller? A neighbour, a psychologist who had created the Holey Soles company, asked Groote for help in writing a business plan. Groote did so and, impressed by what she learned, she invested in the company. When the founder decided she wanted to sell, Groote became sole owner. "We weren't looking to buy the company, merely to invest in it. We wanted to make life simple," she recalls. "But as it turned out, we ended up running it. And once you're in, you roll up your sleeves and get to work."

The new role came with many challenges, not the least of which was dealing with the company's tremendous growth. Holeys shoes were a phenomenon that had outstripped the original founder's capacity to deal with. "Its growth was unprecedented," Groote says. "How do you plan for a phenomenon? You have to put operations in place and create structure. You make a lot of mistakes and learn from them. I'm a strong believer that you need congruency between the head and the heart. You need common sense combined with passion."

Groote had to undergo a steep learning curve while managing a new business in an industry about which she knew little. A trained scientist and leader of associations, she knew almost nothing about manufacturing and retailing. She quickly engaged some shoe industry veterans for their knowledge of the shoe business and the fashion industry in general. "I did have the basics from my MBA training and from my work with associations," she says. "That teaches you transferable skills. But I still needed some real handholding."

Because Holeys was a retailing phenomenon, the company did not have to worry about creating market awareness, often the biggest obstacle facing any new venture. But, while that meant cost savings in the marketing area, it created problems in sales. Groote had to determine which of the many retailers clamouring to sell her clogs would make the most suitable partners.

"When retailers or distributors approached us, at the beginning we were just thankful that they wanted to carry us. As we became more savvy, we quickly moved from thankfulness to requiring them to demonstrate that they had the ability to help brand and sell our products," she recalls.

She also had to deal with organizational challenges that came with rapid growth. While manufacturing had been transferred to China, Groote had to open a new distribution facility, hire more staff and open satellite offices in new geographical markets. The number of employees grew to unmanageable proportions.

"I think at one point we had 70 people around the world. As you grow it becomes easy to lose sight of who does what. Growth also means you have to change the type of people who work for you. At start-up you look for generalists, but as you grow you need specialists. Each stage requires different types of people and it can be a challenge rationalizing all this with your strategy."

As an example, Groote cites the position of the Holeys sales representatives, which at first she treated merely as employees. But, as the company grew, she realized that to be successful the reps needed to be motivated in much the same way as potential customers. They needed to share a passion for the product. Without it, they could never properly represent the product. "We now treat all of our sales reps like customers," Groote says firmly.

Another challenge with the sales force was the nature of the job, which changed as the company grew. As the clog phenomenon grew, Holeys reps were not required to do much selling. They were the equivalent of order takers, which Groote now considers a luxury. But when the original fever for the clogs cooled, the reps had to promote the products more enthusiastically. Some could not adapt to the new reality, or were not willing to do so.

That change began manifesting itself in late 2007 and became very evident in early 2008. Eventually, Holeys began making inroads into new markets with new product lines, many of which grew out of their own designs. The early, neon-bright foam clogs that started the phenomenon gave way to newer, functional and fun footwear products that are now sold in more than 40 countries worldwide. Holeys developed its own technology that combines foam injection with thermo-rubber slip resistant treads to provide new leading edge footwear for many uses. Some still bear the trademark holes that created the phenomenon in the first place. The technology, trademarked as SmartCel, involves the injection of a super-heated liquid foam into a mold. The molded foam shoe has many attributes, including extraordinary lightness, comfort, washability and durability.

Because the shoes are extremely comfortable and supportive they are in great demand from customers who spend long hours on their feet. In fact, one of Holeys' marketing mantras is that "your feet will thank you" for buying the shoes. The Explorer shoe, originally designed as a water sports clog, has evolved into a line of footwear for many other uses. Outdoor enthusiasts wear Holeys to keep their feet cool in summer while also ensuring their toes are protected. Chefs, nurses and retail workers appreciate the shoes for their comfort and foot support during all-day wear. Gardeners use them because they are easy to slip on and off and can be cleaned with a garden hose. Travellers choose them as light, all-purpose sandals that can be carried in a backpack. Sports fans use them for the gym, change room and shower. And, of course, the original target customers, water sports fans, use them because they are such a natural material to use around water. They even float. In fact, much of the shoes' popularity stems from their weight. At five to six ounces, they are much lighter than other shoes or sandals on the market.

Groote's ability to navigate the company through its growth and other challenges has earned her a considerable amount of acclaim, as has her direction of Holeys into a socially responsible company. In 2007, Holeys donated 100,000 pairs of shoes to Soles4Souls, an organization that distributes shoes to third world countries. The company also supported the victims of Hurricane Katrina and the tsunami in Thailand, as well as a number of local causes.

As well as being on Profit Magazine's list of Hot companies for two years, Holeys has also been on the Profit 100 list for two years as an example of excellence in visionary sales leadership among Canada's top women entrepreneurs. Groote's position as finalist in the Ernst & Young Entrepreneur of the Year contests in 2007 and 2008 highlighted her ability to transform a company into a multi-national supplier of lifestyle products.

Having survived her legal battles while growing her company through innovation, Groote has never been content to rest on her laurels. It was clear by 2007 that Holeys had become a different company and needed a different identity. It was still named Holey

Soles, although most customers had long called it simple Holeys. In early 2008, Holey Soles was rebranded as Holeys to reflect its new identity as an innovative company selling not only footwear, but also bags, hats, accessories and children's collections. The new brand identity was aimed at reinforcing the company's position as a lifestyle brand that is playful but at the same time is serious about environmental stewardship, community building, fair pricing, and sustainable business practices. This sense of community is reflected today in the way Holeys refers to its many customers as the 'Holeys Tribe.'

Today, Holeys sells to its "tribe" online, in department stores and through specialty, outdoor-oriented, retailers. This supports its positioning as a company making footwear for those who spend a great deal of time outside and who want comfortable shoes that can handle the rigours of the outdoors. It is also continually fine-tuning its products to fit specialty markets. For example, it has added to its traditional footwear a fleece-lined model for those who want to putter around the house in comfort. Another new product is an ankle boot perfect for working in the garden, walking through wet grass or guarding against the elements. It is 100 per cent leak-proof, ultra-light and washable and, of course, offers legendary comfort. Also, for hunters and wildlife photographers, there are shoes with outdoor oriented designs, such as camouflage.

Holeys has long been in the habit of continually soliciting feedback from its customers and devotees. Its research led it to pursue another specialty market involving children. The company has always valued the safety and comfort of all its customers, but has a special regard for children who wear Holeys shoes. This goes back to before 2006 when concerns about safety for shoe-wearers on escalators came to light. Holeys had already recognized the problem and refashioned its shoe designs with a more narrow fit, round edges and closed toe ends to protect against possible stubs. Holeys' new treads also provide added stability and slip resistance.

Today, Holeys offers children's versions of most of its footwear. In the case of the new rainboot, the children's version was actually launched before the adult one went on the market. Children also appear to love Holeys innovative Critters line, with its family of fun-loving insect characters who promote safety and inspire a sense of community and social values. The line already features Critters shoes, baby crawlers, hats and backpacks, and will soon offer head-to-toe outfits.

Through such innovation and continual transformation, the tiny business that began in a garage in Vancouver in 2002 as a distributor has grown into a multi-million dollar company operating out of an 85,000 sq. ft. facility in Richmond and with distribution centres in Canada and the United States.

With growth of more than 6,000 per cent, the Holeys narrative is about survival and adaptation amidst challenges from formidable opponents. It is also a story of growth based on sound business initiatives and management, continual conversations with customers, an emphasis on functionality and innovation, and a solid track record as a socially aware global citizen. Joyce Groote insists, however, that Holeys' true growth should not be measured in traditional percentage or dollar terms. She is far prouder of what she believes is the company's real measure of success — the establishment of a service-oriented, community minded enterprise that wins over customers through hard work, a big heart and continuous innovation.

INTERNATIONAL ORTHOTIC LABS INC.

Jeff Ayotte, Founder and CEO International Orthotics

Production Lab

One **small step** for man...

✓ Full line of handmade Functional and Accommodative devices

✓ Exceptional cost saving programs

✓ Five day turnaround

✓ Free shipping

NEW! Direct-Milled Pathology Specific Devices

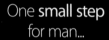

NEW! Trulife Sure Step AFO product line

✓ Free child outgrowth program and much more...

saucony®   Mellow **M** Walk

NAOT

To receive our catalogue or for more information on footwear please call toll free

1-800-887-7138

or fax us at (403) 236-8539

 To view our catalogues online visit our website
www.orthotic.ca

...One giant leap in orthotic selection

INTERNATIONAL ORTHOTIC LABS INC.

6777 Fairmount Drive SE.
Calgary, Alberta T2H 0X6

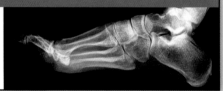

International Orthotic Labs Inc.

In early 2009, when most business people were treading cautiously in the wake of economic turbulence, young Jeff Ayotte was putting in place the first pieces of an expansion plan he hoped would double or even triple his revenue stream within two to three years.

It was an ambitious goal for such uncertain times. But, given the successful history of the eight-year-old company he founded, the Calgary-based entrepreneur had every reason to be confident. International Orthotic Labs Inc. had already been ranked by Profit magazine as one of Canada's fastest growing businesses, increasing its revenue by an impressive 336 percent over a five-year period. The company had consistently recorded annual growth of 20 percent or more. Besides which, demand for the company's product was more or less immune to shifting economic tides.

Ayotte's company manufactures devices designed to support and correct abnormalities of the human foot. Appropriately prescribed and properly designed and built they can free patients from intolerable pain, allowing the muscles, tendons and bones of the foot to function at their optimum potential. Many hundreds of thousands of Canadians benefit from some kind of orthotic device, including athletes, children, geriatric and diabetic patients.

International Orthotic Labs is one of only 34 labs worldwide fully accredited by the Prescription Foot Orthotic Laboratory Association, which requires the company to have the most up-to-date quality and technical expertise available. "We have also been tested rigorously on our depth of orthoses knowledge, and our product process and quality standards," Ayotte says.

"We believe strongly that in order to have a successful company we must have a successful team as well. We accomplish this by empowering our staff to be accountable to each other and to themselves and we employ a 24-step quality control process in which each and every team member participates."

The story of how Ayotte came to create his company is a textbook example of what can be done if you are humble enough to learn from past mistakes, courageous enough to believe in what you want to achieve and daring enough to seize an opportunity that presents itself.

A capacity for hard work helps, too. And as a schoolboy growing up in Victoria, B.C. with his single mother, Ayotte learned very early that "if I wanted things it was up to me to go and get them." At the age of 13, he ran two newspaper routes and later held part-time jobs at Boston Pizza and McDonald's. In high school, he had enjoyed working with his hands. "I always knew I had an ability to learn very quickly and to take on tasks and put in an extra effort to shine," he says.

He was given an opportunity to demonstrate his skills when he was hired straight from school as an 18-year-old to learn the trade at a Victoria orthotics lab, one of only a handful of such labs in Canada at the time. "I took to it like a fish to water," he says. "It suited me very well." New employees were expected to spend their first two years becoming familiar with the five different steps in the process of making the orthotic devices.

"I liked it so much, and enjoyed the process so much, that I learned all five steps in just eight months," Ayotte says.

He had always assumed that after leaving school he would find a job with a company "that I could grow with" and, hopefully, move up the ladder. It happened sooner than he could have imagined. Within 18 months a vacancy arose for an assistant manager and Ayotte, at the age of 20, was promoted to the position. Another 18 months later, the manager himself quit and Ayotte suddenly found himself at the helm of the company.

"Because I was interested in learning and understanding the

business and manufacturing process, including what went into every aspect of the products that we made, it put me in good stead to move up the ladder," he says. "I have always found that by being involved and being interested and just doing your best things will happen."

As the 22-year-old manager, Ayotte was put in charge of an operation that he saw immediately was "terribly unproductive — I set to work over the next year or so, changing that dramatically," he says. Indeed, for so young a person, and one with such limited business experience, it is a remarkable achievement that he was able to orchestrate such a harmonious relationship with both the workers and the owner of the company, a medical specialist who left its day-to-day management pretty much in Ayotte's capable hands.

Perhaps the owner's most valuable contribution was to shower his protégé with an abundance of reading and other material related to modern business practices. Ayotte seized eagerly upon the windfall.

"I'm a voracious reader," he says. "The owner was very good to me. He fed me information tapes, theories on business, on success. I took everything I could get my hands on. In fact, I studied to become a Pedorthist (the art and practice of designing, making, and fitting therapeutic devices for relieving painful or disabling conditions of the feet) all while working full time."

Strolling the lab floor during working hours, Ayotte would have his eyes fixed on the production line while his ears were tuned to a Walkman loaded with instruction tapes. "I got an education that way," he says. "It worked out very well for me. Basically, I was left to my own devices to achieve the goals that I said we could meet. Most employees quickly accepted the new regime, even though they were answering to a man who in some cases was half their age.

"In general, they knew the company was in trouble," says Ayotte. "They knew that we had a lot of waste in a lot of areas. When people see that you are doing things that make sense, it makes sense for them, too. Everyone was older than me, but it wasn't a problem.

In the beginning I had reservations about how I would be treated, and how I would be looked at. But I was in the assistant manager's position for long enough to gain some respect from the staff. They knew who I was and they knew I was the type of person that just wasn't going to accept mediocrity. The people that weren't in line with where we wanted to go — they didn't stay."

For the majority, who stayed with the company, the next few years were a whirlwind of change.

"When I took over, the company was losing money. It was really in rough shape," says Ayotte. "We looked at everything, right down to the core, from how we were making the devices, to the materials we were using, to the machinery we needed to add. And we tried to cut down on waste everywhere."

Adapting during the day what he learned from his books at night, Ayotte analyzed what each worker was doing and how his job might be made more productive. It might involve relocating a machine by a few feet, or making it run just a little faster. "Any little incremental advantage that we could find, that's what we did."

Month by month, the changes worked their magic. "When I took over we had a dismal productivity rate," says Ayotte. "In the next year, we increased it by 316 percent. Over the following two years we achieved more than a 500 per cent total gain over where we started."

As the years went by, Ayotte had good reason to look upon his life with a measure of satisfaction. He was still in his mid-twenties, enjoying a salary that he had only dreamed of, nicely plumped up with an annual bonus that brought his total earnings to more than those of a professional with years of schooling.

"There I was, a 26, 27-year-old kid running a multi-million dollar company and the owner is more or less absent. He was present for only about five minutes each day, asked a few questions, discussed urgent matters and went on his way. Which was great. Everything seemed to progress very well. I thought I was on cloud nine."

Instead, storm clouds were gathering. One of Ayotte's responsibilities was to negotiate a contract with the unionized labour force. "I did all the union negotiations, all of those kinds of things." Early in 2001, when he had been 10 years with the company, Ayotte and the union signed off on a new, six-year contract. "Six years is really unbelievable," he says today. "So we did really well there."

Then came a bitter disappointment. Instead of a reward for the best year in the company's history, and his negotiating skills, the owner came to Ayotte with a proposal to slash his bonus to virtually nothing, more or less cutting his total salary in half. And this was at a time when Ayotte's wife, Jackie, was pregnant and the couple had recently bought a house.

"I said to him, 'Look, if you're feeling the same kind of pain I am, I don't have a problem with this. I will continue on and we will continue on the same track. But you have to show me the books.' But he did not — he would not do that."

Looking back, Ayotte sees that "because I started fresh out of high school I never really asked for or received any kind of contract or very clear remuneration details. It was my lack of experience about what to ask for, and what should have been put in writing.

"Maybe they saw a young guy that didn't have the chutzpah to resist. You know, they thought 'we got this young kid, he doesn't have any formal education, his wife is pregnant and they just bought a house. We got him.'"

If that's what the owner really thought, he had sadly misjudged his manager. Years earlier, Ayotte had been sought out by two Calgary specialists interested in starting an orthotics company in the Alberta city. At the time he had said he wasn't interested. He was loyal to his employer. He had imagined himself staying where he was for many years, possibly even one day buying the company — "it was like my baby to a certain extent."

But now, faced with the owner's turnabout, "it was very clear to me that if I were to roll over and accept what he was trying to give me, then really he would have me over a barrel forever."

And so he renewed his contacts with Calgary, a deal was struck and Ayotte "reluctantly" gave three months' notice in Victoria. A new chapter in his career was about to unfold, although, as he now admits "I had great trepidation that I wasn't going to be able to pull it off."

Ayotte's new partners in the Calgary venture had plenty of ideas but not much of a clue about how to put them into practice. "They needed a doer and I had proven that I could make a successful company," he says.

When he and his seven-months-pregnant wife arrived in Alberta they both went right to work creating a company from scratch. "There are lots of marriages where this might have been a difficult time," he says. "In my case, there was nothing but support from my family and my wife. She believed that, wherever we went and whatever we did, we were going to be successful. She helped me with the logistics of setting up the company."

To secure his majority stake in the company, Ayotte had to borrow against their house. He had learned his lesson about getting things in writing.

"It was important to me to have a majority," he says. "I wanted to be in control of my own destiny at this point. I thought nothing but a majority would be acceptable." Within a couple of months, having secured lab space and stocked it with raw material and machinery, International Orthotics was ready to process its first orders.

And by then, Ayotte's first child, daughter Mya, had been born. Mya now has a younger sister, Katelyn.

Ayotte's partners are specialists who own one of the largest foot clinics in Canada. He knew that orders for orthotic devices from their practice alone would guarantee a positive start for his fledgling company.

Ayotte's initial goal was to reach break-even point. That took just two months. He thought that within two or three years the company could get close to $1-million in revenues. By 2003 it had exceeded that target. "I was very lucky early on to have found some great employees. Both my sales manager and production manager have been with the company more or less from the start. They have been instrumental in our success over the years."

For the first five months of the company's existence, "it was like we were almost doubling sales every month," says Ayotte. "It went from 400 pairs in the first three months, the next year 5,000 pairs, the next year 9,000 pairs and the next year 12,000. Our growth has been exponential; the numbers are always going up. If you were to string together the pain-free steps that patients take on our devices you could walk around the earth nine times, or walk to the moon each and every day."

From the outset, however, the rate of growth was limited by certain fixed principles upon which Ayotte insisted. First, there would be no compromising the quality of the product and, just as importantly, he would accept only orders that he knew could be completed to a specified turn-around time.

Expansion was also staggered because of the need to train every employee from scratch. "They have to learn each process, and it takes time. There is no school where you can go to learn it," he says. "In the first year we had four or five employees and each year we added one or two more. They are slowly learning the process. It takes four to six months for them to become proficient in one area and then they have to move to the next."

As for quality, Ayotte says: "We could have done much larger numbers if we did not care about the quality of what we were pushing out the door. We have always built our products and services around our core values (Pride, Integrity, Teamwork, Performance excellence, and Learning). We really believe in giving that superior quality and service."

It's an unusual business in that Ayotte rarely meets in person the practitioners who prescribe his devices, or the patients who end up wearing them. He can measure his success only by the repeat orders he gets and by the number of devices that get returned, which in the case of International Orthotics is very small.

His focus is on functionality as well as the aesthetics. "Our goal is not to have the patient walk away saying, 'these feel okay I guess.' What we want is for the patient to say, 'this has literally taken away all of my foot pain. I don't have it any more.' Of course this takes some time, the patient didn't acquire their pain overnight and it will not be corrected overnight either, but there should be a steady progression towards pain free ambulation. We are one of the only companies in our industry that will take the device back and refund the order if the patient or practitioner is not happy. We don't want patients walking around on our devices they are not happy with, or that haven't helped their condition. You might think we get a lot of returns. In fact, less than one half of one percent are returned, and that's with a full money back satisfaction guarantee."

Ayotte's insistence on quality means that his devices are not the cheapest on the market — "we believe in charging a fair price" — nor are they made widely available to anyone but professional doctors specializing in abnormalities of the human foot.

"We didn't want to be pushing out devices to whoever wanted to sell them," he says. He accepts that some of his larger competitors will sell many more thousands of devices by catering to "non foot-related professionals." He estimates the market for orthotics in Canada at somewhere in the region of $100-million. "Ours is a niche market in that we are focused on providing the highest quality, most functional devices to those foot specialists who are prescribing them.

"The difference between our competition and us comes down to the fact that each practitioner knows what he or she wants to see from the lab. It can be many things — how professional the devices look, how functional they are, how quickly their orders get returned.

"Turnaround time is a huge aspect. We want to be sure our devices go back when we say they're going back. The patients are in pain, so every day is another day that treatment is delayed. We've designed systems around our manufacturing process that enable us to do that. A lot of our competitors can't do that. They can't organize themselves properly. It comes down to who is building the best device in the most reliable time and to the best quality. We have one competitor, a little larger than us, that we have taken customer share away from because they continually fall off their due dates. They cannot maintain turnaround times. They will go two, three, four weeks without returning the product. The doctor is saying, 'My patient is waiting. They're in pain. I need this device.' And this company can't fulfill that."

Ayotte stays ahead of the game partly by employing the latest technology. There is a shift coming that will see a slow departure away from plaster casts towards 3D scanning. This will enable better turnaround time to doctors across the country or around the world. The practitioner can laser scan the patient's foot into a computer for downloading in Calgary.

"The scan gives us a full representation, with more that 20,000 points of reference on the patient's foot, and we can make our positive cast from that," says Ayotte.

From receiving the image or cast to dispatching the completed device normally takes five days. A core value at International Orthotics is that everyone in the organization recognizes P.R.I.D.E. — personal responsibility in delivering excellence — as a main tenet of the company.

"It may sound corny, but we are making medical devices that change people's lives and we take this responsibility seriously," says Ayotte. "I talk to my employees a lot about this, to instill a sense of pride in the devices we are making.

"I believe very strongly in our products. I tell the employees that they are not just making a plastic insole and shooting it out the door. They are making a medical device that is really going to help someone."

Ayotte knows from close experience the difference his devices can make. His mother-in-law suffered from plantar fasciitis, a painful condition of the heel that many people endure for years. "She would get home from work and crawl around on her hands and knees because she was in such pain," he says. "Our devices can stop that particular condition from causing pain. In fact, now she is an avid hiker who walks many miles each day."

When new employees in their mid-twenties start work, says Ayotte, "they don't see it that way. All they see is a cast and a prescription. They don't grasp that this device is actually going back to Mrs. Smith who is in a serious amount of pain and we're going to help her. It's hard for employees, especially technicians, to feel ownership in the company and to feel as if they are part of something. This is a good way to instill in them that there is more to their job than just the day-to-day ins and outs of working at the lab.

"I say to them: 'You don't just work in a factory or a laboratory. You are just like the practitioner. You're putting your name on what you make, working here eight hours a day. So put your all into it and make sure you are treating it with the respect it deserves.' I have always believed in that and it has served me very well."

For their part, employees share in the success of the company through a profit-sharing program that is paid out three times each year. A 'team-building' lunch is taken on Fridays, when managers provide input on successes and failures during the previous week.

"We believe that solid communication from top to bottom, sales to production, is a key factor in our ongoing success," says Ayotte.

"Another one of our values is to give back not only to the community but also to 'the communities of our practitioners.' A portion of the profits from every diabetic device goes to the Diabetes Association of Canada. And for each child device sold, a share goes towards fulfilling the dream of a child severely in need through the Children's Make a Wish Foundation.

"We are very proud of these partnerships," says Ayotte. "We believe that as good corporate citizens we are making a difference in our own community and in the communities where our practitioners live and practice."

In early 2009, Ayotte saw that his company stood at a crossroads that will be familiar to most enterprises that have gone through a rapid growth spurt and wonder in which direction to turn next.

Does he worry about becoming too big? "I do, actually, because I'm a conservative kind of guy," he says. "I have seen some of our competitors go through the same kind of motions. We have hit somewhat of a plateau with the way that we do things. I had to make a decision. Do I want to stay the same size with the same issues? Or do I want to take the next step and change the way we are doing business?"

For Ayotte, the answer came largely through a "maturation process" he associates with his participation in the Calgary chapter of the worldwide Entrepreneurs' Organization (EO), a forum in which some 7,000 likeminded business owners in 38 countries get together once a month to talk about common issues, personal or business oriented.

"A big part of EO is belonging to a forum group. I belong to a group of seven entrepreneurs that get together once a month for about six hours. We act as an informal board of directors for each other's companies. We hold each other accountable to what we say we are going to accomplish. I have great respect for my forum mates. They are all very successful in what they do and I glean as much from them as I can," Ayotte says.

Ayotte was inspired to join EO after watching a biography of B.C. multi-millionaire Jimmy Pattison who, he says, partially credits his success to his membership in an EO sister group, the Young Presidents Organization.

"I always believed you could pull your own socks up and work as hard as you can and achieve great things, and I think that's true. But, after seeing that biography, I realized, 'Man! Here's one of the richest men in Canada — a tremendously successful businessman — and he's realizing that you can get mired in your own day-to-day operations.' You don't realize that there are other organizations out there going through the same problems you are and that with their help you can overcome those problems and strive to become bigger and better as a person and an organization."

In the course of contemplating his expansion, Ayotte contacted his former employer in Victoria to discreetly inquire whether he might be prepared to sell the business.

"I wrote him saying that I wanted to try to smooth the waters and to express my disappointment with how it had all come down and that I really wished none of it had transpired the way it had," says Ayotte.

"He wrote me back saying he had no intention of selling the company, which was fine, although I still hold out hope that one day I will be able to join the two companies together."

In any case, Ayotte was preoccupied with what he had learned though his meetings at EO. "I realized that as well as we were doing, we could do a lot better," he says. "It opened my eyes to the fact that there's no such thing as a finish line. We're at the point where we're big enough to take the next big step up. I've got enough excellent people and I can add on staff going forward without sacrificing quality or time frames. Over the next two to three years we will double or even triple our size today.

"When you're contemplating growth strategies having great people close to you that you can trust, people who work to always make the company better, is fundamental to future success. I believe that these great people make all the difference in long term success."

To begin that process, Ayotte brought his highly regarded, longtime marketing manager closer into the company's day-to-day operations and hired a sales team to actively solicit practitioners by making office calls on foot specialists in major Canadian centres.

"We've never really done that before," he says. Winning new customers previously depended either on word of mouth or on contacts made at annual professional conferences where the company would demonstrate its products to practitioners.

"We've never actually gone out and forced the issue with customers," he says. "Now, we have a sales team making calls every day. We used to go about our marketing efforts in a bit of haphazard kind of way. We're much more focused now and that's what it takes to achieve any goal, become as focused as possible on it.

"I always saw myself working my way up an organization, learning with it, growing with it, hopefully buying it or taking it over one day and working at it diligently to produce something to be proud of. More or less, that's what has transpired, except for the fact that my company is a start-up.

"I am still a young guy — I'm only 36 — I enjoy the process of business and of producing something I can be proud of. I don't view it as work because there's always another challenge, something new to learn, something to push us forward."

He says he could have opted to keep his company small, but "I think you need to push the envelope and keep on going."

And Ayotte is not unmindful of the financial benefits of growth. "I didn't grow up with a lot of money," he says. "You probably hear this a lot from entrepreneurs who have tried to achieve something. It's the feeling that you would never want to be in a position where you can't live the way you want to live, where you can't pay your bills and those kinds of things. I never want to find myself in that position. Consequently, I've always been a hard worker and on top of my finances. I don't want to be in a position where there's any ambiguity at all in my financial position."

Though his parents, Roger and Elaine, have long been divorced,

Ayotte remains on the closest terms with them. His mother, he says, is "very independent and strong-willed and she passed on those things to me." His father, a former miner, he describes as "very social, a genuinely nice person, I admire both of them a great deal." They are a major influence in his life — along with his sister Jennifer and wife, Jackie, of course.

But there is at least one other person who, if pressed, Ayotte admits to regarding as a special role model: "Although I don't have exactly the same aspirations as Jimmy Pattison, his story makes me believe that anything is possible in business and in life. If you work hard, seize opportunity and keep moving forward, anyone can achieve wonderful success, however they might describe it," he says.

*David Shaw,
Founder and CEO
of Knightsbridge*

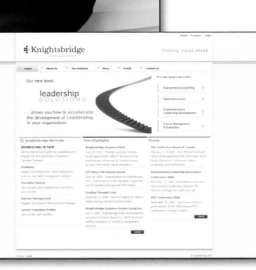

Knightsbridge

avid Shaw was not the most popular guy on the block when he floated his new ideas about how a successful human-capital consulting company should operate. No wonder. Veterans of the profession saw their traditional business model turned inside out. Many of them were running their own little partnerships offering specialist services in areas of specific human capital expertise. And here was Shaw proposing a one-stop-shopping philosophy under which all the many and varied problems of human capital could be addressed in an inter-connected, holistic way.

The animosity generated by Shaw's radical thinking was perhaps not to be unexpected. A comfortable way of life was threatened. "The industry really tried to knock us down when the concept of the new business model got around," he says. The former head of Pepsi Cola in Canada was not to be put off easily, however. "You have to be visionary in these days, and we could see that the customers wanted it, even if the industry didn't." Shaw's vision was the catalyst for the formation in 2001 of Knightsbridge Human Capital Solutions, which in just over seven years has become one of Canada's largest companies dealing in solutions to the full range of human resources challenges.

The word holistic is used with increasing frequency in a wide range of contexts these days so it is worthwhile to consider precisely what Shaw had in mind. In its medical sense, holistic implies a range of treatments that goes beyond addressing the most obvious symptoms. Any semi-competent GP, for example, might prescribe an appropriate medicine to treat a stomach ulcer. But it would require a much more detailed and complex diagnosis to determine the patient's physical, emotional and spiritual condition that caused the ulcer to grow. Translated to the business world, a holistic approach means being able to grasp the big picture behind an organization, not just to view it in its myriad separate aspects. It means that a company with a sickness won't be fixed merely by changing the man at the top. The proper cure requires an overall evaluation of the organization's health.

It should come as no surprise that in building Knightsbridge Shaw went to extraordinary lengths to put together a team of principals and consultants who are at the top of their game. Among the 300 or so professionals in the company's 22 offices across Canada and in the U.S. are men and women — a surprising number of women, in fact — who have authored books and papers considered by their peers to be as authoritative as any in the field of human resources. In their frequent public appearances, Knightsbridge personnel constantly beat the drum for change, citing instances of their holistic philosophy in straightforward language everyone can understand. One frequently cited example relates to a traditional approach of developing leaders by packing them off to retreats to engross themselves in current theories. They come back to their offices pumped up about reshaping their companies' culture only to find the rest of the employees haven't a clue what they're talking about. Their enthusiasm quickly melts away.

"The individual leader, even with the best of intentions and newly developed skills, doesn't have the strength, or the critical mass or the energy to overcome what are very strong forces in the organization," says Liane Davey, a Knightsbridge principal. "It's not that we shouldn't invest in individual skill development, it's that it's not enough."

Another Knightsbridge principal, Vince Molinaro, points to the underlying moral of the story: that no amount of individual leadership will improve a situation unless everyone from the boardroom to the mailing room has a clear appreciation of what policies, what kind of corporate culture, an organization is striving to project.

In an industrial situation, it's relatively easy to gauge an organization's success. Financial numbers tell the story quite readily. But, in human resources, dealing with human behaviour and thought processes, success is not so easily measured. North American companies, for example, spend more than $3-billion a year on training new generations of corporate leaders. But many experts agree that there remains a huge gap between the number of new leaders that are required and what are available. Knightsbridge was formed to help fill that gap by creating a seamless, end-to-end consulting process that covers the full spectrum of human capital solutions.

The company's tag line — "Thinking Moves Ahead" — not only describes how Knightsbridge approaches the consulting services it provides to clients. It also sums up the company's own philosophy that clients should fully understand the trends that are taking place in the market. Only with that information can they determine current and future needs and the responses required to satisfy the needs of their customers.

Founder and Chief Executive officer David Shaw says the company slogan shows that Knightsbridge is always thinking about the future, not only on behalf of its clients, but also for its own benefit. "When we founded the company, we looked for areas in which we could make a difference, where we could satisfy changing customers' needs. We realized the human capital management industry was quite fractured, with providers concentrating on specific areas. This meant that many customers had to seek out different providers for different aspects of human capital management. In turn, this told us there would be an increasing need for an end-to-end solution, and this became our value proposition."

Before launching the company, Shaw carefully researched his idea and canvassed prospective customers and others in the industry about its viability. "We went to several people and asked if this would work," he says. "Generally, people were intrigued and saw the logic, but said that no one had ever had the courage to do it. The fact was we were taking a risk to try to create a new business model. And while that meant competing within the industry, it also meant competing with entrenched businesses with their own brand equity and their people in place. We knew we were creating something brand new — a system where we could provide service to companies for all aspects of their people management, or their employee or organizational life cycle. Most importantly we knew we had to create the glue that would hold the various aspects together."

Shaw's background and corporate experience allowed him to think outside the box in creating Knightsbridge. He is a veteran, not of human resources, but of consumer products. For 22 years, he worked around the world as an executive for PepsiCo, in finance and operations in Canada, then internationally for Pepsi operations in Australia, Southeast Asia (Malaysia, Indonesia and Singapore) and Turkey. Eventually, he returned to Canada to become President and Chief Executive Officer of Pepsi Cola Canada Beverages, a $1 billion company. As CEO of Pepsi Canada, he was responsible for both the business end of consumer sales and strategy, and the industrial end, which involved bottling production, distribution and supply. He gained a thorough grounding in strategy, marketing, and operations. In 1999, when Pepsi Canada's bottling operations were spun off into a separate entity, Shaw left the company to pursue a long-cherished desire to become an entrepreneur. It was new ground for him and he wanted first to understand what it meant to go out on your own to try to construct your own business. He worked to gain experience with a private equity firm that invested in entrepreneurial operations. Eventually, he landed on the business concept that ultimately became Knightsbridge. "Pepsi were very big developers of people," he says. "They were all about stretch assignments, providing their people with opportunities and measuring how they were doing. They were a huge results-driven organization with a culture of winning. As a manager you had to deliver results. They were and are a great developer of people. It's their competitive edge.

"I ended up in human capital because the way in which Pepsi developed their people was in my DNA. I wanted to create a company that had excellence in service, that had tremendous people working together but was also operated in a rigorous style to bring knowledge to clients. Great people working together and focussed on a vision make it an exciting place to work. I had known this at Pepsi, and wanted to create the same culture with Knightsbridge."

Once he had honed his vision, Shaw began methodically building a company that would live and breathe the culture he envisaged. It meant finding investors and making key acquisitions — "four right out of the hat to cover the areas we wanted to work in " — to round out his range of services. "At first, prospective customers looked at our story and liked it," he says, "but they didn't really believe we could make it happen. It was slow going initially, but eventually it reached a point where customers understood we had the capacity to make it happen."

Of critical importance, Knightsbridge had to ensure that the company was governed by a set of values to which all its employees subscribed. This is no easy task when managing a company that employs consultants, who traditionally tend to act independently. Having made the initial acquisitions, the company took a calculated breather over the next two years to integrate Shaw's vision and values into Knightsbridge. But it was essential, he believes. "We spent a lot of time building a team culture," he says. "We needed a brand that would resonate in the marketplace and that means a strong value proposition. To get that brand recognition you have to have people galvanized behind that proposition and who live the brand day in and day out and who pound their chest with pride when they tell people they work with Knightsbridge. We embedded courage as a core value. We had the courage to construct a new business model and that takes a certain type of individual, one who knows how to deal with ambiguity."

Shaw recognized, for example, that such a company would need people who understood the tensions involved between operating a successful company and providing first rate consulting services. Knightsbridge spurns "lone wolves." All those connected with the company are acutely aware that they are part of a team and that the group rises and falls on each member's contribution. It means that the consultants it employs are able to perform equally well in as many roles as are required.

"Everyone here is very effective at lead generation and spotting opportunities and knows how to move those opportunities around the group," says Shaw. "We have many stars in the system but they are interested in only one thing — doing their work as a team in front of the customer. They want to be able to look their customers in the face and say they can help them with a particular challenge and have the comfort and trust knowing that their team-mates would be providing the level of service that they themselves would give. It's all about knowledge and sharing best practices, no matter what the discipline."

Shaw's passion for his business strategy was a positive factor when he set about raising the initial $7 million he and his then partners needed to make the company happen. He also faced one of those frightening moments familiar to many would-be entrepreneurs. In Shaw's case, the moment was the realization that as an entrepreneur he was taking a far greater risk than he ever did as the chief executive of a billion-dollar company. And it's not only the financial risk; it's also your reputation that is on the line.

The reality of his position struck home after Shaw had acquired a human resource management unit from the giant consulting/accounting firm KPMG. "I handed over the cheque to buy the business and realized I had only $10,000 left in the bank and had to make payroll within two weeks," he says. "I learned several lessons right there and then.

"The first was that in the corporate life I never had to worry about cash flow but that in an entrepreneurial venture cash is king and that's where most problems lie. I now tell people who are interested in becoming an entrepreneur that the first question you need to ask yourself is always: 'do you understand cash?' There is only one focus required and that is daily cash management. I still look at our cash three times a week and some would say even that is not enough. Frankly it's your measure of health and success.

"The second lesson is that having a good relationship with your bank is an imperative, regardless of whether things are going well or not. It's a fundamental of building an entrepreneurial venture. Never underestimate this. You need a large measure of trust and a level of transparency with your bank, especially if you have personal guarantees on your home. Nothing keeps you more focused than that."

Another lesson Shaw learned was that the first few years of building a vision takes 150 per cent of your focus. "It's your reputation that is on the line and your personal guarantee to many employees that your vision is correct — and that they will get paid every two weeks. You have to have the ability to balance all the different components with setting up a business, maintaining a positive attitude and being able to manage under stress as well as you do when things are going well. Finally, you need the ability to communicate what you are doing and how you are doing it, so people can understand where you are going."

Of all the lessons learned, however, perhaps the most important is to stick with your vision. Shaw wanted Knightsbridge to become Canada's finest human capital solutions firm, a $100-million company that would sit at the top of the human capital management industry. Believing in your vision, he says, is sometimes the only thing that keeps an entrepreneurial venture going in the tough, early building period. Unfortunately, having the vision is often missing from the strategic planning process of many entrepreneurial operations, he says. "Your vision allows you to focus on the future. You need a beacon so that when you get knocked off the road — and you will

— you can get back on. With a vision, everyone knows where he is heading. It's just so important."

Shaw's vision was for Knightsbridge to offer an impressive array of services designed to deliver "integrated, sustainable solutions to complex human capital challenges." Today, these services include assessment of leadership potential and coaching of individuals, how to attract talent and how to build organizational and leadership capability and capacity along with career management and transition. Knightsbridge has recently moved into workforce deployment, assisting companies to enhance productivity and efficiency by implementing and aligning processes around scheduling and time management of their labour force.

Many items on Knightsbridge's menu of services are the result of judicious acquisitions and alliances. The company has been relentless in assimilating quality firms in its drive to the top. Early on, it acquired the Canadian career transition practice of KPMG Consulting LP, Herman Smith Search, a boutique executive search firm in Toronto. This was followed by the acquisition of GSW consultants and Bussandri Macdonald Groupe Conseil (Quebec), firms that provide executive assessment, executive coaching, organizational development and leadership capability services, including succession planning.

After a period of integration and fine-tuning, Knightsbridge in 2006 acquired the leading independent executive search firm in Toronto, Enns Partners, to increase its level of executive search. And in 2007, it signed a licensing agreement with the HR Chally Group, a U.S.-based assessment services group, for the use of its web-based selection and development technology. In June 2008, it acquired Belle Isle Djandjii Executive Search Inc., a leading Quebec executive search company, to strengthen its market presence in Quebec and enhance sectoral expertise.

In the next month, it acquired Axsium Group Inc., North America's leading consultancy in workforce management solutions. Axsium delivers business and technology advisory services to companies with large workforces, primarily in the retail sector. Workforce management is the nuts-and-bolts of human capital management in large organizations because it uses technology to automate the time, attendance and scheduling of its people.

"It's an extraordinary business," says Shaw, " that is simple to understand. For example, in the retail sector, having employees properly scheduled so that when consumers come into the store shelves are stocked and a proper level of cashiers are at their checkouts is crucial to maintaining customer satisfaction. The beauty for an organisation is that not only do they improve productivity and efficiency, but they also increase customer loyalty, employee satisfaction and top line revenues. Otherwise you risk losing these customers.

"Axsium Group is a perfect strategic fit that uniquely positions Knightsbridge to further build its breadth and depth of human capital services in Canada and to expand our reach into the United States," Shaw says. "It adds exceptional workforce management domain expertise to our arsenal of integrated human capital solutions consultants, expanding the reach, depth and speed at which we manage customers' workforce and talent challenges."

By understanding competitive strategies and customer needs, by identifying market trends and the changing nature of industry, Shaw has ensured that Knightsbridge is on track to achieving his original vision of a $100-million goliath in what has been essentially a small-firm market. By offering services that help companies at all stages of their organizational life cycle, Knightsbridge is two-thirds of the way to that goal. Today, it is considered to be Canada's premier human capital solutions company, with many large organizations counted among its clientele. "We were the first in this industry to apply a holistic approach to human capital management," Shaw says. "We have always had a mission to move people and organizations to greatness by reshaping how the market unlocks its human and organizational potential."

Integrating the work of many different consultants offering many different services is no simple matter. There is much potential for overlap and redundancy. Knightsbridge approaches this complex task by ensuring that its people have the opportunity to become knowledgeable around several practice areas. This allows for personal growth of the individuals who are the fibre of Knightsbridge. And the company has always worked to ensure that its people have a broad view of the organization and of its role.

Inevitably, that role adapts to meet changing circumstances. The economic decline of 2008/09 sent many business executives into crisis mode, desperate for inspired leadership to guide them through the downturn. As Knightsbridge consultants Stephanie Paquet and Bryan Benjamin pointed out in a paper written in 2008: "In today's increasingly volatile business environment, it has never been more important to have the right talent in the right roles." Their paper posed some key questions, such as:

Which leadership positions are most critical to the organization? To what extent is there a plan to mitigate risk against critical positions? What is being done to accelerate development to ensure ready-now talent pools of leaders are in place for critical leadership positions?"

As a different Knightsbridge paper says, "What makes this downturn especially challenging is the fact that many of the people leading organizations today have not been at the helm during similar turbulent times. In fact, most leaders and employees in the workforce today have not directly experienced this type of economic crisis in their working lives. For most of the workforce this is new territory."

Knightsbridge consultants believe they can offer practical solutions to organizations wrestling with these unfamiliar issues, alerting them to possible pitfalls. A common response among some executives facing tough times is to over-react, the consultants say. This can leave them immobilized by fear. Another is to under-react

— "there is no shortage of leaders with their heads in the sand, just waiting for the crisis to pass." The Knightsbridge consultants advise a middle way — "to react productively, to roll up one's sleeves and get to work." Recognize that the crisis is a test of individual and collective leadership and that it can create opportunities. "Have people in your organization develop plans for how to capitalize on opportunities created by stresses in the system. Then strike while the iron is hot."

It is easy to imagine a troubled corporate executive turning for comfort and solace to a Knightsbridge consultant offering solid advice based on decades of experience and being challenged with the words: "Leadership will be judged not by how a leader excels during the good times, but rather by her resilience during tough times. As a leader, what is your personal resolution during this crisis? Are you ready?"

Knightsbridge is certainly ready for anything. "It's really quite simple," says Shaw. "We help get people on the bus. We keep people on the bus and help them be more effective from a standpoint of leadership. We help organizations deploy their people in a much more efficient manner. And finally we help them get off the bus when the time arises and help them think through the next stage of their personal career."

Knightsbridge's premiere service, and its strategic wedge, is in the area of organization and leadership development. The goal is to align a company's structure, people, culture, skills, processes and systems to ensure that human talent and organizational solutions are in concert with its overall business strategy. Knightsbridge consultants work with organizations to develop visions and identify core values.

In the area of developing leadership, Knightsbridge provides a service that is increasingly in demand. As Managing Director Vince Molinaro has said: "Building leadership capacity — ensuring an organization has the right talent to fill future leadership roles — is critical for businesses these days." The problem is exacerbated by the sobering statistic that between 40 and 60 per cent of today's leaders are nearing retirement age. Candidates with the necessary knowledge, experience and leadership capability to replace them are in short supply. To address this problem, Knightsbridge designs and delivers award-winning leadership development programs based on the central concepts of its best-selling book, The Leadership Gap (Weiss & Molinaro, 2005, published by Wiley & Sons).

Knightsbridge principals Molinaro and Liane Davey have since collaborated on a second book, co-authored by David Weiss, entitled Leadership Solutions: The Pathway to Bridge the Leadership Gap, a work that elaborates on the holistic approach to HR adopted by David Shaw. The book has been widely and favourably reviewed. One reviewer wrote in the Canadian HR Reporter: "The authors have capably tackled a complex and pervasive mission critical challenge that has eluded clear understanding, effective implementation and crucial outputs. The book is no less than a detailed handbook for crafting near-term solutions to produce longer-term results." The same reviewer also hailed the book's "thoroughly defined" explanation of what holistic leadership is all about, saying that "in retrospect it appears to be the keystone for the entire framework, ensuring employees have 'an integrated view of the enterprise and can focus the organization's resources on creating customer value.'" Another reviewer welcomed the authors' "practical approach" and their inclusion of "leadership culture, organization practices and leadership behaviour as key cornerstones of their holistic leadership model." While the primary focus had traditionally been on leadership behaviours, "the new model represents a more balanced approach for transformational change and sustained results."

When professionals with decades of experience in human resources deliver such positive opinions about the Knightsbridge holistic philosophy it is evident that David Shaw has proved his vision to be an inspired one. In a few brief years, the former Queen's

University commerce grad has transformed Knightsbridge into one of Canada's largest human resources firms. He appears to be enjoying his success. It's been said of him that he is "having too much fun running this business."

But he can be deadly serious about the challenges facing business leaders: "The successful organizations in the future will be those that understand where the labour market trends are and understand the need to be adaptive to the people who work in their organizations," he has said. "I don't think people will recognize the work force between today and 10 years from now in terms of . . . the way we work, the people who are engaged in the work force and the work that people are doing. I think every organization should be looking at doing things very differently . . . knowledge workers can migrate very quickly." Such key questions explain why Knightsbridge is so closely aligned with the Canadian Business Hall of Fame, with which it works to identify the leadership challenges of the future.

Away from his Toronto office, Shaw is active in the community. He is a former chairman of the North York General Hospital Foundation and a former member of the hospital's board of directors. He is chairman of the Stratford Chefs School and has also served on the advisory board of the Schulich School of Business. He currently sits on the board of Queen's School of Business. At work, he is a director of Amrop, a global alliance of executive search firms of which Knightsbridge is a member, and he sits on two public company boards.

LEAGUE

**INTERGENERATIONAL
WEALTH™**

Adam Gant and Emanuel Arruda, League Assets Corp. Founding Partners

League Assets Corp.

I t seems entirely probable that the economic recession that roiled across Canada in late 2008 will eventually rebound to the benefit of businesses that observe such old-established virtues as financial transparency and that adopt the highest ethical principles. So much of what had occurred to undermine confidence in the old economy was due either to moral turpitude or unapologetic greed — and, often enough, a toxic combination of both. Is it too much to expect that the massive task of rebuilding business confidence, launched in the early days of U.S. President Barack Obama's first administration, might be harnessed to the birth of new corporate morality — one in which top executives begin to attach more importance to issues other than the bottom line?

The notion is not so impossibly altruistic. Leaner times stiffen competition. When there is less demand, those who would supply it must exercise greater discipline — offer more for less — if they are to survive and prosper. Citizens who were appalled and shocked by the behaviour of the grasping financiers who brought Wall Street to its knees might in future demand greater accountability. Corporations were, perhaps, put on notice that more would be expected of them in areas not just of customer service, but in matters of social conscience, a sustainable quality of life and in particular of the environment.

There were already examples of entrepreneurs who had early on recognized the value of adopting such high-minded principles, even before the global recession began to take its toll. The success of one of the fastest growing private real estate equity investment companies in Canada, League Assets Corp., shows how capital and conscience can work in harmony for the benefit of all. The firm, based in Victoria on Vancouver Island, and now active across the country, was founded on the solid premise that commercial real estate is a reliable long-term investment whatever the current state of the economy. But the co-founders of the company, former Canadian national oarsman Adam Gant and Emanuel Arruda, son of Portuguese immigrants to Canada, developed that premise with the goal of making the opportunity for profitable investments in real estate available to ordinary, middle-class Canadians, not just the extremely wealthy.

With a minimal investment — people have become "Member-Partners" in League for as a little as $1,000 — you can buy yourself a stake in a multi-million-dollar shopping mall offering both a monthly return on your money plus a stake in the growing value of the equity. Since League was founded in 2005, its investors have been rewarded with enviable returns. They speak highly of League's accomplishments, in particular of its commitment to long-term wealth creation for future generations of investors' families — what the founders call Intergenerational Wealth™. In fact, their real estate investment trust, the IGW REIT, is named for this very goal.

Like many young couples, Jonathan and Cindy Goosen spent everything they earned when they were first married. Planning for their retirement was seldom on their minds. The Dartmouth, Nova Scotia, couple were still paying off their own student loans while they raised four young children. They now face the cost of their children's education while still pursuing Cindy's dream of one day purchasing a small farm. Through investing in the League, the Goosens hope to accomplish twin goals — to teach their children "to be comfortable with money and to understand the power of investing in the future."

League co-founders Arruda and Gant regard their investors almost as "family." The company chooses deliberately not to employ "traditional" salespeople, those usually identified in the public's mind as hard-nosed, heavy-handed types bent on selling something you don't need. Instead, League responds to inquiries by directing people to its "Blue Book, the company "bible" that sets out its aims and principles and explains how the company's syndicated real estate investments work — including its private REIT and Limited Partnerships — and why its model is so successful.

"The Blue Book allows investors to see what we see in every opportunity so that everyone can make a truly educated and informed investment decision without needing an investment 'advisor' to 'explain' it to them — for a fee, of course," Arruda says. When someone calls, League employees introduce the Blue Book to them. "We tell them that if they are interested after reading the book they can call us back. Most investors like this because everyone gets the same treatment, even if they don't enjoy equal wealth. That's a tenet of our credo. Every Member-Partner shares the same enrolment experience and there's no pushy salesman breathing down your neck."

The company credo embodies the spirit of everything the company does. It is read at the beginning of all company meetings and its values are non-negotiable. It is a remarkable document, penned by Arruda himself during a period of personal reflection. Among its 22 cardinal points, the credo states: "We will do for others as we would have them do for us." It stresses qualities of leadership: "We must be bold, prudent, and above all, free from the fear of making an honest mistake." And when mistakes are made: "We will acknowledge them openly, correct them immediately, and look upon each as an opportunity to gain valuable lessons." In a section devoted to the company's dedication to its customers, the credo declares with high-minded confidence: "With each investment we initiate, and each new Member-Partner that we help to achieve Intergenerational Wealth, we add strength to the fabric of our free society." League's Member-Partners, it says, are "comprised of extraordinary individuals who are deserving of respect."

It was the Blue Book that caught the attention of Joshy Kallungal, a retired professional engineer living in Aurora, Ontario. To ensure that he and his wife, Esther, could afford to do the things they enjoyed, they needed to supplement his pension. "I do have other investments that I manage myself," he said. "I haven't used a broker in years because, frankly, I have not known one who can do better than I can." But Kallungal was intrigued enough to invest with the League and two years later says his investment is doing about 50 per cent better than his other equity investments. The couple are having a "wonderful time" playing tennis, travelling, golfing and reading — "all things I didn't have time to do when I was working. I'm very happy with the results to date. What was promised was delivered."

The potential of an investment that would go on paying back into the next generation was what first brought Montrealers Tom Kalmar and Leslie Cameron to League. Many years previously, Leslie's grandparents had acquired an oceanfront log home with a spectacular view near the picturesque Vancouver Island community of Lantzville. When the couple came to consider making an investment, their primary motivation was to ensure a way of keeping the seaside haven in the family for generations to come. Today, they say their investment with the League has made it possible to guarantee that legacy for their four children. To those thinking about taking the plunge with League, Tom and Leslie have this advice: "Just do it!"

What is the secret to League's success in the volatile commercial real estate market? For one thing, it's Adam Gant's eye for a bargain. Gant's countrywide network of brokers is briefed to alert him to what are recognized as League's specialty — "ugly duckling" shopping malls in dire need of a makeover but which are, nevertheless, producing a positive cash flow. Typically, says Gant, they are properties with a "negative emotional reaction." In blunt terms, that means they're the kind of malls shoppers might be inclined to pass by. The previous owners may have been "milking" the mall for whatever cash it could generate, even with high vacancy rates and maintenance that may have been sorely neglected. When Gant looks at such a property, his first thought is: 'how much better it's going to be when we get our hands on it." Some potential buyers, he says, walk away without considering the real value, meaning League gets a good opportunity at a good price.

League doesn't think only of the property itself. The company's philosophy goes beyond slapping on new paint or jacking up the rents. It takes into account the impact that improvements might make not just to the property itself but also to the immediate community. Says Gant: "While all improvements made to the properties must impact our bottom line they must only do so without negatively affecting their communities and without harming the environment. Our aim is to enhance the properties such that they rate best in their class and provide quality working environments for our tenants."

It's an honourable goal, but what makes it a practical one from the investors' perspective is that their interests come first. League charges a small "acquisition fee" — recently reduced even further — for negotiating the purchase of a property. The ownership itself goes 100 per cent to the investors. The company mostly profits, along with investors, as its improvements to the site increase the overall value of the property. From the outset, the company opted to do something virtually unheard of — not to take a piece of the ownership, or cash flow, up front. Instead, the company earns it incentive share only after investors' value has increased when it takes a 20 per cent cut of the value added as a result of the improvements made. Investors share the rest.

The founders describe their philosophy as a "more equitable form of group ownership for larger investment properties." As partners in a private company, Arruda and Gant pride themselves on their direct dealings with investors, whom they look upon as friends as well as investment partners. Investors are referred to as "Member-Partners" who have contributed to the building up of a League Assets Corp. portfolio of Canadian commercial and retail properties with combined assets approaching $300 million. Add in the estimated build-out value of its other investment pools, including the development of a four million sq. ft. city centre in Colwood, B.C., and that number will eventually swell to around $2 billion.

Arruda's effective communications strategy and innovative management of client services, combined with Gant's savvy spotting of distressed properties and talent for value creation, have propelled the company's continued success despite the recent downturn in the financial markets. Gant points out that League's real estate investment trust provides investors with a stable portfolio of income producing properties whose values, unlike the stock market, don't go up and down from day to day. "Typically, we buy to hold indefinitely," he says.

The value of recently improved properties in the IGW trust is assessed every three months and at each quarterly re-evaluation period any increase in net asset value is added to the unit value of the IGW REIT units. Annually, a third-party appraiser re-values the entire pool and verifies the unit price. As of January 2009, the results from the trust outstripped the five-year results of all publicly traded Canadian real estate trusts. The publicly traded REITs were being influenced by stock market trends from which League, being private, is largely insulated. As of February 2009, despite the downturn in world markets, the unit value for League's IGW REIT increased to $1.117 per unit. The total annual return for the preceding 12 months was 14.04 per cent. The annualized return since February 1, 2007 was 15.74 per cent, which includes the cash distributions plus an 11.7 per cent increase in the unit value since inception. In a real estate market that was taking a beating, League's redevelopment and leasing efforts proved enough to offset adverse local market conditions.

Apart from the financial returns, League offers other attractive incentives to investors. In the IGW REIT structure the value of your ownership stake grows, tax-deferred, until you decide to sell your units. When you do finally sell, just as with direct ownership of real estate, Revenue Canada treats the increase in value as a capital gain, which means it is taxed at 50 per cent of your marginal tax rate.

Surveying the economic outlook in early 2009, Arruda said: "Where others would be tempted to throw up their hands and blame the markets our team has redoubled their efforts to help us reach the targets we set while times were still good." He emphasized that League has never missed a distribution payment to Member-Partners. "We're proud of the fact that no Member-Partner has lost money investing with League."

Gant and Arruda have largely shunned any focus on themselves as personalities, choosing instead to focus on their ideals and the League's attention to sound fundamentals, its determination to succeed and its distinctive corporate philosophy. But the two co-founders have interesting, though different, stories to tell.

Arruda was born in the Portuguese island of San Miguel. He was 18-months-old when he moved with his family to Toronto. Like many who hail from the Azores archipelago, he brims with "simpatico," – a Portuguese word that denotes a demeanour of ready smiles, engaging humour and refreshing honesty. The young Arruda first learned about real estate from his father, who worked as a superintendent of apartment buildings in Rexdale, Ontario for 24 years. At age 10, Emanuel began assisting his father, including showing suites to prospective tenants on his own.

"I come from the school of hard knocks," he says. He says his entrepreneurial streak first manifested itself while studying science at the University of Toronto. He then turned to the business world, giving up an earlier ambition to become a surgeon. He started by doing sales on the street, armed with an attitude that said, "Nobody gets by you. If you screw up, learn from it and use what you learn for the next opportunity you have." Then came a stint as owner of a boutique advertising and marketing firm. But it was a personal incident — the break-up of a marriage — that uprooted him from Toronto and brought him West.

"We sold the house and in two days sold everything we owned. My ex, an actress, was away 10 months of nearly every year we'd known each other, and we hadn't seen each other for more than a week in nearly two years. But when everything was sold and gone we decided to take one last road trip together. It was then we realized that we'd made lots of cash flipping houses "by accident," so why not do it on purpose? We decided to buy an RV so we'd have a clean place to eat and sleep while we fixed and flipped our way across Canada," he recalls. It was an adventure, he says, but, as the Rockies opened the way to the breathtaking beauty of British Columbia, his immediate thoughts were, "I want to stay here."

He spent some nights in the parking lot of a WalMart on Vancouver Island before finding a more permanent home for his RV near Port Alberni. "At times then I thought myself to be a dumb ass — 'you don't have a house . . . you don't have a car'. But I remember the lesson I learned selling everything I owned in two days on my front lawn: The things you own, end up owning you." He met up with a realtor who introduced him to the concept of real estate syndication. He realized that his instincts and experience made him a natural for the business.

Using the RV as his rolling headquarters, Arruda worked on his first two properties and it was then that he met Adam Gant. The two began talking business and partnership. "I was sure about Adam," Arruda recalls. "The man is incapable of guile." They found they shared similar morals and ideals as well as a desire to create lasting wealth with a social purpose. But still he felt he needed time to cement plans for the future.

"I literally disappeared into the woods for 40 days to search my soul," he says. Like the biblical Moses descending from Mount Sinai with God's commandments carved in tablets of stone, Arruda emerged from his wilderness retreat with a noticeably longer beard and the broad outlines of his proposed enterprise engraved on his heart. As well as the basis for the Blue Book, he had sketched out tenets of what became the company's credo.

"I wanted to make sure we all knew the ground rules and that we all shared the same definition of honesty, among other things," he says. "Our credo is the basis of our partnership and our business. It is what gives our investments a better chance of success relative to the competition."

Arruda's partner Adam Gant is the kind of guy you might feel equally at home with on Wall Street or strolling along Victoria's colonial waterfront. He grew up in the B.C. Interior city of Kelowna where his family ran a commercial chemical supply business. He had first thought of a career in engineering or physics but life offered a different opportunity. With a build of a pro-basketball player, the 6-ft-6-in. Gant set impressive numbers on the campus rowing machine when he went to the University of British Columbia in 1999. "Rowing is 25 per cent about your back, 60 to 75 per cent about your legs and 5 to 10 per cent about hands. I guess I was built for it," he says. As the records fell, Gant was scouted for Canada's national rowing team. In the summers, meanwhile, he returned to Kelowna to work on his house-painting business. "I drove around looking for dilapidated houses and offered to paint them. I set records for my franchise area doing painting jobs," he says.

Around this time, the real estate bug caught him. "When looking for painting jobs I would tell myself (about a particular building), 'it's so ugly, I love it.' I started reading business books and read stories about B.C. entrepreneurs and real estate deals." It was at university that Gant met his future wife, Tara, who was training to be a teacher, but who shared her fiancé's interest in real estate. When he and Tara closed their first real estate deal in Victoria in 2002, Gant was away in Italy representing Canada at the under-23 world rowing championships. "Soon we bought a second property," he recalls. "The timing was great, interest rates were coming down and there was extreme liquidity. It was the perfect storm," he says.

And then he met Arruda.

In the business of real estate syndication, sad stories outnumber the happy ones. Manuel Arruda and Adam Gant know this. They have lived it. What is different about these two professionals is that they have developed a company credo and they live and breathe it. So does each and every one of League's employees. It is their shared belief in the principles of honour and transparency and their ongoing commitment to improving the quality of life for families in Canada and abroad that sets them apart.

An unusual symbol of their credo is the heraldic crest that adorns the League's web site and its promotional literature. The granting of a Coat of Arms is a significant honour bestowed on select Canadian institutions by the Heraldic Authority of Canada under the authority of the Governor-General. The Chief Herald determines when a grant can be made and in the case of a corporate body this requires that its finances are in order and its activities are "responsible."

"League's Coat of Arms symbolically represents everything we stand for," says Arruda. The icon is intended to reinforce the tenets of the company credo. "If a future leader of League ever tries to take the company in the wrong direction — investing, say, in weapons manufacture — I hope that the employees and the board members will point to the Coat of Arms and say 'that crest says we don't do that.'

Just as the name 'League' was chosen to reflect the company's principles of "positive inter-dependence" and Member-Partnership, each element in the design of the Coat of Arms embodies an aspect peculiar to League. "It is our seminal statement of values and states what we as founders of League wish to accomplish," he says. The crest conveys the company's commitment to security and strength, alluding to secure investments while symbolizing the principles that the co-founders put in place to protect investors and investments.

Other elements on this heraldic signature include a flame that refers to the light of knowledge and League's commitment to educating and informing its Member-Partners. A helmet with an open visor denotes transparency of information as well the founders' dedication to growing a company built on solid systems, and not just on their leadership. A lion and an ox depict courage, leadership, industry and strength. A chain refers to the linking of investors in common goals. Perhaps the most significant aspect of the Coat of Arms is the motto that Gant and Arruda live by: "My word is my bond; my honour is my glory."

Words and symbols do a lot to showcase a business. But it is action that determines success. Chuck Desjardins, a certified journeyman machinist from Edmonton, says he was attracted to League "by what is said in League's written communications. The values and goals are aligned with mine," says the father of three sons. "There are a number of things about League and the way it does business that give me confidence." Key among them is "the fact that principals earn their share at the back end, alongside me, when the profits come in, so my investment is not diluted at the front end the way it might be with many other investments."

League traditionally has looked for distressed properties to rejuvenate, thereby attracting higher-paying tenants preferring locations made desirable by the improved use of space, signage, parking and other assets. An example is in Campbell River, a Vancouver Island town subject to cycles of boom and bust depending on the demand for the region's abundant natural resources. League acquired the Tyee Plaza in June 2007 for about $14 million, just as the community was emerging from an economic slump. Shoppers Drug Mart agreed to occupy 17,000-sq.ft. in the rejuvenated plaza. With such a prestigious tenant League was well on its way to achieving its goal of increasing the value of the property by $7 million by year's end 2008.

The Colwood project on the fringes of Greater Victoria represents a different departure for League, transforming the company from manager of assets to a real estate development finance company. The 13.89-acre site currently includes two strip malls and some houses. But the plan is to replace these with a new city centre, including as many as 11 high-rise buildings that will tower over the fairways of the Royal Colwood Golf and Country Club and 400 acres of lush greenery owned by Royal Roads University. This pioneering proposition, amounting to an eventual $1-billion redevelopment on the western shore of Vancouver Island, is by far League's biggest and most ambitious undertaking.

Over a 15- to 20-year span, local developer Les Bjola of Turner Lane Developments will work with League as its banking and finance partner to create City Centre Colwood, comprising 3.5 million square feet of office and residential buildings, a shopping, dining and entertainment district and substantial underground parking. This "green" development is to be financed through the Colwood City Centre LP, a League-controlled limited partnership. Since multiple buildings are planned for the site, Gant says there is potential for each to be financed by separate groups of investors. The goal is to create a new urban environment for the city of Colwood and, in harmony with League's social conscience, it is proposed to include some social housing.

"This is not a project which we will build and hope people will be attracted to it. It will be a planned and staggered development where each part will be tailored and focused to meet the needs of investors and tenants. Prevailing market forces will determine what is best for the site," says Gant.

For developer Les Bjola, who has been in the Victoria real estate industry for over 25 years, that is music to his ears. "If you're looking for instant gratification, you're not going to get it with this project," Bjola has said. League, he said, understands that it's not an overnight event, but rather a long-term relationship.

"They've got a very solid understanding of how they have to go about it. They have done smaller projects that show me they understand it's a work in progress; it's not a one-time thing."

Social responsibility looms large in League. "We are committed to playing a leadership role in bringing about social change," says Arruda. In this regard, in December 2008, League announced the formation of the League Charitable Foundation, a newly formed philanthropic arm of League Assets. Its principal objective is to tackle homelessness and poverty at home and around the world. The fund was announced along with an inaugural gift of $200,000 to the Greater Victoria Housing Society. Since 1956, the Society has been dedicated to providing affordable rental housing for seniors, families, and persons with disabilities.

League has also partnered with the Ontario-based Absolute Leadership organization to bring hope and relief to impoverished individuals around the world. Through a program called Hero Holidays young Canadians have an opportunity to travel to developing nations to build homes, schools and medical clinics. League is a principal supporter of Absolute Leadership along with Home Depot and WestJet airlines. "The Hero Holiday program is a vehicle for teenagers to learn the value of work, money, friendship and service to others," says Arruda. "These experiences will be especially important to the children and grandchildren growing up in the "inter-generationally wealthy" families of League's Member-Partners. We want to help them raise value-centred citizens, not materialistic brats."

The corporate responsibility shown by League and its Member-Partners has helped open the world to Canadians such as Rosana Morales, a nursing student at the University of Western Ontario. Morales was a Hero Holiday participant in 2007. The following year she organized a group of fellow students to facilitate medical clinics, health seminars and building projects in the Dominican Republic.

In 2009, League planned to help young Canadians in the Hero Holidays program to build houses in Mexico, assist a community of Haitian families and construct water pipelines in the Dominican Republic — among other things. Firm believers that actions speak louder than words, Gant and Arruda sent a quarter of League staff members on Hero Holidays last year. "We're trying to build an organization that no one would want to see fail," says Arruda. "That begins with showing our staff what League is all about."

On a rainy day in Victoria, with dark clouds hanging low over the city, Arruda and Gant gathered their staff together at their Oak Bay Ave. office to talk about plans for 2009 and lay out their vision. Their plans are ambitious. They want to achieve $80 million in new capital and enrol at least 700 more Member-Partners by mid-year. Their remarks to the staff were stirring: "We are building an organization that will create an evolutionary step in the advancement of human civilization . . . We are building a group of people who are driven to improve their own lives and the lives of those around them . . . We are building a team that will become a force of nature — moving with strength and purpose in fulfilling our goals."

Arruda and Gant then unexpectedly announced that they were giving up their respective roles as chairman and chief executive officer and from then on would be known simply as "co-founders" of League. "We intend this change to flatten our organization so that no one ever feels they must leave the company to seek advancement elsewhere. There will always be room at the top."

What is refreshing about League Assets Corp. is its wholesome conviction that the fair and successful acquisition of family wealth can be achieved within the context of a philosophy devoted to a sustained improvement in the quality of human life. The company's famous credo says it simply, but powerfully: "We must endeavour gradually to bring about such a reconstruction of society that poverty and its attendant evils shall cease to exist. We must do our part to ensure that future generations inherit from us a world that is cleaner, safer and happier than the one we know now."

As a business philosophy, it may be unique. It certainly deserves the success it has already achieved. And League Assets seems destined to continue that success in the coming years.

M & R Environmental
President and Founder
George Mate

The M&R board of directors
(l to r sitting) Barb Winberg
and Dani Mate
(l to r standing) Harold
Winberg, Rahmat Vefghi
and George Mate

M&R Environmental

George Mate takes his seat at the head of the M&R Environmental boardroom table and splays his fingers across its gleaming mahogany surface. "I want two things from this," he says. "I want to explain how this company was built so that other entrepreneurs can learn from my mistakes. And I want to give credit to the people who helped make it happen."

At 50 years of age, George Mate puts on no airs. He's dressed for comfort in worn Levis and an open-necked shirt under a sturdy jacket. What's appropriate on his waste-plant floor is equally good for the office. It's not the label on his suit that counts. In 1993, when he founded M&R Mobile Plastigrind, the company that would become M&R Environmental, he didn't set out to create new standards for the recycling of waste in British Columbia. But that's essentially what has happened. After years of heartache and sweat, his personal impact on the waste business has been extraordinary, particularly from an environmental perspective.

Mate confesses to making mistakes along the way, mistakes that cost him dearly. Given the chance to start over, he isn't sure he would. But he's being hard on himself. What enduring success isn't built on stiff lessons? As it turns out, in going toe-to-toe with national and international competitors for more than 16 years, he and his partners have helped define an industry standard for service and technical leadership. They have established a thriving enterprise for the collection and recycling of waste and the distribution of environmentally friendly products. They made, and continue to make, a difference.

M&R Environmental is tucked away in a Burnaby, B.C. industrial park and it's not exactly what you might expect. Across the street is a manufacturer of vitamins; a golf course borders the property. The facility is spotless and state-of-the-art. There are no waste oil drums rusting in the back corner of a fenced compound, or unpleasant odours. From the street, M&R Environmental looks more like a manufacturing plant than a hazardous waste treatment facility. Its 43 employees include licensed professionals, maintenance staff, business development managers, trained drivers and field personnel. The company did $10 million in sales last year and it dominates the Lower Mainland of British Columbia in each of its product and service categories.

The M&R story begins in 1982. At the time, 24-year-old George Mate and his wife, Dani, had been married for two years. He had spent a semester at the University of Haifa in Israel and was attending classes at Langara College. But he was not finding school an easy experience. This was a period of major economic recession with bank interest rates hovering around 18 per cent and unemployment at post-World War 2 highs. Mate decided to take a break from books. He sought advice and help. A family friend and peer, Larry Vinegar, said he could use a young man with a strong back and a willingness to learn. His firm, MasterWash Products Ltd., was in the used-oil collection and solvent tank rental business. It was a small, family-owned concern that manufactured the tanks and made money from changing solvents.

"I grew up with that company," Mate says. He was taught how to wash parts and ensure they were in working order, but his experience in other aspects of the business was limited. The firm had a division called Vinoco Oil that blended oil and produced lubricant for supply to auto shops. Marketing the products was the responsibility of an employee who drove a stocked truck throughout the Fraser Valley doing door-to-door sales and deliveries. When the man was convicted of a DUI charge and lost his license, Mate got the job. "I'd been a parts washer service rep and didn't see myself in sales, but Larry convinced me to give it a try and I discovered I had an affinity for it. I found I was able to identify with the customers and did quite well at it."

By 1991, the Vinegar family had tired of the hazardous waste business. They sold out to Laidlaw Environmental. Mate went along as part of the corporate assets. He found himself a cog in a much larger corporate machine where he was put in charge of the parts washer division. "I grew that business from 1,100 units to about 1,850 units in three years, but through that time I really hated working for a corporation. I just hated it." He preferred the previous family environment. "It was more personal. I didn't like working for a large, publicly traded company because I saw stupid decisions being made every day that weren't in the interest of the company at all."

During three years with Laidlaw, Mate helped the parts washer division grow to include other services such as used oil filter recovery and spent antifreeze disposal. Because of what he was doing for Laidlaw, he says, "I ended up stumbling on to an opportunity which is what put me into business on my own. I was trying to get Mr. Lube's business for their used oil filters, as they were dealing with another company at the time. They said, 'we have a bigger problem that no one has a solution for. We're throwing out thousands of used oil bottles every week and they are just going into the landfill.'"

Mate, then 34, recognized the problem as a business opportunity, but found Laidlaw unwilling to respond to the challenge. "It's my opinion that big corporations don't want to be pioneers in anything," he says. "They're happy to try to horn into an existing market if they think they can find a profit, but they're not much for innovation."

Since he and Aaron Rahn, another Laidlaw Environmental employee, were both dissatisfied with their jobs, they agreed to try setting up an independent business. They founded M(ate) & R(ahn) Mobile PlastiGrind with a staff of four. They bought a granulator in Los Angeles and leased a five-ton truck to carry it.

"The biggest challenge you have collecting plastic is that you're moving a lot of air and not a lot of weight," says Mate. "We thought it would be innovative if we could grind the material on the spot and then go on to the next customer." It wasn't long before they faced their first challenge. When they tried to put the granulator on the truck, they found it was too tall. "We figured that was no big deal. We could just cut it down to size," he says. But the granulator was engineered that way for a reason. "When you cut it down and make the throat shorter it doesn't work properly. You toss the stuff in and when it's grinding it wants to toss it all back out."

Mate shakes his head at the memory. It was just the beginning of his problems with the 'simple' recycling idea. Customers for the oil-bottle service were given bags in which to collect and store them, but inevitably the bags ended up stuffed with all kinds of other waste. "We thought we could just take the bags we collected on site and grind them right there, but the customers tossed in spark plugs and wrenches, oil filters and garbage. We learned the hard way that we had to take the bags to a sorting facility first."

And that presented a further difficulty, because M&R didn't have such a facility. The company was still operating out of a small, shared warehouse in Richmond, B.C. "One of the first things you need to establish when you get into the waste business is what you are going to do with the material after you collect it," says Mate. For M&R, the question involved two commodities — shredded plastic and residual discarded motor oil.

Finding a market for the plastic became a priority. Mate had negotiated a contract with an Ontario company to accept the waste, but at M&R's expense. "I sent it off to him at my cost. It was terrible. My profit was flying out the door bit by bit by bit."

Mate turned to Tony Moucachen, operator of the recycling company Merlin Plastics, which had a plant in Delta, B.C. The company had developed expertise in granulating, washing and reheating plastic materials that it turned into a resin, formed into pellets and resold for industrial use. "Tony said if I could figure out a way to get the oil off the plastic, he could reprocess it. We tried to set up a solvent wash system to remove the oil from the containers, which was a nightmare. Then we tried a water wash system. That was also a nightmare. Finally, we stumbled onto the idea of centrifuging the plastic and spinning the oil right off it by injecting heat."

The process worked. Merlin agreed to buy all of M&R's recycled plastic material and the relationship continues to this day. The waste oil was not a problem, as local companies such as Newalta would happily collect it. Meanwhile, M&R had left its shared warehouse space and moved to a new industrial home on Horseshoe Way in Richmond. That same year, 1997, Rahn decided to leave the business and sell his share. Lacking cash, it meant Mate had to agree to repay Rahn's $90,000 contribution to M&R's start-up capital out of future revenues. It was a tough commitment to make, for his wife Dani, his family and himself. He says he had faith in himself, but he had no idea how long it might take to meet the obligation to his former partner.

Mate had to dig deep to persevere. On a cold, rainy November afternoon not long after Rahn's departure, his commitment to the business was sorely tested on a personal level.

George and Dani had brought their children with them to work at their Richmond plant site. The couple's task that morning was to grind five-gallon water cooler bottles. "In those days we didn't have a facility big enough to handle our mobile grinder, so all the work happened outdoors," Mate recalls. With their three young daughters waiting inside the family car, Dani and George slogged through the muck in the work yard and lined up the bottles that had to be fed to the grinder.

The task was not difficult. But, every once in a while, one of the large plastic bottles would drop into the granulator incorrectly, jamming the machine. When that happened, Mate had two options. He could shut off the equipment and open the machine from the bottom to clear the blockage. That was time-consuming and difficult to do alone. Or, he could climb into the apparatus and manually free the bottle from the top by hand.

Mate was impatient that morning. Wet and cold, with the kids waiting in the car, he opted for the swiftest solution. After locking down the power so no one could accidently start the machine while he was inside, he shinnied up the conveyor belt. Standing on the rotor that fed the granulator's maw deep within the machine, he went to work to free the blockage. Unfortunately, he stood on the rotor in the wrong way. One set of blades spun and pinned him inside the equipment at the shins.

"The blades sliced though my pants and cut me quite significantly," he recalls with a shudder. "I was screaming in pain and Dani was standing outside in the rain completely powerless to help me."

Pinned and bleeding, Mate cursed his luck. "I couldn't believe the jam I'd gotten myself into. I'd walked away from a safe job that paid me in the mid-$70,000 without a worry and here I was pinned in a granulator, bleeding and practically penniless and I was doing it all for what? Sure, I had my own company but I was seriously wondering if it was worth the effort."

Weakened by blood loss, Mate was eventually able to free himself. He crawled out of the granulator into Dani's arms, cursing. "The accident was just one more thing I had to endure. There I was, virtually alone in the business, and badly injured. It was a traumatic moment for me.

"Nowadays, when I sit with employees and I share the history of the company, I try to help them understand what I had to endure alone in order to get to where I am now. It is all part of what it takes to win."

Another practical challenge he faced was that British Columbia had no stewardship program in place to govern the recycling of oil containers, or the hazardous waste oil the used bottles contained. When M&R approached potential clients to discuss fees for taking away their waste, they would say: 'Why should I pay you to do this (take away the used oil containers) when I can just put it in the garbage?' "What many of these people didn't realize was that the provincial hazardous waste regulations clearly stated if a container had more than three percent oil by weight in it you were not actually allowed to landfill it."

The problem was that the regulations were not being rigorously enforced and Mate found he had to fight for every customer. In 1998, he decided he'd better go on the offensive or he would soon be out of business. Again turning to a friend for advice, Mate hired Evan Stewart, a media relations consultant, to lobby local municipalities. The strategy eventually paid off and led to the Greater Vancouver Regional District inviting Mate to address its solid waste committee. With dramatic flair, the recycler gave the committee members an in-the-face lesson about the realities of used oil container recycling.

"I took a bag of oil bottles. If you stand with a bag of oil bottles long enough, all the residual oil will drain to the bottom of the bag. As I spoke it did exactly that. I held up the bag and said: 'this is what you're allowing into the landfill. Forget about the solid waste for a moment. Look at the hazardous waste you are allowing to leech into the water table. Not only that, you are allowing it contrary to provincial regulations.'"

The presentation galvanized the committee. Its members agreed to alert oil companies and commercial operators of automotive repair facilities to their responsibilities. They sent out a letter specifying how the companies were to handle the issue of used oil containers. If they could prove they had drained each bottle for at least one hour to accumulate all oil residues the GVRD would allow the plastic bottle in the landfill. If not, they had to find a designated service to recycle their bottles.

"It was not quite as good as a ban," says Mate, "but in part that is how we grew our business, because then the oil companies came on board. That letter provided us 200-odd more locations with a fee-for-service in the Lower Mainland. Unfortunately, we had already spent a lot of money and we were tremendously underfinanced." The challenge lay in securing the necessary resources to fund the company's growth.

There was one regular source of good income, but that, too, was soon to be put in jeopardy. M&R PlastiGrind was recycling five-gallon water cooler bottles, made from polycarbonate, normally a very expensive material with tremendous value in the recycling market. M&R had contacted all the major bottled water companies and built a market where it would bring its mobile grinder directly to their facilities. Previously, the water industry had landfilled all their cracked and broken five-gallon bottles.

"We had become quite dependent on the revenues we were generating from those companies," says Mate. "But in 1999 there was a great amalgamation in that industry. As certain companies grew larger through amalgamation they realized they were giving up a potential revenue stream by having us grind their polycarbonate bottles. So instead they bought and installed their own granulator and began grinding their bottles themselves. They then marketed their own waste material back into the plastic recovery markets. I lost about $60,000 in revenue overnight which is quite significant when you are only doing $400,000 a year. I was seeing stars."

And then there was the case of the underhanded competitor. As Mate tells it, a Richmond company called Waste Not Recycling was in the paper and cardboard recycling business. Its manager decided he could compete against M&R in the plastic oil container business. "He was running around town undercutting me by 50 per cent. I lost a fair bit of business to him. I kept saying, 'they can't do it for this amount,' and I questioned whether they were really recycling anything, but it didn't stop the stampede of customers."

At the time, Mate was managing the M&R operation from his home. "The phones kept ringing to cancel, cancel, cancel and it got to the point where I didn't want to answer. I literally was in tears when the phone rang and Dani just kept saying, 'It will be okay, we'll work it out.' Believe me, there were moments when she had the strength that I didn't."

Mate was proved right about the rogue competitor. An expose in the Richmond Review newspaper eventually showed that Waste Not Recycling was doing an abysmal job and was actually delivering waste oil containers to the landfill as garbage. But the damage to Mate's company had been done. "When I lost the water business, and other container contracts, it was devastating," he says. "I really had to re-evaluate what I was doing. I decided I needed to go back and start doing the things that I knew best. That included oil filter recovery, antifreeze recovery and parts washer sales and service."

Once Waste Not Recycling went out of business, M&R had no local competition in the plastic container side of the recycling business. However, there was ample national and international competition. "Up to then I was afraid of taking on the big boys like Laidlaw and Safety Kleen, but switching strategy meant I had to do it," Mate said. The evolution at M&R also meant the company had to invest capital to buy the barrels its customers could use to deposit the oil filters and the antifreeze for subsequent collection.

"Every time I went out to set up a new customer it was $120 out of my pocket." But the change in strategy worked. "We weren't making a profit, but we were starting to grow the business." In 2002, M&R's six staffers processed 2.5 million pounds of plastic and the company was doing $600,000 in business. During that year, former partner Rahn's investment was paid back in full.

While M&R now had better cash flow, it was still not sufficient to fund essential elements of growth. The company was collecting a huge number of oil filters but they still had to be processed to produce income. Arthur Weinstein, owner of Allied Metal and Salvage, was willing to accept M&R's used filters once they were cleaned of oil and crushed. But a crusher suitable for the purpose had a $100,000 price tag, beyond M&R's immediate resources. So Weinstein offered his friend help. He agreed to finance the purchase, generously allowing the loan to be repaid in kind with steel material.

Mate was still determined to build his business around used oil recycling and he was soon to recognize an opportunity waiting to be seized. There were then two chief competitors in the used oil business in B.C. One was Newalta, an Alberta firm that has since become one of Canada's leading industrial waste management and environmental services companies. (Today, Newalta transforms waste into $400 million of reusable products). The other competitor was Mohawk Oil. The two companies competed ferociously in Western Canada until Newalta bought out Mohawk in September 2002. Mate knew the Newalta people well because they had been among his former bosses at Laidlaw Environmental.

Once the takeover of Mohawk happened, he says, "there was essentially no competition for them in the used oil business and I started wondering whether there wasn't an opportunity for M&R to be an alternative in the marketplace."

That suspicion led to a phone call to a former workmate at Laidlaw, Rahmat Vefghi. Mate and Vefghi had a cordial history. Vefghi had worked for Newalta, where he played a significant role in expanding used oil markets. "I asked him to tell me about the used oil business. What would I do with used oil if I were to collect it? How would he deal with it? What had to be done to it?"

Mate offered to hire Vefghi as consultant, but Vefghi countered with his own offer to become a partner in developing a used oil division for M&R. "I thought I could do a good job collecting used oil and figured I had enough contacts in the marketplace to generate a good amount of business if Rahmat could find a place to sell it," Mate says.

M&R now needed a permanent storage location for its used oil. Acting on a suggestion from his old friend Larry Vinegar, Mate turned to Jim Wilson, owner of Active Chemical, who was processing bunker oil from Alaskan cruise ships transiting Vancouver's port.

With Vefghi's assistance, he was able to persuade Wilson he should take M&R's oil and process it with the bunker oil to produce a saleable blend. In February 2003 the three formed a company called PacWest Resource Recovery. Three pumper trucks were added to the M&R fleet through 2003 to handle its growing waste oil service business.

Meanwhile, Newalta's takeover of Mohawk had further unforeseen consequences for M&R. Until then, waste oil had been collected from customers without charge. But, following the takeover, Newalta began to impose collection fees amounting to six cents a litre, with a minimum invoice charge of $60. One of Newalta's major customers, Mr. Lube, baulked at the new levy, providing M&R a potential new client opportunity.

Mate knew the government and oil industry were discussing the terms of a stewardship program for the collection of used oil and oil products such as oil containers and oil filters. He also knew the program would likely become law in late 2003. He went to Mr. Lube with an offer to pay them two cents a litre for the million-plus litres of used oil that Newalta was charging them to collect.

M&R was already handling the collection of Mr. Lube's plastic containers. Mr. Lube gladly accepted the offer. "We felt that was an equitable thing to do — but yes, I was trying to tip the scale with that offer, and I did," says Mate. "We had a couple of trucks collecting 300,000 litres of used oil a month. There's a market of about 1.8 million litres of used oil available on the Lower Mainland monthly, so we were getting about 16 per cent."

During the summer of 2003, on the advice of a used oil recycler named Les Harper, then the owner of Little Dipper Holdings in Lloydminster, Alta., Mate leveraged his success with Mr. Lube. Through a radio advertising campaign created by media consultant Gary Chomyn (recommended to Mate by a customer), he managed to jump the gun on his competition. He advertised his willingness to pay for used oil two weeks before the stewardship program commenced.

"My phone started to ring off the hook. Our office was still in our home at that time and Dani was answering from 6:30 in the morning to 10 o'clock at night. Dani was literally up until midnight every night entering new customers into the computer and setting up service cycles and everything else." To handle the exploding challenge, Mate in 2004 rehired an old friend and former co-worker, Harold Winberg, as Sales and Marketing Manager. Winberg had gained impressive sales and marketing experience with Pennzoil Products Canada and quickly applied his skills with M&R.

"Harold took a different attitude about growing the business. Understandably, as a new company entering an established market, we were not well received by the competition. In our industry there is a lot 'smoke and mirrors' and plenty of mud gets flung. One of Harold's first observations was that we had to be transparent." Winberg's first strategy was to design a new M&R website replacing the former, single-page billboard site.

"We put every bit of information about M&R we could on the website, like our government permits and insurance information. It was all about being transparent to our staff, customers, prospects and the competition," Winberg says.

"All the mud that was being slung at us, we answered with facts on the website. Then I had to get people to the website, so I started an Internet-based contest in which customers could win gift cards every month. It was a huge success. I had never seen anything like it. The redemption rate was 35 per cent. At Pennzoil, we thought three to five per cent was excellent. We've had a web-based contest for our customers annually ever since."

In April 2004, M&R added the word 'environmental' to its name to better reflect the nature of its business. That year, it processed 20 million plastic containers, three million oil filters, 480,000 litres of antifreeze and nine million litres of waste oil. None of the waste ended up in landfills. By March 2005, the company had moved to its current 18,000-sq.ft. home in Burnaby.

Up to this time, M&R had been taking its used antifreeze to a small recovery business run by Bob Edmiston. Now Mate convinced Edmiston to come to work for M&R Environmental. One of his first tasks as manager of the glycol division was to find a better way of recycling used antifreeze. A company in Denver, Colorado, was making a mini, vacuum distillation processing plant that M&R purchased and installed that November. The company was now able to develop its own recycled antifreeze product, called Eco-Freez. Mate expected to sell 800,000 litres of recycled antifreeze in 2009, requiring well over one million litres of waste.

Among other major changes to the company in 2005, Mate & Vefghi ended their working relationship with Active Chemical and Harold Winberg and his wife, Barb, were invited to join Mate, his wife and Vefghi as partners in M&R Environmental.

"If I have had an ability to do anything it has been to recognize my shortcomings and to bring in the right people," Mate says. "Today we own about 52 per cent of the local used oil recycling market. We collect about 70 per cent of the waste antifreeze, 85 per cent of all the plastic oil containers and 60 per cent of the oil filters."

Winberg points out that M&R Environmental provides "full circle service and more products than our competitors." The company has 4,300 customers in its database and the list has grown by about 400 new customers a year since he came on board. "We're a dynamic company," he says, "particularly in caring for our employees. People here really matter."

Mate's choice to work in a family-like environment is one he does not regret. "Every year we have a blow-out Christmas party for the staff," says his wife, Dani, now comptroller for M&R Environmental. "We give a significant bonus and everyone heads home with a really nice gift. Last year we took 35 staff and their partners to Disneyland, just to change things up a little."

Running a successful enterprise is not all about the money, her husband maintains. "If you are resourceful and willing to persevere you will find a way. It's very much like me having a filter crusher for $100,000 financed by Arthur Weinstein. You find a way. When we were really struggling in 1996 and 1997, I asked Tony Moucachen for help and he lent me $50,000. I was willing to give him a percentage of the business, because I had to stay alive. He never asked for a contract or a legal agreement. He just handed over a cheque. I repaid it all. Our business is very much built on a lot of long-term relationships, and I don't bail on them."

MetroBridge Networks Corp.

A visitor must ring a buzzer to gain access to Dorian Banks' offices high above Georgia Street in downtown Vancouver. That way, says the president and co-founder of MetroBridge Networks Corp., he is more comfortable. He doesn't appreciate the thought of a stranger stumbling uninvited onto a business opportunity he or a member of his staff might have scribbled on an office white board.

And that could happen because, as Banks proudly says, he has at least one new idea "every few days" and "at least one a month is okay to do, and one per quarter is feasible and should be done." An entrepreneur since his schooldays, it's an understatement that Banks has a fertile imagination when it comes to creating new business.

Banks has done 'the deed' on a shoestring and as an agent of global companies. He has personally made millions, and lost them. He's gone from couch surfing in friends' homes, with a wallet flat as a haddock after a business failure, to living in five-star luxury. And it has happened more than once.

Dorian Banks has done business in easy economic conditions and in tough ones, like the recession the world experienced in 2009. He's gained a certain surefootedness that allows him to deal confidently with tough challenges. And, at age 39, he has acquired a suave demeanour honed by experience in North America and Europe. His acute sensitivity to opportunities is so ingrained that he looks at the world differently from most people.

His is the quirky perspective of an inventor devising new business services and products. Half the time, he says, he stumbles onto his best ideas. An example is his first lucrative entrepreneurial experience when he was in Grade 10. During Canada's major recessionary period in the mid-80s, role-playing was a popular fad among students and Banks was no exception. Dungeons & Dragons was in vogue then, and he found himself wrapped up in the schizophrenic world of avatars and strategy games. It was precisely the time when computers were beginning to make inroads as an entertainment tool.

"I got together with some other kids a little older than me at school to try to start a company," says Banks. "This was when we used 8 1/2-inch floppy disks and we were programming in Pascal. We started our business making a 'play by mail' game for kids without computers. People from all over the world subscribed for $9.95 a month by cheque. They would submit their move on a sheet of paper and we'd put it in the computer and run all the turns against each other. It was really a very complex version of Risk (Hasbro board game) because it was a world domination game. We called ours Balance of Power.

"We ran that business for a year. It's absurd to think people would play by mail but they did and it was a big thing back then before the Internet. We made a lot of money with it but eventually it was taking too long to process the turns. Our computer was just too slow. We ended up skipping class so we could spend time on the computer running the mailed-in moves. Eventually our attendance records showed and we got in big trouble at school, so we sold the company."

Chris Crawford, who had formerly worked for Atari, transitioned Balance of Power to computer. It was the first game he wrote as a freelancer and has been called the ultimate Cold War simulation. Of course, Dorian Banks had no idea just how meaningful the re-crafting of his game idea would become in a computer gaming environment that would grow to global proportions. The original computer version of Balance of Power was made for black and white Macintosh in 1985, ported to the Apple in 1986 and to Amiga and AtariST in 1987. It is nearly impossible to find now.

"I remember finding a copy in a second-hand game shop," Banks says fondly. It helped him realize that business ideas have a limited shelf life. Though his corporate adventure as a teen may have tarnished his scholastic performance, Banks says his mother gave him her full moral support. With various self-employed careers, including wedding planner, interior decorator and real estate developer, she passed along an acquired taste for entrepreneurial risk. He remembers she often helped him face off in discussions with his more traditionally minded father about the merits of using time for business ventures versus homework. He's still grateful.

It wasn't long after the game venture was sold that the youngster succumbed again to the lure of self-employment. He created a teen club in the basement of a restaurant in his hometown of Kitchener, Ontario. Called The Back Door, "it was a full on, full blown nightclub except that there was no alcohol and it was for teens only." The venue proved popular, so much so that Banks was forced to hire the high school football team as bouncers.

"We made a lot of money on that idea," he says, "but looking back I realize all the things I didn't do right, or do at all. No permits or inspections. No insurance. But you have all these turning points in life, the small moments that can change everything, and that club idea was one of them for me. My partner was Mike Kubenk and neither of us wanted to DJ. We just wanted to chat with girls. So to settle things we flipped a coin and Mike became the resident DJ while I kept the place running."

From that time on, Banks' destiny was to be business and his friend's became music. Kubenk, now known internationally as DJ Czech, has had a prosperous career since his days at The Back Door in 1989. A resident of Vancouver for the past 13 years, he has an extensive touring schedule and is one of Canada's leading DJs for up-front electronic music. He has played prestigious clubs and massive raves throughout Europe and North America for the past five years and is building his own music label, with two other partners, called Futuristic Funk Records.

After high school, Banks decided to pursue a business degree at the University of Western Ontario. His plan was to attend the Richard

Ivey School of Business there, but after a subject failure was noted on his transcript, the business faculty refused him admission. Perversely, his failing grade was in math. After taking remedial classes during the summer, he overcame that hurdle and eventually earned his B.A. His post-graduate goal was to get his business degree.

Banks' personal life took a dive in the last of his first four years at university. When a girlfriend who had been attending Richard Ivey got a chance to transfer to the London School of Business, she dumped him. "I was incredibly depressed over that," he recalls. School suddenly held little interest for him. He came close to being expelled for skipping classes. In an attempt to buoy his sprits, his mother had gathered pamphlets from various post-graduate schools and encouraged her son to apply. He did. But he remembers that first summer after graduating in 1988 as bringing a long series of rejections from universities around the world.

One day, however, his sister, Lara, handed him an envelope from Harvard. "I'd made it through the first round and needed to submit a $500 non-refundable deposit — which I didn't have — for my application. My dad said I'd already spent enough on school and that I should get a job. My mother, however, secretly wrote a cheque for me. I eventually got in, and then my real problems started."

Banks says he needed about $25,000 US to cover the costs of his two-year, post-graduate program and his bank account was dry. His father, then a vice-president with Dana Auto Parts, was not wealthy, but had a "comfortable income." Banks knew his father could afford to help him get to Harvard and he prevailed upon him to do so. "Eventually my dad said if I earned and saved half of what I needed over the summer, he'd pay the rest. That left me with a huge price tag and only two months, but I had no choice but to try. I wanted to get into Harvard."

In his high school days, Banks had taken photography courses at a community college and that training helped him land a day job at a photography studio. He would work all day there, come home to sleep for a few hours then head over to the Home Hardware distribution centre where he had a job as a forklift operator, working until 7 a.m.

It was a long, hard summer, but lack of sleep wasn't a problem for the energetic young man, who has a tendency towards insomnia. The hardest part of the job at the distribution centre was functioning in a union environment. It starved his entrepreneurial spirit to have to play by the union rulebook, he says, though somehow he managed to hold his tongue that summer. His bank account bulged with $8,000 before the fall, enough to persuade his father to pay the balance of his budgeted Harvard expenses.

During the next two years, Banks studied and earned his business degree, graduating with one of the highest marks in his class despite his weakness in math. His performance encouraged his professor to hire him as a teaching assistant in 1992. "I worked very hard and they paid me $2,000 a month in salary. It was essentially no money, because I worked 120 hours a week marking papers and helping to teach. But it looked good on my resume." Banks was asked to return again the following term and he accepted a post as a senior teaching assistant. When he arrived in Boston, however, he learned that two of the lecturers in his program had not been able to obtain working visas.

"They promoted me to lecturer, much against my will," he says. "I had to prepare lesson plans and teach in an amphitheatre with 90 students, many of them older than me. I did that for a year, and it was probably the biggest learning experience of my life. It had more of an impact on me than all of my previous university experiences put together because, essentially, I had to know more than all those students every day."

Fortunately, his lectures used a case-based method that made the process easier for all concerned. Shy by nature, Banks says that standing before the students was an excruciating experience. He got over that, too. "Now I can speak to a crowd of 5,000 without notes. Back then though it was very different."

Banks moved back to Kitchener knowing he did not want to pursue a career in academia. "I realized teaching wasn't for me. It had shaped my life, and that experience is like a strobe light on my resume, but I knew I wanted something different."

To take a mental break and think about his options, he moved to Grand Bend, Ont. where he and a friend, Jeff McCormick, opened a store selling trendy beach-wear clothes to the mostly student tourists. The clothes they stocked were popular and they branched out into making shirts for the serving staff in local bars. They took part of the payment for their shirts in beer. One evening, while doing his bar 'collections,' Banks heard a Tragically Hip tune — 'Fifty Mission Cap' — playing on the jukebox. The bartender said the song was his favourite, so Banks scribbled a logo on a napkin and said he'd put it on a baseball cap.

The ballad about Toronto Maple Leafs player Bill Barilko has become a Canadian hockey classic. Four months and five days after Barilko scored the winning goal in overtime to clinch Toronto's sixth Stanley Cup in 1951, the plane he was travelling in went missing on a flight back from a fishing trip in Quebec. His distraught team mates insisted his equipment be kept in his locker during training camp that fall, in case he showed up. He didn't, but it was as though the team was cursed that, unable to claim another Cup victory for the next decade. In 1962, however, helicopter pilot Ron Boyd found debris from the plane about 100 kilometres north of Cochrane, Ont. Barilko was buried in Timmins and, as if blessed from the beyond, the Maple Leafs beat the Chicago Black Hawks that year to reclaim the Cup.

"I made 100 of the hats and they all sold out the same day at $20 each," Banks remembers. "It was a license to print money. And, lo and behold, I heard that the Tragically Hip was going on a national tour and that they would be stopping for two nights in nearby Markham."

Banks and McCormick decided to set up a booth at the concert venue to sell clothes and the Fifty Mission caps he had designed. "We scraped enough money together to make 2,500 of the hats. They had Mission 50 on the front and No. 5 Barilko on the back. With Jeff, Dorian's sister Lara, and a couple of friends, the troupe of entrepreneurs arrived at the Embassy Suites Hotel in Markham to check in. Banks' credit card was declined and the group had only $300 in cash, enough for a single night's accommodation.

They set up a stall at the Markham fairground with the Fifty Mission caps as their centrepiece. "They started flying out," says Banks. "We had line-ups, so we started taking some of the colours away to slow down our sales. We were stuffing the $20 bills into shoe boxes." After selling several hundred caps, Banks felt nervous about having so much cash on hand and decided to take it back to the hotel. There he found his key card no longer opened the door to his room. "The manager wanted me to empty my room and I said I would, but first I wanted a safety deposit box." The manager allowed his scruffy-looking guest the request and watched in shock as Banks shovelled handfuls of cash into the tray. Needless to say, his room key was soon functioning again.

Back at the fairground, McCormick had run into problems. Two members of the Tragically Hip's organization were claiming that the Fifty Mission caps were an infringement of the group's copyright, even though the Tragically Hip logo had been deliberately left off the caps. "They said that if we stopped selling the caps they would not press charges. And they took away the 200 we had on display. We were really depressed because we still had 2,000 of these things in the van and we had no idea how we'd unload them. A couple hours later this guy in Bermuda shorts and white socks almost to his knees comes up and asks me to take a walk with him." The stranger turned out to be in charge of Tragically Hip's licensing. He said the band liked the hats (they were actually wearing them on stage) and he offered to sell them back for $5 each. Banks said he could afford to buy back only 100. But for every 20 hats he bought back his team smuggled another 200 out of the van. By the end of the concert they had unloaded their entire stock.

Their success did not go unnoticed. The licensing company invited Banks and his partner to work with them to pursue the sale of band accoutrements in shopping malls across the country. It was an innovative concept for the time and the young men accepted, taking on groups like Pearl Jam and Nirvana. "We started out making subtle logos on ball caps for the rock band 54.40. But because of the cost to produce samples that band members invariably rejected we soon realized this was going to bankrupt us." Banks decided instead to try to use his connections with four wholesale clothing lines from the U.S. that were not yet in distribution in Canada. "We ended up representing 14 major clothing lines in Canada."

They scored big time, representing for a period companies such as Dragon Optical and Sessions, one of the top snowboarder wear companies in the market. Sessions founder Joel Gomez enticed Banks to join his team to run the company in Santa Cruz, California in 1996.

"It was interesting. I'd never snowboarded in my life, even to this day, and here I was running a snowboard clothing company. I'm running a professional snowboard team and eventually a professional skateboard team, starting a skateboard clothing line and then a record label called Sessions Records. It was interesting doing all those things from scratch and actually having money behind it. I was definitely becoming a start-up entrepreneur."

Management conflicts forced him to resign from Sessions and in 1997 he moved to Vancouver. He floated from job to job, doing work as an IT consultant and working for a company called Fibron Machine. "They made conveyors that helped re-thread printing machines. They asked me to help them modernize their company to prepare it for sale, so I revamped their computer system and innovated with things like digital imaging."

A German engineering company called Voith AG purchased Fibron and wanted senior management to come with the acquisition. Banks said he wasn't interested. "They didn't like that answer from me and they asked me to go to Germany and do for their company what I had done for Fibron. Now, Fibron was doing $15 million in business and Voith was a $7 billion company. I wasn't going to do it, but they kept flying me over to Ulm and showing me things. Then they showed me what I was going to get paid and I decided to go," he says with a laugh.

Banks spent the next few years "endlessly flying around the planet" visiting Voith AG's 177 offices and "basically modernizing and globalizing the IT structure." He found the transition difficult. The various divisions of the company operated autonomously and were fiercely independent. "It was very frustrating and eventually I realized I wasn't happy being employed in this massive company, even though I was making $250,000 a year. So I phoned up one of my buddies and told him I was heading back to Canada."

Before he could leave, however, a colleague, Jan Roy Edlund, who was working as a $400,000-a-year consultant in Zurich, Switzerland, said he would quit his own job if Banks would stay in Europe and work with him and another friend to develop a dot.com start-up.

Banks agreed. He moved in to Edlund's apartment and met his roommate, Pablo. "Pablo had agreed to quit his PhD studies at the business school in the University of St. Gallen to join us." Between the three of them, they had foregone nearly $1 million in annual incomes to work together. "Every morning we would go down to this little restaurant, eat hardboiled eggs and brainstorm. We'd stay there all day and have lunch and draw on placemats. We would have at least eight new ideas every day. These two guys were brilliant. We finally thought we were on to an exciting one — streaming events on the Internet in real time. Back then it was a revolutionary idea."

That idea went nowhere. But one day at the restaurant, says Banks, "the bill came and only Pablo had money. It occurred to me that it would be really convenient if I could just beam him some money using my cell phone." Before long the three men had developed a working outline for using texting to send money. "In a few months we had a complete system built that would allow you to send a text message to anyone on the planet with a dollar amount, a currency, in it. And even if the recipient didn't have an account with us, they could open it." The three men purchased the moniker MyCash.com. "Our idea was to make money on the currency exchange. The earning potential was incredible and all you needed was text messaging.

"So we developed the platform and we had people like Credit Suisse Bank and BMGMusic interested. BMG was looking for a way to do micro charges for downloads on songs. We would go into presentations and I would ask for someone's cell phone number and send them cash right there. It was really quite cool."

After millions had been invested in the concept, for equipment, legal bills, corporation expenses, filing of provisional process patents and research, the MyCash idea bogged down. "We had settled to take money from BMG to build the system out. We wanted to do the richest countries in Europe first and then go to North America. Just as we were about to be funded the NASDAQ crashed. On the following Monday it was like the ice age hit." The team tried to modify their plan to be more conservative, to roll it out more slowly, but the dot. com implosion did them in. "We went through all of our cash and beyond to the point we couldn't pay rent or buy our groceries." Banks had to ask his parents to wire him his plane fare home.

The year was 2000 and he was back in Canada with no prospects. A friend, Jason Hebesy, invited him to stay in Vancouver and look for work "where at least the weather was good." Banks scrounged more help from his parents and, with a one-way ticket to the West Coast, made another move. He connected with a steel fabrication company that needed an IT consultant to help with the acquisition of new computer equipment. "They were hesitant because they had no high-speed connectivity. I told them not to worry, that there was high speed everywhere now."

The company, George Third & Son, took his advice and spent $300,000 on computer equipment, only for Banks to discover there really was no access to high-speed connectivity in the area. "I had my foot in my mouth big time," he says. "I struggled to find providers, but no one could do anything because of the company's location, so I ended up researching Wi-Fi on the Internet."

Eventually, Banks purchased some Wi-Fi devices and began experimenting with connections over distances that seemed to work. He rented space on a rooftop in Burnaby and installed antennas. Using the Wi-Fi gear, he was able to supply George Third & Son with the connectivity he had promised. He set up a broadband wireless network solution that used microwave technology to transmit data, instead of a physical cable connection.

That was the genesis of AirCelerator Wireless in 2001. "I wasn't trying to start a company. I just wanted to solve their problem." A week later, Banks had an inquiry from Accurate Effective Bailiffs, and then another from Modulok, both neighbours of George Third. The number of connections kept growing, with customers volunteering to pay for the development of new service areas. Banks was ploughing the money customers paid him back into the business. "I still basically had no money to my name." He remembers going in to a coffee house and trying to pay for his coffee with a bankcard. "The coffee cost $1.71 and I had no cash in the bank," he says. Through a haze of embarrassment, Sarah Morten, a former girlfriend who had been standing behind him, volunteered to pay for his drink. "It was a pretty humbling moment."

Banks resorted to a simple subterfuge to make AirCelerator appear bigger than it really was to companies interested in his services. He leased two cell phones, answering one using his own name and the other posing as an accounts and installation manager.

It was a desperate ploy, but it worked. Until 2003 Banks worked alone, but that year Stan Walker became his first employee. Walker continues to work with Banks at MetroBridge today.

The AirCelerator team soon ran into competition. Equipment to operate the wireless broadband connectivity was becoming cheaper and easier to access. One company in particular, Universco, became an aggressive, competitive threat. "I used to call up the boss at Universco and we'd yell at each other because he was always undercutting me," says Banks. By late summer in 2003, however, the two competitors began talking about a merger. In the fall they joined forces, renaming the partnership MetroBridge.

The company has done well.

MetroBridge Networks has become the largest broadband access provider in southwestern British Columbia. In each metro market it serves, MetroBridge has diversely located multiple gigabit upstream connections to Tier 1 international network operators (e.g.: Level3, Above.net, Bell). In addition to Tier 1 upstream, MetroBridge has many direct peering relationships with companies and networks such as Microsoft, Google, Akamai, PCCW, Speakeasy and Limelight. MetroBridge has now become in international concern. With the acquisition of Utah Broadband LLC, a Salt Lake City-based company operating in six countries, it generates about $8 million in annual sales.

As he continues to work to build MetroBridge, Banks is also involved in "a million side things." Under the banner of New Ventures BC, for example, he agreed to mentor Air Games Wireless Inc., a company that in 2001 won the first annual New Ventures BC Venture Competition. From a field of 170 entries, it captured the $50,000 Bank of Montreal grand prize. Banks has stock in the company and an ongoing involvement with Air Games and its 140 employees.

As an entrepreneur, he looks at things that "are a pain, or have an unreasonable cost" and tries to come up with a solution. "I'm always looking for industries to organize. I want to come up with something that hasn't been figured out, rather than fitting into an industry that's the same as everything else." He has pet projects he is developing, projects as diverse and different as delivering gardening products effectively, to IT pay-as-you-go services that make technology deployments easier and more affordable for small and medium enterprises.

These days the entrepreneurial bachelor spends time in Salt Lake and Phoenix every month, cities where MetroBridge has operations. His also devotes hours to other he mentors, advises or is creating. "Business start-ups are somewhat of an addiction for me now, I guess," he says, with a charming modesty.

Lisa Shepherd

mezzanine consulting

perspective you can depend on

Lisa Shepherd accepting the Profit Hot 50 award from Ian Portsmith, editor of Profit Magazine

The Mezzanine Team

Mezzanine Consulting

There were enough people telling Lisa Shepherd she was dreaming the impossible that a lesser person might have given up. But Shepherd doesn't quit easily. And, in proving her critics wrong, she sets a prime example for would-be entrepreneurs that — given the passion — gender, age or experience need not stand in the way of achieving the most ambitious individual goals.

The Vancouver-born Shepherd is today, at 36, the sole proprietor and chief executive officer of Toronto-based Mezzanine Consulting, a thriving business that was named one of the fastest growing companies in Canada and boasting a prestigious roster of blue chip clients. In eight short years, the company she heads has evolved from the crucible of a tiny, part-time summer business run by a handful of students at the Richard Ivey School of Business at the University of Western Ontario in London. As part of their learning experience, five or six students a year got to try their hands at some real-life consulting work for local businesses.

Shepherd learned of the student consulting group when she returned to Ivey in 2001 to complete her MBA after five-years' working overseas. She enthusiastically accepted an offer to join the small program. It was a risky job, with no guarantee of a salary unless the group secured clients. It was a case of "eat what you can kill," she recalls. At the end of that summer, Shepherd, at the age of 28, knew she had found a promising opportunity that she was determined to pursue.

"I thought, 'This is a really neat business opportunity, but it's not well structured as a business.'" One problem was that the consulting group operated only in the summer. And the changing mix of students each year guaranteed a lack of continuity. On the plus side, the Ivey name had enormous cache, not just locally in London, but in a much wider sphere across Canada. Clients were proud to boast of their connection with a school of such grand reputation.

Emboldened perhaps by the innocence of youth — or, more likely, driven by her strong willpower — Shepherd buttonholed the supervisor responsible for the Ivey Business Consulting Group (IBCG). Why not turn the enterprise into a full-fledged division of the Business School, she suggested? There were all kinds of advantages, she said. There were Ivey graduates out in the working world who would be happy to reconnect with the school for help in research and consulting, she pointed out. Existing Ivey students would have greater opportunity to obtain real-life experience. Ivey faculty, too, might get involved in consulting work to enhance their real-world experience and become better teachers. And finally, Ivey, by leveraging its established brand, could expect to create a valuable revenue stream for the School as business grew.

It was a bold presumption, but Shepherd's irrepressible enthusiasm impressed the university authorities. Go ahead and draw up a business plan, they said. Work with one of our executives-in-residence as a mentor. Enter Brian Harrison, former head of the Canadian division of the global consulting firm A.T. Kearney, at the time acting in retirement as consultant to Ivey. For the next year, Harrison and Shepherd worked together, meeting with the heads of departments to go over plans and staging workshops to demonstrate how a new, permanent, full-time operation would work. It was a "wonderful experience," Shepherd now recalls.

In the end, however, the timing wasn't right. The Ivey authorities told Shepherd she had a great idea but that it was not a priority for the School and they would not finance it. "Essentially, I got a pat on the head from the school," says Shepherd, with no trace of bitterness. "They told me, 'If you want to, you're welcome to continue your role with Ivey Business Consulting Group. But you won't have a salary from the school, and we won't financially support the business." Though disappointed at the time, Shepherd says that in hindsight she can accept that her plan for a super-sized Ivey Business Consulting Group "just wasn't a fit with the School's direction and objectives at the time, and understandably so. I look back on it now and I understand where they were coming from."

There was a silver lining to the cloud, however. Ivey may have declined to back the business financially, but they had given her the chance to pursue it if she wished. "It would have to be totally self-sustaining," Shepherd says, "and I imagine they thought I would walk away to get a 'more normal' job. But I didn't. For the next two years, I continued to run the consulting group at Ivey, with limited oversight from the School." In those first years, the financial rewards were not huge. In 2001 IBCG had revenues of $80,000, in 2002 about $150,000 and in the third year about $250,000.

"You graduate out of an MBA program and you believe that you're worth a cool half-million a year, and you quickly realize that you aren't," says Shepherd. "It wasn't what I thought I'd be making, but we were doing alright."

By late 2004, the ties between Shepherd and Ivey were beginning to bind. Though the enterprise still bore the Ivey name, it was to all intents and purposes Shepherd's business. The previous year, she had opened an office in Toronto to be closer to potential clients. And she began to hire permanent employees, in addition to the students from Ivey and other schools she would take on each summer. It became clear that to really give the business a chance, more changes had to be made. Changing the name of the business, though, was no easy decision. "We had clients in the early years who loved the Ivey name, and we were a little bit scared when we changed it," says Shepherd. But once the business was renamed as Mezzanine Consulting, IBCG ceased to exist and Mezzanine took flight. Shepherd explains the choice of name: "When you stand on a mezzanine you can see the situation around you very clearly. And that's what we do; we give our clients a better perspective on their landscape."

Shepherd's gain could be seen as Ivey's loss. But she is generous in expressing her gratitude to Ivey for giving her an opportunity she might not have found elsewhere. "I wouldn't have this business if it hadn't started under the auspices of Ivey," she says. "Lisa Shepherd hanging out a shingle and presenting herself as a consultant would have been a very tough go." Even so, the first four months of life in the Toronto office were "incredibly difficult . . . when we moved to Toronto we had a barebones client list. We had only one project and it was an incredibly difficult time."

And always on the sidelines were those doubters who gave a young woman of limited experience little chance of succeeding in what was an essentially all-male world. "Those first few years I had a lot of people around me, whom I respected, who were very skeptical and questioned what I was doing. It was just sheer pride and stubbornness that got me through those first three years. In fact, year one was easy, because you're so excited at the start-up. It was years two and three that were really tough.

"I didn't realize when I started doing this how unusual I was. As a relatively youngish, female CEO I'm often met with skepticism by many male CEOs who are most commonly in their forties, fifties and sixties. That's a reality you can't do anything about. All you can do is meet them on their level and through the course of your dealings with them they come to understand that you're capable, that you're dealing with the same problems they are, and that you actually may have some things to teach them." Ultimately, however, it was the force of her personality that made the difference. "I had tons of energy, and clients really liked the fresh perspective and the new ideas. They liked that we were young. They would not have hired us if they weren't okay with that notion."

Those early years were invaluable as a wake-up call to the realities of being an entrepreneur. "With an MBA, I was theoretically well prepared to be a consultant," she says. "But a Master of Business Administration is very different from a Master of Business Creation, or Master of Business Start-up. To administer a business is a very different exercise than to get a business going. In her talks to students today, Shepherd emphasizes the need for "being nimble and adapting and listening to your customer. These are the most important things that you can do in those early years." She stresses that businesses must make it a priority to have proper structures and processes.

But there's more to it than that.

"If all they do is put processes together they're going to be missing the reality of what the customer wants. You have to be very fluid." An MBA program, says Shepherd, is invaluable. "Two-thirds of what I learned in the MBA program has been absolutely vital to the success of this business. But one third is not. It's up to the entrepreneur to figure out which is which in every situation. For example, an MBA doesn't teach much about people and their emotions. "The MBA has classes in human resources. They try. But nothing replaces experience," says Shepherd. "Looking back to my first few years, I see that I had a lot to learn. I worked hard and we did some very good work. Our success speaks to the work that we did in those early years. Clients referred us and kept coming back to us."

Experience also taught her that adhering rigidly to orthodox methodologies doesn't always work. "Sometimes now I look at those methodologies and I think, 'Ugh, that would have taken months to do,' and really the answer lies in just spending a couple of days over a short period of time with the executive team of the company involved. And the answer will be clear."

There have been dark moments in Mezzanine's growth that threatened both the company and her position within it. Shepherd was always aware that the majority of professional services firms are structured as partnerships with individual partners responsible for bringing in their share of revenue.

"I've seen them; many run as mini-fiefdoms," Shepherd says. "Instead, I decided that I would offer equity in the business to very good people." Finding candidates who were "smart, personable, dynamic and able to establish relationships with clients" proved difficult. When Shepherd believed she had identified a good candidate, "I made him a deal for a percentage of the company, based on selling $500,000 worth of consulting in his first year. Unfortunately, he didn't hit his target, but — foolishly, in hindsight — I still gave him the equity."

Later, she brought two more people on board on similar terms, both of whom she considered to have skills that would complement her own. "I'm the one who likes to go out and meet with clients. I like bringing in the deals," she says. "But managing the projects and making sure the work gets done on time, and dealing with all the people — that's where I needed the help."

Shepherd came to see that having multiple partners at the table presented unforeseen difficulties. "It was apparent that we all had different visions for where we wanted the business to go. By 2006, it was all falling apart; the atmosphere in the office was tense." Worse, Shepherd discovered to her deep disappointment that the three individuals were plotting to take over the company and force her out.

"They wanted to oust me from my company. It was devastating," she says.

She was saved by her foresight in including a "shotgun clause" in their contracts stipulating that any shareholder could name a price at which the shares could either be bought or sold. "That's what happened to us. The other three named a price and the price was a great deal for me to reacquire their shares. Much to their surprise I said, 'Thank you very much and goodbye.' They left the company in 2007. It's a tumultuous story, but it's something that happens in a lot of businesses." It was a traumatic experience.

"Now it's ancient history, but at the time it was overwhelming and emotional. In business, we like to remove the emotion, but being an entrepreneur means that you are emotional about your business.

I had invested so much time and knowledge in these individuals. I think they were surprised that I turned the deal around on them." Ivey has invited Shepherd to write a case study about the incident so that future students might benefit from it. And she's ready to do it. "Lots of people want to hear the good news about growing a business," she says. "The reality is that there is so much more that goes on behind the scenes. Entrepreneurs need to know about the tough parts too, or they might think they are alone in their difficult experiences."

In her frequent speeches to student audiences, and others, Shepherd usually begins by deconstructing the myth of entrepreneurship as a hugely glamorous enterprise. "Being on the PROFIT 100 is exciting, and everyone loves a growth story," she says. "But you reach a point where everybody thinks you walk on water. Drink too much of that Kool-Aid and you forget what made you successful in the first place: caring about your clients, working hard and constantly adapting."

Nevertheless, Shepherd is justifiably proud of the success she has achieved with Mezzanine. Revenues increased by a whopping 715 percent in her first five years in business. The company was named one of Canada's fastest growing companies in 2008 by PROFIT Magazine and Shepherd herself was the youngest female CEO on the list. She has also been nominated for the 'Top 40 Under 40' Award and the RBC 'Canadian Woman Entrepreneur of the Year' Award.

Bell Mobility, the major communications company, was the first large firm to work with Mezzanine, followed by credit card leader Capital One Canada. "By having a couple of big names on the roster, we could then go and talk to others. Now, it's not so difficult to open the door to new clients." Her client list now includes Hewlett Packard, Research in Motion of BlackBerry fame, Hbc, Celestica, MSN Sympatico, Intel and Philips.

Shepherd says it was the result of a "domino effect . . . we've worked with Intel, HP, and Capital One, and so if I talk to Cisco tomorrow, they'll be like, 'Okay, that's fine. You've got a track record.'

For any young entrepreneur that's the biggest challenge, getting the credibility. In the first two, three and four years it was hard. People wouldn't hire us because they didn't know if we knew anything, and they didn't know if the company was going to stick around."

Shepherd also had a clear idea of the niche she wanted to fill in the competitive world of consulting. She was aiming somewhere between such global giants as McKinsey and Co. and, at the other end of the spectrum, independent consultants capable of tackling only small-scale projects in limited, specialized areas. "We fit somewhere in the middle," she says. "We wanted to bring the best of the thinking from the big consulting firms, but also the nimbleness and flexibility, and the price-point, of the independents. It was a good fit, but it was a tough go initially because we had to educate the market that we existed." By 2005 though, Mezzanine was "reaping the rewards" of its strategy.

In the pivotal year of 2008, Shepherd faced the economic upheaval that was challenging companies everywhere, big and small. It triggered changes at Mezzanine too, where the downturn had an early impact. "We saw a lot of clients holding off on making decisions, a lot of clients pushing back on budgets," she says.

"We started to see, possibly before many other businesses, a big change from the incredible level of activity that we had in 2006 and 2007." As a result, Mezzanine Consulting went from pure market intelligence and consulting work to also offering out-sourced marketing management. This meant that Mezzanine began assuming the marketing function of companies with revenues ranging from $3 million to $25 million. "It's very difficult for such companies to get good marketing," she says. Shepherd sketches out their dilemma. They might hire a full-time but inexperienced marketing manager for between $40-50,000 a year. But they end up "throwing their money away." Why?

"Because that marketing manager is in charge of a $100,000-plus marketing budget that very likely will not be spent to the company's best advantage because of the inexperience of the manager." And the answer is not to hire a more experienced individual at $100,000 a year. "Frankly, they don't need that level of full-time expertise. They need a combination of the two. They need this $100,000 person for one day a week, and they need this $50,000 person for a few days a week to execute the plan. "What we've done is make that possible. Companies pay us between $40,000 and $80,000 dollars a year and they get a high level of expertise, the power of a team, continuity, and most importantly results and confidence in their marketing."

This side of Mezzanine's business has "helped us get through a rough consulting year," says Shepherd. "Consulting is a high or low business. You've got tons of peak demand and then no demand. You need to even it out with something, so we've evened it out with this."

Another new development is for Mezzanine to invest in promising businesses that urgently need the consulting help they are too small to afford. "I really like growing businesses. That was the whole point of this," says Shepherd. "Once in a while we will find a company that we think has a really neat product, or a really great opportunity. However, they may not have the money to hire us and to market themselves the way they should. So, we'll make an interesting arrangement with them. We'll actually invest in that business. We're doing this right now with a company whose CEO is an inventor, a chemist. He is the first to admit he doesn't know much about sales and marketing. I look at him and think, 'Oh, wow, you need to spend some money. You've got something really great.' But, he doesn't have the money to do it. And he doesn't want to take out big loans to do it."

Shepherd takes particular pleasure and pride from investing energy, imagination, time and money in these promising ventures. "In the earlier years I didn't have the money so I had to get paid for all of our work. But now we're in a situation where we can consider it. It's fun. It's this whole dynamic of constantly changing the model and doing different things which gives us stability, because we are diversifying."

Shepherd finds the experience of promoting promising ventures rewarding in more ways than just financially and she expects to do more of it. So far, such work has been done on an ad hoc basis. "These companies came along. It's serendipitous," she says. "Maybe over time we'll want to make it more structured and planned." Still, "it's a balancing act. How many different things can we be doing and doing well?"

Though Mezzanine has grown substantially in terms of revenue, Shepherd is happy with current staffing levels. "We have seen that growing a consulting business, a professional services firm, is expensive and difficult," she says. "We would rather grow our clients' businesses and keep a small core team. I like the size of the team right now; it's manageable and delivers high quality. It's also less stressful for me. As CEO you have to figure out what's the right balance for you. I'm balancing what's right for the company, but also what's right for me. I have the luxury of making that decision."

The luxury of being free to make her own decisions is something Shepherd never underestimates. "The most important message I like to get out is that being an entrepreneur may be tough, but it's worth it. I look at my professional life now and I feel so lucky because there is nothing in the world that I cannot do. If I decide tomorrow that I want to open up an office in Calgary, I can do it. If I want to do a project for some neat little company I can phone up the CEO and say, 'Here's what we do; here's where I think we can help you.'"

The power to control her own destiny is personally valuable to Shepherd, who treasures her good fortune in being able to decide on the nature and diversity of the work she takes on. "I'm lucky with that. Companies don't hire consultants to solve easy problems, so we are dealing with strategic issues in many cases. The diversity is fantastic. We'll be working with a health care client one morning and a software company in the afternoon. The continual change is what keeps us fresh and energized."

"I feel so lucky now," she says. "It's been 14 years since I graduated with my undergraduate degree and I honestly feel that the professional world is my oyster. That's such a wonderful thing for an entrepreneur, or for anybody to whom autonomy is important, and who thinks they have a lot to give. Sometimes you have to take matters into your own hands and create those opportunities yourself. Not everybody will give you those opportunities. You can't let gender or age stop you from achieving what you believe your potential to be. Entrepreneurship is about individuals saying, 'I can make something happen. And I'm going to show the world that I can do it.' Do it, and don't think twice about it."

While Mezzanine Consulting has continued to grow, it is hard to place a monetary value on the company. Shepherd says, "The only way you can value a company is if someone makes you an offer." Not that her company is for sale. The inestimable value of Mezzanine lies in the skills and talents of its CEO and, without her, it wouldn't be the same business. Don't expect her to relinquish that role soon.

"I love my role because I get to work with smart and talented people and we in turn get to work with CEOs and senior executives on their big business problems," she says. "I'm not just a consultant. I think there's a lot of skepticism about consultants, but I can relate to small business CEOs who are running small $2-million to $10-million businesses. Because I'm dealing with the same challenges: It's 'How do I finance growth?' Or it's, 'How do I deal with an individual who wants equity and I'm not sure I'm ready to give them equity?' I love sitting at the table, solving those problems."

Dwayne Stewart and Phil Goddard, Founders of Pacific R.I.M.Services

Mexx

Cactus

Tilting

Staples

Pacific R.I.M. Services

Entrepreneurship can occasionally be an occupation fraught with peril. Most entrepreneurs' early years involve continued adversity — start-ups are invariably small, inexperienced, and under-resourced. As they grow, that adversity continues, although it takes on new forms: Each life stage of a company produces a new set of problems and situations to be resolved. Given this reality, the companies most likely to survive and prosper over time are those led by people who can remain flexible and creative enough to cope with the blows that business naturally produces. They learn lessons from operating close to the edge, and integrate them into their business methodology, which must also be rooted in a strong business culture based on sound principles, a clear philosophy and transparent ethics.

At Pacific R.I.M Services, a fast-growing construction company based in the Fraser Valley city of Abbotsford, in southwestern British Columbia, such a commitment has been at the core of the company's culture since its inception in 1993. The name R.I.M. refers to Renovation, Improvement and Maintenance but could equally well stand for Respect, Innovation and Motivation — qualities on which the founders decided they would build their reputation.

Chief Executive Officer Dwayne Stewart, and Chief Operating Officer Phil Goddard, based their philosophy in part on the Rockefeller Habits, as developed by Verne Harnish. In his book, 'Mastering the Rockefeller Habits,' Harnish describes "three barriers to growth" common to growing companies. They are: "the need for the executive team to grow as leaders in their abilities to delegate and predict, the need for systems and structures to handle the complexity that comes with growth, and the need to navigate the increasingly tricky market dynamics that mark arrival in a larger marketplace."

Harnish emphasizes the need to build a strong team focused

on a shared set of goals, to create accountability throughout the organization, to properly communicate company goals and practices and to "align top management with the entire company."

Of course, even the most tested template for organizing a successful business is redundant if it is poorly implemented. In the long term, the example of those at the top determines the outcome. At Pacific R.I.M., Goddard and Stewart have gone to great lengths to make believers of their 35 employees.

The two co-founders are good friends, though from different backgrounds and different generations. Stewart, the youngest of the partners at age 37, is the son of a Fraser Valley dairy farmer. An outgoing personality with a flair for computers, he runs the administrative side of the business. Goddard, born in Victoria on Vancouver Island, grew up in the Metro Vancouver area and trained at the B.C. Institute of Technology. He has more than 30 years' experience in commercial construction, and is chiefly responsible for field operations. Both men emphasize that each other's responsibilities can and do overlap.

Certainly, their beginnings as business partners didn't point to a great future. Goddard was a small independent homebuilder who foundered in the recession of the early 1990s, as did many other independents. Stewart was a youth of 20 who had spent some time in the restaurant business and knew that farming was not in his future and thought he might try his hand at construction.

For the first several years' of its existence, the company operated out of various premises attached to one or other of the partners' homes. The two men were doing most of the work themselves, though occasionally their wives would lend a hand with painting and other tasks. The story is repeated often of how, at the outset, the company's capital consisted of a Student Visa card with a $500 limit, a Canadian Tire store card and an aging Chevy Cavalier.

Pacific R.I.M. has today grown into a full-service commercial construction company able to build a new facility from the ground up, carry out renovations and updates for existing tenants, and furnish ongoing maintenance as required. Using its carefully nurtured contacts with the trades, suppliers and designers, it offers one-stop shopping from blueprints to ribbon cutting.

Early on, the partners made a conscious decision to go after "clients of excellence" — brand-name companies with a presence across Canada — instead of spreading themselves among a variety of jobs as do most small construction companies. Although they didn't realize it completely at the time, the two had adopted a strategy that was to guide them for the next 15 years: commonly referred to as "working a vertical." In the partners' case, the vertical was to specialize in construction of stores in and around malls.

Their first breakthrough came when they persuaded an expanding pizza business to give them a contract for a $16,000 renovation of a restaurant in a Langley mall. "We worked overnight, night after night," Stewart recalls. "We completed the whole renovation in less than 10 days. They were so happy with the quality of our work that they became our biggest customer."

The profit for Pacific R.I.M. on that job was a miserly $20 — but the client, Panago Pizza, was so impressed they came back. "We got to the point where they just couldn't use anyone else," says Stewart. "Wherever we went, they would check the numbers and we would be the least expensive and the most efficient — even though they tried numerous times to see if our prices were remaining competitive."

The company was still relatively tiny — working at this stage out of an office in Goddard's home basement — but its ambitions were large. "By the time we were given a second opportunity with Panago," Goddard recalls, "we had figured out what they wanted. That's when we first identified that what commercial clients want is a job done as quickly as possible, so they can start the cash registers running again."

Over the next four years, Pacific R.I.M. worked on no fewer than 52 Panago pizza projects across B.C. and Alberta, gaining valuable insights that helped steer its future success. But, in 1997, the relationship ended. Panago, although delighted with Pacific R.I.M.'s work, decided for internal reasons to take its construction work in-house.

Stewart recalls being at his young daughter's birthday party when he received the telephone call from Panago. Suddenly, a client that had been the mainstay of his business for four years had withdrawn. "I heard that we had lost the next job we were bidding on," he said. "That was the job that was going to pay the mortgage. It hit me right there that we really only had one customer and it was gone."

It is not uncommon for entrepreneurs to reach a low point in business life when they are figuratively standing at the edge of a cliff and staring at the abyss below. It is how they deal with such a frightening experience that usually marks how they will operate their businesses from then on. In Pacific R.I.M.'s case, this was the partners' first time facing this painful, sinking feeling. And they learned a lesson from it. "We realized that though we were our own bosses, we weren't yet a real business," said Stewart. "It was at that point we learned not to have all our eggs in one basket."

Stewart and Goddard determined to remedy the problem by launching an aggressive marketing campaign to broaden their client base. They set out to woo mall managers and tenants with face-to-face contacts and a broadly distributed promotional CD the size of a business card that for its time was a technological marvel. Their tactics worked. Reitmans, the women's clothing retailer, had a bad experience with a contractor it was using. A mall manager recommended Pacific R.I.M. and the deal came together. R.I.M. has since been involved in more than 200 projects for Reitmans in western Canada.

The basis for this lasting and mutually beneficial relationship is no secret — it lies in consistently delivering a superior quality of work in a reliable way, done to strict timetables and with the utmost financial transparency. It became a model for how they now conduct their business — a consultative approach in which they partner with clients to ensure the best possible result with a minimum of fuss.

"From day one, we show the client a cost sheet for every job we've done," says Goddard. "It makes the process transparent. If they want the job done more cheaply, we can say, 'Which of these numbers would you like to take out?' It becomes evident to them. By being open and honest with the client we involve them in the process. By educating them, you become a true partner."

The partners knew that if they were to attract other clients in the same league as Reitmans they would have to aggressively seek them out. The major apparel retailers all were based in Ontario and Quebec, and traditionally, these companies had used eastern construction firms to build their western projects, even though travel costs were high.

Stewart and Goddard thought they could change that. They booked flights to Toronto and Montreal. "We made appointments," says Goddard, "we said, 'well, if we're going to go there, let's talk to all of the main players in Canadian retail.'" And they did — Moores, La Senza, The Gap, Tommy Hilfiger, La Vie en Rose, all the big names. The two partners stayed in a cheap motel, but there was nothing cheap about their presentation. "Many of these potential clients said they had never had anyone fly out from the West to sit in their office," says Goddard. "We weren't real to them. By going there, it had a powerful impact. They saw that there were companies in B.C. that were capable of doing their work cheaper and better. It was the beginning of the end to that eastern mindset."

The trips to Eastern Canada were also a turning point in the growing sophistication of Pacific R.I.M. The partners saw that "business development" was as important to what they were doing as actual construction. They brought in a consultant to help formalize their business structure and management practices. And they began rigorously applying what they were learning about managing a business.

"Construction is still an industry that isn't flexible naturally," Stewart says today. "It seemed pretty radical then to look at contracting as a service business rather than just a business that manufactures a product. But it's how we approach everything. We decided that we had to customize to the client as in any service industry. Speed, quality, and market pricing is expected, but we consult with the client to deliver what they need particularly."

As an example, Stewart points to a magnificent effort Pacific R.I.M made for the Tim Hortons restaurant chain in 2008. The company wanted to renovate 160 stores but didn't want the renovations to disrupt business. After it contacted Pacific R.I.M., the partners realized that the largest problem involved time. Traditionally, a renovation would involve several days' of demolition and careful rebuilding. But the company wanted to minimize downtime in each store and for the chain as a whole. Like true problem solvers, Goddard and Stewart decided to change tradition.

They put together a team of seven "shock troops" who were all cross-trained in different skills so they could fill in for each other and work together at the same time. In traditional construction, one tradesman would complete a job before another could begin. The "shock troops" were housed in RVs and went from location to location to conduct the renovations over a six-month period. The team would go into a store, cordon off areas for renovation so business could continue, and then rapidly perform the renovation. The entire process averaged less than 12 hours per store and in one phenomenal effort the team managed to renovate a store in just six hours.

"We learned after losing our first big client how to systemize our business, and this was an extension of it," says Stewart. "With restaurants, the client's biggest concern is minimizing closing time and we worked on that for some time. Also, we could do it cheaper than most people because we had developed a very good relationship with tradespeople by helping them out when they needed it. You have to understand your clients, and develop a custom process for each one. It's what makes us unique."

It was thinking like this, plus glowing testimonials from satisfied customers about the company's reputation for excellence, that created an all important, word-of-mouth campaign about Pacific R.I.M. Throughout the middle part of the first decade of the 2000s, the contractor attracted such prestigious clients as Mark's Work Wearhouse, the office supply company Staples, the Cactus Club restaurant chain, Tim Hortons, and Boston Pizza. The company recorded consistent sales growth of more than 20 percent per year, culminating in a hugely successful 2006 when business increased by a staggering 68 percent. For four years in succession, the company was listed as among the top 200 fastest growing companies in Canada as determined by PROFIT Magazine.

In 2006, Dwayne Stewart won personal recognition when Business in Vancouver magazine named him as one of its brightest business stars under the age of 40. He told the magazine: "Good systems and processes are the glue that holds together the fabric of our lives, and those systems have to be bigger than you, or your fabric breaks."

That same year, the company finally quit its succession of temporary homes to move into a 6,000 square-foot purpose-built office and warehouse in a business park on the outskirts of Abbotsford. For the first time, the company could boast of a physical presence that matched its new clout in the B.C. construction industry. Five years previously, the business was still based over a garage at Stewart's home but by then, the company was employing almost a dozen people and about to embark on several years of exponential growth.

One thing that has not changed, however, is the relationship of the principals. Despite the difference in their ages — "we're of a different era," admits Goddard — the two men project the image of a well-honed team. In addressing a meeting, each will add to the other's views. The atmosphere they create is one of harmony and trust. Clients have taken note of this fact. "People have asked us about it," says Stewart. "They say, 'You have different personalities, but they complement each other.' It works because of our differences."

Both men are constantly vigilant over their "core values" and their dedication to the principles they believe give their company an edge over the competition. The key elements are passed on to employees in a way intended to make them feel they are a part of a family. "Humour and enjoyment of work and life" is one core value and, even in serious discussions, a light-hearted moment is never far away. The company's legendary Christmas parties are a highlight of the year, eagerly anticipated by employees.

"We've been able to attract excellent employees by making them part of the process, using good communications and rewards in a family-like, yet professional corporate atmosphere," Stewart once told an interviewer. All staff are encouraged to further their careers by taking appropriate courses that will add to their skill levels and prepare them for future advancement.

As the growing extent of the economic downturn became apparent in late 2008, difficult staffing decisions had to be made. They were handled with considerable grace. After much "soul-searching," the partners concluded a half-dozen or so employees would have to be let go to ensure the company's continued viability. "We had to make tough decisions," Stewart said. "We didn't enjoy doing that. But it's what has to happen." Stewart made a point of providing those who left with glowing testimonials, and in fact some are now back working with the company as fill-ins for vacations. Stewart also reassured the remaining staff that: "Your positions are safe. We are going to fight to make sure all of you in this room succeed as a team through this difficult period."

It's straight-talk like this that has a discernible effect on employees who have come to understand that their bosses are not reciting texts from a how-to manual, but are saying what they really mean, and what they think is important.

Says Goddard: "Respect is part of our culture, and I believe it starts at the top. I have a lot of respect for Dwayne, and I believe he does for me. Our dealing with hiring and firing is based on these core values. The deciding factor in the staffing decisions we have made is that it's absolutely necessary."

The requirement for respect extends out on to job sites where employees are expected to show courtesy in dress and manner among themselves and with everyone from tradespeople to landlords. "Every person is equal and deserves that respect. It's not negotiable," says Goddard.

Pride in one's personal appearance and demeanour is equaled by the passion that Pacific R.I.M. invests in all its projects. The company strives to leave the impression that it cares, not just about the physical structures involved, but also about the skill with which they are put together, and the lasting quality of the work.

"We like to say to the client, 'Good luck in your sales,' when we turn over a store," says Goddard. "We've built some of the highest quality stores, and they stand up. That's success. When you look at two different projects in the same mall, one built by us, one by a different contractor, and one looks three years old and ours still looks basically new — that's success. It's a huge part of why I get up in the morning. I'm driven by the success of our clients."

Keeping staff in the loop, and in tune with management's thinking, is not left to chance. Stewart constantly asks his employees: "Why am I here? Why are you here?" He tells them "it's because we are creating a future for our clients, and thereby creating a future for ourselves both in the office and out in the field."

Again drawing from the Rockefeller Habits, the company has regular "huddles."

"They really provide a good rhythm to keep us moving along," says Stewart. The purpose is so that each member of staff understands what their priority task is for that day, where they will be working, if they foresee any roadblocks — or perhaps merely to share some good news. Quarterly meetings are also a part of the yearly calendar, when senior management shares news on corporate developments, reinforces core values, outlines challenges and identifies opportunities for the immediate and long-term future. "Everyone should always know what's going on at the top, and at the bottom," says Stewart. "That's why we do this."

Goddard wonders at how companies "far bigger than us" function in the workplace without such meetings: "How do people working in such companies know what the people at the top are saying?" he asks. "How do people get to know each other? How do these companies function? I scratch my head."

This continuing communication extends to Pacific R.I.M's marketing. By concentrating on winning "clients of excellence," the company is consciously aware that it is setting the bar extraordinarily high. Brand-name retailers and landlords with prestige properties can take their business where they choose, while still demanding the highest levels of quality and service. This fact keeps Pacific R.I.M. on its toes. The company is always prepared to go one step beyond to ensure client satisfaction. This includes a willingness to accept small jobs in the hope of winning more substantial contracts in the future.

"By doing the small stuff for them, we can gain their trust," says Stewart. In fact, the partners have frequently found that new clients will respond to the company's willingness to do the little jobs. "Once they have confidence in us, they'll tell us, 'You made my life easier, so now I'm going to give you a shot at something bigger.' As a result of that we haven't had to step out of our comfort zone all by ourselves."

He cites the example of a clothing retailer that decided it needed an urgent change to its decor. "They had a pain. They phoned us and we were the Aspirin," says Stewart. It was a small project, but there will be something bigger soon." In another case, they were asked to board up a retail location whose windows had been smashed by a car. Normally, the job wouldn't have been worth bothering with, but Pacific R.I.M. did it, knowing that it was good client/relationship building to perform a minor chore, and not treat it as an annoyance.

An overriding goal of the company is to build a stable of a minimum of 100 "clients of excellence," and inevitably this may mean expanding the reach of the company. This is a challenge, because putting an ad in the Yellow Pages in Saskatchewan or Manitoba is not the answer. Word of mouth has proven to be by far the most successful route to bringing in new business. And once contact has been established, says Stewart, "what works for us is when the two of us sit down eyeball to eyeball with the person we want to work for and convince them that they want to work with us."

The bigger the territory any company tries to cover, the more stretched its resources become. A huge advantage of working in the Metro Vancouver region is that its geography concentrates populations, and the businesses they support.

It's one reason Stewart has confidence that whatever twists and turns the economy may take, the fact that his company is located at the heart of the diverse region is one guarantee of its future prosperity. "The number of people here will always generate a dynamic economy. It's always been that way here. That's why we're here."

This does not mean that the company is content to play only in its own backyard. Stewart and Goddard are constantly looking at expanding their operations. "There's three-quarters of the country that we're not paying any attention to," says Stewart. "There's lots of business available. We are in the process of going national with the work we do."

The two partners recognize the obstacles that face any enterprise seeking to break out of its home territory. Setting up a regional office requires substantial capital. There's the challenge of getting your name out in front of would-be clients who do not know you. And there can be difficulties making contacts with the right people in the trades ready and able to commit to your high standards.

Even without a national presence, however, Pacific R.I.M. benefits from the fact that the West Coast itself is increasingly attractive to national companies.

When a top-line clothing retailer based in Ontario made contact in 2008, Stewart and Goddard tried to put themselves in that company's shoes — in effect, "to think like an owner." And what's uppermost in such a client's mind? "They're looking for a contractor who, when they have a job underway, the client doesn't have to fly out here once a week to make sure things are going well. They want a contractor who knows what's needed and can provide it," says Stewart. "So that when the client does come out West, he can come with confidence that he is being fairly dealt with, that his costs are under control and the work is being carried out in an excellent manner. Then he can move on. That's what we've offered and that's what we've proved we can do."

Of course, Pacific R.I.M's business changed in late 2008 just as it did for many companies as recessionary winds blew through the continent. At the end of 2008, what had been a strong vendor's market suddenly became a buyer's market. Where previously contractors might expect to bid successfully on 75 percent of all jobs, in the new, depressed economy they'd be lucky to take 30 percent.

But, while he has no illusions about the challenges that change created, Stewart remains optimistic, knowing that the company is flexible enough to navigate them. As a result, Pacific R.I.M. is moving to maximize the effectiveness of its traditional practices while becoming more thoughtful and more creative in securing new work. "We're no longer pursuing four jobs and getting one," explains Goddard. "We're pursuing six or eight jobs and getting one. It means we have to be better than the competition."

One challenge is that clients, hard-pressed for capital and trying to keep expenditures in line, could be tempted by low-ball offers. But the partners believe that as a result of the solid relationships they have developed with clients over the years, Pacific R.I.M. is better placed than most to ride out this challenge. "We stood by our clients in the vendor's market and gave them excellent service, no matter what," says Goddard. "We did some things for nothing. And those clients have come back to us, have looked at us across the table, and said: 'you guys stuck with us and we appreciate that. Now that it's a buyer's market, we're not going to treat you badly. You are going to have our business and our continued support through the tough times'."

While he appreciates customer loyalty that was carefully nurtured over years, Goddard also recognizes that Pacific R.I.M. must change to cope with new times. "We can't continue to do business exactly as we did before," he explains. "Our clients expect us to give them better value, quicker completion of projects, and ways to save money and make sure that every dollar is well spent."

This kind of flexibility in the face of adversity extends to Pacific R.I.M's own operations. It is placing new emphasis on internal cost controls, looking for ways to save on materials, rentals, fuel and travel charges and demanding greater accountability from staff in getting paperwork done on time. It also means using the right number of staff on the right jobs at the right time and generally learning to work in a more intelligent way, even down to such mundane issues as employees giving timely notice if they have to take a day off.

Running a tighter ship, streamlining administrative procedures, honing the bid process, eliminating waste in material and human effort, ensuring jobs are done to schedule while still paying attention to company culture and client experience — this is how Pacific R.I.M. Services is arming itself for a sustainable future.

Ever the optimist, Stewart was claiming at the start of 2009 to detect "a lot of positive energy" in the marketplace. Potential clients told him they didn't want to be left sitting on the sidelines and be unprepared for the inevitable turnaround in the economy.

That's the kind of thinking that mirrors Pacific R.I.M's own plans.

It refuses to sit on the sidelines. Instead it is continuing to be flexible and is preparing itself for that turnaround.

*Kerry Shapansky, Pareto
CEO and Founder*

PARETO

Helping you sell **more.**

Pareto Strategy Council

Pareto Strategy Council

*Shapansky family build a
school in Kenya, 2005*

Pareto Corporation

In the 19th century, an Italian economist by the name of Vilfredo Pareto observed that 80 percent of the land in Italy was owned by 20 percent of the population, or, more broadly put, 80 percent of total wealth was owned by 20 percent of the people. This equation has since become more commonly known as the 80/20 rule, also dubbed the Pareto principle in the 1940s by business management thinker Joseph M. Juran. Aside from having a melodious ring to it, the Pareto principle has proven itself a rule of thumb in everything from business — 80 percent of sales come from 20 percent of clients—to daily life situations whereby most of us will spend 80 percent of our time with 20 percent of our acquaintances and/or wear 20 percent of our clothes 80 percent of the time, and so on.

You might wonder what a successful, modern-day company president and CEO such as Kerry Shapansky could have in common with the 19th century Italian economist Vilfredo Pareto. Well, for one thing, Shapansky was so impressed with Vilfredo's principle he borrowed his last name for his marketing company.

Because Pareto Corp. is a company that focuses on the execution side of marketing rather than being all about advertising, and because Pareto has forged itself a solid niche in measuring and delivering quantifiable results for its clients, Shapansky saw the Pareto principle as being "the perfect metaphor" for what he was trying to build.

"We were about helping you reach out and grab your most important client relationships and deliver more value to them," says Shapansky, sitting in his Toronto office and taking a break to discuss the story of how he got here and how Pareto was born.

"If we could help companies recognize that the Pareto principle is what they should use to focus their marketing spend, then they could get a much bigger bang for their buck."

To that end, Pareto directs its clients to focus on the 20 percent of relationships that make the most difference, rather than, as Shapansky puts it, "trying to boil the ocean through advertising."

And if there was any doubt that the Pareto principle was no more than some sexy-sounding maxim, Pareto Corp. has proven the worth of its name in short order. Under the expert guiding hand of Shapansky, Pareto currently boasts revenues of $80 million with over $8 million in profit, a dramatic ascendancy from its lowly beginnings in 2002, when Shapansky took on the losing proposition then known as the Caxton Group.

"Sounds like the noise a cat makes when it gets a furball stuck in its throat," Shapansky says drily, referring to the original name of the company.

Perhaps anyone would make that kind of noise if they were swallowing a fledgling public company with less than $2 million of revenues and $2.5 million worth of losses. But not Shapansky. For him, this was the perfect opportunity. Not only was he able to afford to buy into the company with his "budgetary constraints" of the time, it gave him a blank canvas on which to realize his vision. And he didn't waste any time laying down his first stroke.

Within three months after taking the helm of the newly named Pareto Corp., Shapansky had steered the "little wee mess of a public company" from a money-losing position into a cashflow break-even situation. A scarce seven years later: $80 million in revenue, with no end in sight for growth potential. Shapansky attributes the company's success to a combination of two things: a handful of smart acquisitions and good old-fashioned organic growth.

"If you're not growing organically, I don't think you can sustainably grow your business through acquisition, at least not in our industry," Shapansky says, noting that if people aren't buying more of what you're selling, there's something fundamentally wrong.

Or, as he succinctly puts it: "If the dogs aren't eating the dog food there's something wrong with your formula."

Once he found himself with a public marketing company on his hands — something he had not initially intended — Shapansky set about studying the beast. What he discovered about most public marketing companies was that they were trying to do rollup strategies; buying different companies, aggregating them and thinking "bigger is better." But, in his industry, Shapansky saw a problem with that thinking.

"We don't have factories that produce what we do; we have people who produce what we do. And companies don't own relationships, people own relationships. So you think that because you buy somebody's company, you own the relationships of that company? Don't kid yourself. Those relationships will walk out the door as soon as those people who you alienate and stick a bunch of money in their pockets walk out the door."

To that end, Shapansky has been extremely careful about choosing both the companies and the partners brought into Pareto. The selection process is not, Shapansky says, merely about finding a company with the right financial and product attributes.

"It's about 'I need to make sure that I've spent enough time with this person across the table who's going to be joining our team so that I'm confident that their addition is not going to mess up the flavour of our soup; and they're committed to something beyond just getting a cheque in their pocket.'"

Granted, Shapansky concedes this selection process with its canny scrutiny, nurturing and compromise is more difficult and time consuming, but finding the right fit pays off in loyalty and commitment. In fact, Shapansky got it right the very first time he tried it his way, as evidenced by Naylor Event Management, their first acquisition in 2002. To this day, seven years later, Kim Naylor is still one of Shapansky's right-hand people in building Pareto, currently holding the title of Executive VP responsible for much of Pareto's business development activities.

Aside from Naylor and others who are in it for the long haul, so too are Pareto's clients. Shapansky is deservedly proud of the fact that Pareto has retained 100 percent of its retail clients even in the current economically troubled times. To illustrate, Shapansky recalls a recent conversation with the senior marketing executive with one of their largest clients wherein the VP told him they were slashing spending across the board.

"She said, 'We're slashing our ad spend, we're slashing our flier spend, we're slashing our branding spend, we're squeezing expenses in every area, but I'm going to spend more on the things we do with you because I can measure the degree to which they drive sales results.'"

And that is the key. Being able to measure results may sound obvious, but it's what sets Pareto apart from other marketing companies or ad agencies. In fact, Shapansky says Pareto is likely viewed as an anti-agency, because they've taken a different approach from a traditional creative ad agency to solving the same problem. Not for them the glossy ad campaigns or sexy slogans. For them, it's all about execution.

"We frankly believe that a B-quality idea with A-quality execution will beat a great idea with shoddy execution every time," he says, adding that his clients typically don't suffer from an absence of ideas, merely their execution in the marketplace.

"We define ourselves as being in the business of helping you sell more. What that gets at is we really believe if you can't measure it and you can't quantify the impact that it has, you probably shouldn't be spending a lot of money on it."

It's a strategy that's been proven time and time again, much to the delight of Pareto's clients. In 2008, Pareto did a multi-million-dollar project with a grocery chain that was able to quantify a return on the investment in less than three months. In other words, the grocery chain was making more money than the project had cost them inside three months.

"When you can deliver those kinds of results, even the most myopic executives will say, 'You know what? Maybe we need to spend more money here because it's a pretty safe bet that we're going to get a fast return,'" Shapansky notes.

When first launching his business in 2002 and wondering how to "create a better mousetrap," Shapansky says he tapped into what people were frustrated about with the status quo. What he heard consistently was that clients were being bombarded with glossy ideas and great pitches, but when it came down to implementing them and measuring the degree to which they made a difference, they didn't make the grade.

"That sexy, brand-building TV commercial that they got to spend four days in the desert shooting is often tough to quantify sales lift on. But if I do an in-store promotion, I can measure the impact of that promotion in one store versus another store that doesn't do it and absolutely quantify what the lift is," Shapansky says. "So, part of it is the discipline of measuring it and part of it is being willing to be held accountable to the results."

While Pareto is steadily racking up loyalty points from without and within, Shapansky's loyalty lies proudly and squarely in Canada. A sixth-generation Canadian and self-described "fierce Canadian nationalist," Shapansky says his hidden agenda is delivering competitive results to companies operating in Canada and helping them be the best they can be. Because most of their clients are multinationals, Shapansky recognizes that the home office has already come up with a brand strategy. His job, as he sees it, is to "Canadianize" the strategy and make sure it sings in this market. In order to facilitate strong regional market knowledge, Pareto has people in every province, territory, and community of any size from coast to coast so they can adapt things to the local market rapidly and responsively.

"Feet on the street," Shapansky says simply. "That makes a huge difference."

Another thing that makes a difference is the fact that Pareto carved out a unique space as a retail-focused marketing company, as opposed to hitting up the manufacturers — "the Cokes, the Pepsis, the Procter & Gambles and Krafts of the world" — as almost every other marketing firm was doing. Early on, Shapansky was aware of what he calls the "Wal-Martification of retail" whereby retailers were starting to take back control of their stores.

"We made a decision early on that, as opposed to being the 101st marketing company focusing our efforts on manufacturers and trying to get in their door, we'd focus on the retailers. We discovered that there was almost nobody focused on the retailers."

Another unique approach that sets Pareto apart from its marketing brethren is that they are not exclusive to one company in each sector. Because Pareto is all about execution, Shapansky says that although they have specific client-dedicated teams, they will work with everybody. This distinct approach of working with clients' competitors makes Pareto "industry experts," a position that only benefits the retailers.

Because of these farsighted and intuitive decisions, Pareto now counts many of Canada's top retailers as its best clients and is in conversations with virtually every other major retailer in the country.

What is the source of Shapansky's creative vision? According to the affable CEO himself, he was born into it, inheriting a non-traditional way of doing things from his entrepreneurial family. His grandfather, a Saskatchewan-born farmer with only a Grade 4 education, became a significant landowner and a respected leader of his community in such roles as chairman of the local Credit Union and Reeve of the Township. These accomplishments, his grandson says, were attributable to his grandfather's creativity and ability to work with people to get things done.

Shapansky's own father followed suit. With little formal education and humble beginnings working in a body shop, he subsequently rose through the corporate echelons to become head of sales and marketing at Mutual Life of Canada, responsible for 2,500 people. Shapansky attributes his father's success not to academic learning but, like his father before him, to his people skills and his ability to rapidly discern whether a given situation made sense or not.

"Or, as he describes it, 'a good gut', in terms of being able to make the right kind of calls," Shapansky says.

With that impressive lineage behind him, one might expect the younger Shapansky would also eschew academia for the thrill of entrepreneurialism. But, in a rebellious turn, Shapansky decided to opt for the traditional. First step, a university education. Next step, become a lawyer on a political track. All was going according to plan, with Shapansky comfortably ensconced in his second year at the University of Waterloo. Then came a fateful day when his professor began to discuss the teleology of Socratean philosophy versus the non-teleology of Aristotelian political philosophy. Shapansky describes his memory of that life-changing moment: "I thought to myself, 'I am never going to use this crap as long as I live. I stood up and I marched down the hall and I went to the Registrar's office and I withdrew. I had no clue what I was gonna do next."

While his family and friends were shocked by his decision, particularly since he'd been excelling in the academic arena, Shapansky says he was simply itching to go out into the world and make it on his own.

Freed from the bonds of academia, he found himself at a loose end. When a buddy who sold dental supplies suggested Shapansky join him at a dental convention in Chicago to help man his booth, the 20-year-old university dropout eagerly agreed. While there, walking around the trade show floor, Shapansky found himself interested in all the computers and the management software systems on display. The year was 1984 and computer-automated offices were relatively new. Being of a curious and agreeable nature, Shapansky chatted up one particular company from Albuquerque, New Mexico, that was featuring "what looked like the sexiest system on the floor."

"I said, 'Who sells this stuff for you in Canada?' And they said, 'We've never sold a system in Canada.' And I said, 'Well, I'd be interested in potentially getting the distribution rights for Canada.'"

Naturally, it didn't phase Shapansky that he had zero knowledge about computers or distribution and even less about dentistry. What he did have was an idea and determination to see it through. Soon enough, he had secured the Canadian rights and within 18 months was selling more systems in Canada than they were in the United States. Humble, yet entrepreneurial beginnings. And, much like his forefathers, this first foray into the working world also involved some heavy lifting. The computer system of the day weighed 70 pounds and filled the entire backseat of Shapansky's car.

"So, I was shlepping this thing literally across the country in the backseat of my Audi and showing up at dentists' offices just praying it wasn't a three-storey office with no elevator because I was gonna have to carry this enormous computer upstairs," he recalls.

Shapansky quickly discovered that selling a product wasn't nearly stimulating enough to keep him motivated. The fun part had been coming up with the idea in the first place and then being able to convince the Albuquerque people to hire him.

"But once that was done, it wasn't a very creative environment. So I decided to move into the world of training and consulting and making a difference."

Shapansky began to realize that his true inspiration came from his mother. Unlike the male members of the family, his mother was a stranger to working outside the home. But the positive impact she had on other people's lives reached far beyond the walls of her own house. On more than a few occasions, Shapansky recalls coming home for dinner and finding an extra plate set at the table for a stranger his mother had "adopted on the streets" and brought home for a meal.

"She was an incredible mother — just an amazing salt-of-the-earth woman who really ingrained in me that it's not what you do, it's how you do it that matters," he says.

When his mother's life was cut tragically short by breast cancer at the age of 47, more than 1,500 people lined up to attend her funeral. Shapansky heard story after story from people he didn't know, heartfelt anecdotes about how his mother had touched their lives, how she had reached out to them and made them a better person. That, he says, was inspiring.

"Here I kind of thought I'd been chasing after my old man — who is a great guy, by the way — but he was a traditional business person and had success in a corporate environment.

"All of a sudden, I realized, no, no, no — I'm much more inspired by this idea of making a difference and having an impact on people's lives and having an impact in the country we live in than I am inspired by selling computers or making a dollar or having more traditional success."

From the looks of things, Shapansky has managed to inherit qualities from each of his parents, embracing his mother's sensibilities along with his father's entrepreneurial motivation. But it took a few years of various corporate experiences before everything gelled. His first gig, post-computer sales, was to teach classes for six years at a training company called Wilson Learning, an experience he did find stimulating.

"I found that it was scratching at a little bit of what my mother put in me, where I was helping people become better people and that was flipping a switch in me."

Inspiring as this experience was, the irony did not escape Shapansky that he was "just a kid who had dropped out of university" who was teaching senior executives about team building, management skills and running corporate vision workshops. The experience helped assuage any lingering doubts he may have had about dropping out.

"I'm not a quitter, and this decision to do the big march-out in the middle of poli-sci class probably was one of the things that drove me just a little bit harder, To say, you know, you've gotta prove you're smarter than the rest of them, you've gotta prove you are ahead of any of your buddies from university who followed a more traditional path.

"So, this being able to sit in front of rooms full of MBAs and teach them maybe helped to feed the monkey a little bit."

After Wilson Learning, Shapansky was recruited into the world of Xerox in 1993 to start the Xerox Consulting Group, a job that lasted two and a half years. The job had one major outcome: he met Mandy, the woman who would become his wife and the "love of my life." She still works at Xerox as CFO. A second marriage for both of them, it brought together four children — two from each previous marriage.

If the Wilson Learning experience was all about his mother's inspiration and Xerox was about his personal life, Shapansky's next move reflected the more traditional influence of his father. In 1996, he became president of the Canadian division of a U.S.-based company called Maritz, working out of offices in Mississauga, Ontario. There, Shapansky oversaw the company's growth over a six-year period from $12 million to $120 million in sales. The only downside to the success was that he was still only "a hired gun," unable to fully utilize his creative side while working for somebody else.

One day a good buddy and successful entrepreneur named Michael O'Gallagher "literally grabbed me by the lapels and said, 'Shapansky, what the hell are you doing working for somebody else? You're an entrepreneur. Everything I see inside of you is me. You've gotta grow some balls and get out there and do this on your own and stop working for somebody else. You'll be much, much happier and much more fulfilled when you do.'"

O'Gallagher was a self-made man who had created an immense fortune, He had worked with Shapansky as part of the Young Presidents Organization that helps educate and train young CEOs. Shapansky had tremendous respect for him. But what really added weight and urgency to his words was that O'Gallagher had cancer, and eventually died at the age of only 47. It was a turning point, a sharp reality check that drove itself home with a powerful impact.

"Right there and then I decided I was getting out," Shapansky said. "I was making a tremendous amount of money and had the job down to an art where I didn't have to break a sweat, but it was melting my brain."

Shapansky marched through the corporate hallways to Steve Maritz, the owner of the company, and told him he was leaving. After fulfilling various obligations, an amicable departure ensued. Shapansky was once again at large.

He says he convinced his wife to take a six-month sabbatical to travel the globe with their children and have "an early midlife pause." They spent two of those months in Greece, where Shapansky said the trip helped them "get in touch with who we all were and what matters in life. And then I set about trying to figure out what I was going to do next."

"When I left Maritz, my thinking was, 'I've gotta do something bigger.' But what I concluded was, 'No, that's not what matters most to me. What matters most is being in an environment where I can really paint the canvas and have some freedom to create the kind of company I really want to create."

While pondering his future, Shapansky became involved with a charity called Altruvest Charitable Services. Altruvest ("altruistic" + "investments") theorized that one should spend as much time thinking about a charity investment as one would about a stock investment, thereby ensuring an investment into a good organization. One day, while seeking a "handout" for his charity, Shapansky walked into a

Bay Street banker's office in Toronto and met a fellow by the name of Kingsley Ward.

The banker, after graciously giving Shapansky a donation for his charity, asked him what he did for a day job. An idle question perhaps, but if it had not been asked, Pareto Corp. might never have been born and a longstanding friendship and partnership might never have come about. Shapansky explained his situation and that he was in the process of looking to buy a business and start a marketing company, He omitted only one detail: "I never quite mentioned to him that I didn't have the capital to be able to buy much of a business."

Fortunately for Shapansky — and for Ward — the meeting couldn't have come at a more fortuitous time. Shapansky needed a business and Ward just happened to have one that had just gone public, a little furball of a company called the Caxton Group that was losing more than it was making. Because it had just gone public and had some financial backing, everyone was committed to making it a success.

"So, Kingsley said to me, 'Is there any chance you might be willing to take on and lead this little Caxton company and use this as your platform to grow your business?'" Ward then added this nugget: "I'd be so grateful that I'd be prepared to back this in a significant way financially."

After some analysis, aided by his wife ("there's no question about who holds the pursestrings in our house") Shapansky took on Caxton, changed the name to Pareto and was in possession of the blank canvas he had coveted.

"But it was better than a blank canvas because it was a canvas that had some committed investors behind it. I knew I wanted to do something on my own, but I knew it wasn't hanging a shingle and sitting in my garage by myself. I needed a few people to be able to work with."

From its humble beginnings in 2002 to its current success,

Shapansky's canvas has evolved according to his vision both by acquisition and organic growth. He says his success is attributable to "a little more luck than foresight," but his earlier experiences had a powerful influence.

At Wilson Learning, for instance, he learned the importance of creating a culture inside an organization and this belief helped shape Pareto. When Shapansky talks about culture, he dismisses "the value statements that you shmear on the walls and then don't operate that way." What he's talking about is actually finding a way to live by a different set of principles.

"I'm a huge believer in the fact that our assets walk out the door every night and go home," he says.

"If I can't find a way to tap into the passion inside of our people and have our people feel like, 'this isn't just a job for me, I really feel I'm part of creating something unique and special,' then I'm not tapping into half of what those people can deliver to our organization."

Wanting it is one thing, but making it happen is quite another. As far as the latter goes, Shapansky found his culture muse in Michael Dell, of Dell Computers. According to Shapansky, Dell prefers the term "aspirational attributes" as opposed to "values." To that end, Dell adopts these attributes under the umbrella term 'Soul of Dell.' This was the essence of what Shapansky was seeking for his own company.

"So, I stole it," he says with a grin.

Thus, the 'Soul of Pareto' was introduced early on, including five elements that the company passionately cares about and believes in. The five elements might mirror those of other companies — "things like caring, integrity, results matter and clients first" — but the difference lies in the aspirational attributes tag. In other words, Shapansky explains, "We don't think we're there yet and we work hard to try to catch each other doing things right."

When someone is identified doing something right — demonstrating a 'Soul of Pareto' attribute — they are duly recognized and rewarded. Everyone in the organization can identify someone for recognition. This system "really works," says Shapansky, who is proud of Pareto's extremely low turnover rate in a company of 250 full-time and 1,000 part-time employees.

Shapansky acknowledges that most people will say they want to work for a caring company, and, to comply, most companies will say they care. "But, what does it really mean?" he asks.

In Pareto's case, it means the caring extends beyond the corporate world into the Third World. In the fall of 2009, for instance, Pareto planned to send 20 employees to Kenya to build a school. The selected volunteers were to lead their own fundraising project, enabling them to travel to Africa and erect their school. Pareto has also partnered with the Free the Children charity, providing expertise and skills to help them be more effective. Underlying all of these endeavours, whether corporate or charitable, is the Soul of Pareto, which has no borders and no limitation, much like caring.

"I think the outgrowth of that is people go home and say, 'You know, my company cares, my company matters, I'm proud of what we do and I feel like we're making a difference.' And then when the times get tough, that's the stuff that gets you through."

Having proven himself in the business world on his own merits, Shapansky has never forgotten how he got here and who helped him along the way. Asked what advice he would give entrepreneurs, he doesn't talk about business plans or bottom lines, strategies or skill sets. He only mentions people.

For the payoff, choose your capital partners wisely. In his own case, meeting Kingsley Ward was an ideal connection.

"He is a man of integrity; he does what he says he's going to do. He knows what he knows, but at least as importantly, he knows what he doesn't know and doesn't try to pretend he's an expert in areas where he's not. His undying gratitude and loyalty to me has been a huge enabler both for me personally and for Pareto."

Joanna Track, Publisher and
Founder of Sweetspot.ca

Sweetspot.ca

The sweet smell of success. It's unmistakable, albeit indefinable. Canadian entrepreneur Joanna Track captured its essence in her business, which works on the premise that we all need a little 'sweetness' to enhance our daily lives. That sassy, self-assured, and slightly saccharine notion has led to the slice of pleasure known as Sweetspot.ca.

"The idea was to create something for people who want to be in the know — people who care about trends and lifestyle. Covering only the most novel products and services, celebrating creative talent, uncovering hidden gems. But, it's also about the attainable: as we always say, we like to be aspirational but attainable," Sweetspot's founder and publisher Joanna Track explains.

She knows a thing or two about aspiring to a lifestyle. Only a few years ago, the shopaholic spent more time window-shopping than actually shopping. "Sweetspot was born out of my own personal passion for 'stuff.' I've always been someone who had a thing for fashion and beauty, even though I really had no money. But, I could look at the magazines, and I would find the less expensive alternative," says Track.

"That was the whole essence of the brand. You might not be able to afford a Louis Vuitton purse, but that doesn't mean you don't care about knowing what the latest design is. You read the magazines and you want to be 'in the know.' But, you can still go and find a similar style bag. So, that's always been our brand; to be funky and cool, but not too sophisticated."

Upon its launch in June 2004, Sweetspot.ca started by e-mailing its subscribers a daily fix of 'Sweet Nothings' — an electronic, Toronto-based newsletter sent to inboxes from Monday to Friday and then archived on the website; brightening dull days with the latest trends, beauty tips, décor ideas, and the coolest restaurants and places to go.

Thus, whether you're savvy like Carrie from 'Sex and the City' or looking to put your finger on the pulse of what's hot, Sweetspot satisfies all tastes. "We make sure we combine local content from four major cities — Toronto, Montreal, Calgary, and Vancouver — with national content, which means that our newsletters appeal to anyone across the country. So, that's how we try to balance it," says Track. As a result, today the newsletter reaches 75,000 subscribers nationwide.

Billed as 'Canada's first online trend-spotting lifestyle guide' this Internet venture has loyal readers, eager to stay up-to-date on "all things fun, fashionable and just plain fabulous" — something that wasn't overlooked by Rogers Communications, the largest media company in the country, which snapped up a piece of the Sweetspot pie in 2006. Now Track's company is sitting pretty under the 'digital media publishing' branch of Rogers' umbrella.

Of course, plenty of growing companies have vanished into the machinery of a "corporate behemoth," as Joanna affectionately refers to the media empire that came knocking at her door. Rogers often simply 'acquires' magazines that grab its fancy. In fact, they own 70 magazines to date. Yet, Joanna was far from looking to retire, so the savvy thirty-something singleton found a way to not only remain the publisher-in-chief but retain creative control, which works to both her and Rogers' advantage.

Brian Segal, CEO of Rogers Publishing, first contacted Track to discuss cross-promotional opportunities, which led to a flattering offer of Rogers taking a minority stake in Sweetspot. Track knew that she was onto a good thing when she built her company, but her feelings were validated by this impressive nod from the big boys.

"I had been approached by a few other media companies before," says Track. "But it was never the right thing, and that was when I was more, let's call it, 'desperate.' Because I was still really struggling — it was myself and one other employee by that time. And I hadn't been paid in 15 months, I'd burned up my RRSP, and I had borrowed money from my brother." Soon, she was in debt to the tune of $70,000. "But then, things started to turn around, we were starting to make money. So, when Rogers came along, I actually wasn't desperate anymore, but clearly intrigued."

Unlike the potential investors of the past, Segal told Track something different. "They said, 'we like what you've built and we don't want to mess with that.'" This mutual respect has been a cornerstone of the relationship between Sweetspot and Rogers.

Ultimately, the backing from Rogers Publishing meant being able to hire new employees — from a staff of two full-time employees in March of 2006 Sweetspot's staff now totals 25. "We have a few departments. So, I'd say seven of our employees are in editorial; that's all the writing, the content. We've got four people in marketing, but marketing also includes our creative team.

"Then there's our Tech Department of four people, because there's a lot of programming involved. The good news about the Internet is that you have a low overhead, but there's still tons of coding. And you always have to stay on top of technology. I didn't come from a 'techie' background and that's what I've learned. There's always a new advancement and if you're not on it, you're behind," notes Sweetspot's founder.

Out of Sweetspot's team of 25, there are 24 women, and one man — it's a 'woman's world,' evidently. "I think he feels lucky. He's in touch with his feminine side," laughs Joanna. Of course, far from being sexist, she explains, "It's partly 'the brand' and partly self-selection because the people who want this kind of job are women, mainly. From the editorial side, you really have to be the audience to want to write about that type of content. And then, even the marketing, it appeals to women, so they're the ones who tend to step forward.

"It's funny, because when we went to hire our Director of

Technology, I thought for sure it was going to be a guy. That sounds stereotypical, but I just thought, 'it's technical, it's going to be a guy.' We interviewed a handful of people and a woman came through the door and she was just the best fit. So, is she the best fit because she's female? Maybe partly, but it was her skill set combined with fitting in. We did have one or two guys in the past who have since left the company. And we always joke, they just couldn't cut it — you don't hire a man to do a woman's job! Seriously though, we don't discriminate. It just happened."

Rogers' support also led to a spacious new office on trendy Bloor Street in Toronto. Not too shabby when you learn that Joanna initially started Sweetspot in her apartment. "I guess day-to-day I accept it as my reality, but still pretty often, I'll walk in here or I'll be in a meeting and I'll think, 'I can't believe this is really happening!' We just moved into this office at the start of 2009, and I joke, 'Who are all of you people? How did you all get here? I can't believe I pay all of your salaries!' That still blows my mind."

Sweetspot ranked 20th on the Profit Hot 50 list of Canada's Emerging Growth Companies in 2008. "It's a whirlwind," Joanna admits. "And a lot of entrepreneurs will tell you how it's stressful, it's this and that, and it is all those things. But where I've been really lucky is, my stressful period was short. I got over that hurdle in an exceptionally fast way.

"Now I have different stresses, but they're not nearly as bad. Before, you know, I was worrying about paying the bills, whether I was going to stay in business, I don't have any advertising contacts — the fundamentals of keeping it afloat. Now, my stresses are things like cash flow, week to week, but nothing like 'are we going belly-up?'"

In addition to relieving financial burdens, Rogers brought marketing power to the mix. In the first year of their alliance, Sweetspot's subscribers tripled from 18,000 to over 50,000, and shortly afterwards the site's annual revenue exceeded $1 million.

They've since attracted big name advertisers like Holt Renfrew, Cadbury and L'Oreal, and negotiated campaigns worth as much as $200,000 apiece.

"In order to expand my revenue opportunities, I really had to look at Sweetspot differently, rather than just being a newsletter. That's when we decided to expand the website component. It's no longer just an archive, it's a destination, so that way, we are now selling eye-ball traffic there."

This includes movie 'tie-ins' such as a recent promo for Disney's 'Confessions of a Shopaholic,' which dotted the website with eye-catching 'banner' ads. "Our sales department, over the years, has become bigger. It used to be a lot of pushing, trying to get in the door, and tell people who we are," Track says. "There was a lot of education, too, because what we were doing was new. And now, it's still a lot of pushing, but there is also demand; those who will come to us and say, 'We want to work with you.' We have a great relationship with Disney. So, they came to us regarding a campaign to launch their new movie."

Most of Sweetspot's advertisers are targeting this female demographic. "That's our audience — 97 percent female," says Track. "I always joke that the rest of them are my relatives. But, no, there is definitely a male audience, especially when we write about restaurants and 'non girly' stuff. Although, we specifically target women — that's what we're good at, and that's what we know."

From a labour of love to a (currently) $2 million company, now the future is looking as sweet as the hard candy offered in her office reception lounge. She risked everything to publish a free e-newsletter, quitting her cushy Account Director position at international advertising agency Ogilvy & Mather.

"For about six years, I was involved in the direct marketing side of advertising. Before that, I was in a few other marketing jobs, including working at Air Miles (The Loyalty Group). So, my work background is marketing, but I actually started off interested in math and finance. Which is another twist — I always had an aptitude for numbers and I majored in math in university." Joanna holds a BA in Mathematics from the University of Western Ontario. "Then I went MBA at York University (now the Schulich School of Business) and majored in finance."

Her defining moment came during the summer of 1994 between her first and second year at York. "I worked at Merrill Lynch on the trading floor as my summer job and at the end of it I thought, 'I'm so not doing this for the rest of my life.' But it wasn't the stress that got me; it was the culture. I realized I am not made for this. I cannot wear nylons. I can't just go to work everyday and the whole topic is money. Money can be the end result, but I need something tangible; there has to be something more than just how many different ways you can make money.

"So, I went back to MBA second year and dropped all my finance courses, and here I am. My husband says I'm a socialist. Me and Obama," she smiles. (She is a big Obama fan.)

Joanna's change in direction eventually paid off in spades when Rogers threw their money into the pot, taking her entrepreneurial dreams to the next level. She notes, "When I first started Sweetspot, I was still working full-time at Ogilvy and I started it on the side, but I always wanted to turn it into a business. It wasn't like I was caught off guard that it actually turned into a business. I always had a strategy of wanting to grow it big and sell it. Although, where I was surprised was how fast it happened. I kind of thought I would be in it for at least five years before anyone was interested. And Rogers came on board after two years."

But before solidifying a relationship with the media giant, Joanna Track made sure that she had completed her due diligence. She asked around to ensure she was getting a good deal, and hired a lawyer to join her during negotiations with Rogers' executives. As a first-timer, it could be intimidating to sit at a boardroom table with honchos who already "know the game."

Both she and Rogers remain 'mum' on the details of the resulting deal that made the private company a subsidiary of Rogers Publishing. But, Joanna acknowledges that she has kept an autonomy that puts her in a place that she herself calls "the sweet spot."

"My life has dramatically improved in a pretty short period of time," she explains. "Rogers are mostly hands-off. They're more involved in the back-end. It's mainly on the financial side of things. Their accounts receivable department manages our receivables. They do our monthly reports. They do our taxes. As far as content, marketing strategies, sales strategies, they have no involvement at all.

"Basically, once a year, I go to them with a budget and say, 'these are my plans.' And then, that's it. From a day-to-day side, someone in my marketing department might call someone at Rogers — maybe they want to work with one of the magazines, Lou Lou, Flare or Chatelaine. But, there's no mandate and no, sort of, rules of engagement there."

Joanna laughs, "I always liken it to having a 'sugar daddy.' You know, because they're not going to let us go bust, but at the same time they're not around and they don't pay a lot of attention."

Ultimately, Track is aware that "I kind of got the best of both worlds. In the beginning, Rogers bought a 30 percent stake. So, I was still the majority shareholder and they did it based on a strategy of 'we're going to invest some money, to see where this company goes,' and if it went well, they had the option to buy the rest. As it happened, it went well, and the deal was supposed to expire in July of 2009, but somewhere around the middle of 2008, Rogers realized that this was going really well. They knew that once they owned the whole thing, I might leave. Because I didn't sign-up to be 'working for' Rogers."

As a result, Rogers asked Joanna to stay onboard in her current capacity and extended the deal until 2011. "As well, they bought another stake, so now they own 70 percent. Even though I'm the minority, they still set it out that I manage the company. So, we're like an investment to them."

When asked about her plans 'post 2011', she's not entirely sure. "I don't know what happens after they've bought the rest. I'll retire?" she jests. "I will never work for anyone else again. That's for sure. I've learned so many lessons, and whether I am here or doing something else, I will always do things on my own terms. Whatever happens, any of those past insecurities of 'can I do it?' are out the window and I can be that much more confident because now, I know I did it."

In the meantime, as long as she's at the helm, Sweetspot will remain true to its roots and continue to offer its free newsletters in a funky style that's all its own.

Following in the successful footsteps of the Sweetspot brand, the company is in the process of branching out with new sister sites 'Sweethome.ca' and 'Sweetmama.ca.'

"While Sweetspot was the original property —it's the real catch-all for lifestyle information across Canada — fashion, beauty, restaurants, all that. Then what happened was we realized that we were getting all this content information about things that were more for moms, such as cool maternity wear, diaper bags, funky kids' clothes.

"For a Sweetspot audience, if you're not a mom, you don't want to read about that. But, if you are a mom, you would." Joanna Track is keenly aware of this, as an expectant mom herself: "Yeah, I'm going to be a 'sweet mama.'"

She notes, "There's a whole other host of advertisers who would want to focus on the mom audience, so we created Sweetmama in 2006 as a further niche, where we could just dedicate content to that target group." The Sweetmama newsletter has, to date, 27,000 e-mail subscribers.

Track continues, "Where we differentiate ourselves from the competition is that there are a lot of mom sites but they are mainly about advice. You know, 'what do you do with a colicky baby,' or 'my kid won't sleep.' That's not our business. We're about, 'this is the coolest diaper bag,' 'here's a kid-friendly restaurant.' And so, our tagline for Sweetmama is: 'Raise them fabulous.' It's the consumption side of parenthood."

Meanwhile, Sweethome was launched in early 2009 with a similar philosophy, focusing on 'cool' home décor and entertaining. "If you're on Sweetspot and you just want to know about things like the latest jeans, maybe you don't want to know this really deep design-related information. Which is why we're launching Sweethome, based on that same theory as Sweetmama. We're creating this other niche, for people who have that specific interest.

"I've always been someone who operates in simple, digestible chunks. This way, it always remains manageable to us and to consumers," explains Track.

"Both of these new sites are still within our same broader target audience, so we're not all of a sudden going out to target 60-year-old men. They fit with our readers. We know what we're good at, instead of venturing out into something different. People ask us all the time: 'Are you going to do a men's website, just for the guys?' And we always say: 'Not right now,' because that would be a whole other story."

With added sites on her plate, she will also soon be juggling the working world with her new foray into motherhood. "I will be taking a little break but, of course, as an entrepreneur, you have this passion, and I don't want to be gone.

"I have a good life now, and I'm very much a proponent of work-life balance. Now I'm married with a baby on the way (due in July 2009), my goal is that I'm going to be off for a couple months, but 'off' means that people will still e-mail me and call me, I just won't be here every day. And then I'll ease back in. I've promoted a culture here that is very flexible. People work from home, and they come and they go, so I'll just be doing the same thing."

Delegation is key. "I actually feel and, maybe I'm unique, but I've set it up in such as way that there is a balance. Sure, I can probably make more money and do more things here, yet I've hired other people so that I don't have to work as hard. Maybe I could have not hired them and do all the work myself, but I'd rather give up that money and have a life. I'm not a workaholic, but I could plough through stuff, I could come up with new ideas, new angles, I could be working 80 hours a week. I've chosen not to.

"Of course, I think the reason we've had continued success at Sweetspot is the people. I give myself credit in finding the right people and teaching them my way of managing work. But, they are all amazing and every one of the people who work here treat this like it's their company, too."

Sweetspot's image as a 'feel good' company extends to keeping these great employees happy. "I think we've really gone the distance to make it the most incredible place to work. Especially because we're tied to Rogers, we see the stark contrast — not to bash them, but they're the ultimate corporate behemoth culture. And here, it's the opposite.

"It's not like a free-for-all by any stretch. People will tell you they work harder than they've probably worked at any of the other jobs they've had. But they care and they're treated well."

Instead of working for 'The Man', Joanna can see the benefits at Sweetspot. "Personally, I've worked in some big corporate cultures, and I always performed well, but I always had questions, like, 'Why does it have to be that way?' The answer would always be: 'Well, just because it is.'

"So, I created Sweetspot with the mission to start a business for all the entrepreneurial reasons but also as my own little human nature test. To see if I could build a culture where you do let people have certain liberties and still be successful. And I've proven that it can work. It takes a lot of give and take, and a lot of trust, but it works."

With a turnover rate of only one employee per year for the last three years, Sweetspot's staff apparently agrees. "It's the little things — like get-togethers, regular 'J-Tea Time' (one-on-one time with Joanna), and making sure my door is always open. And the flexibility of being able to work from home; everybody has a laptop. Also, we invest to let them go to training sessions."

Moreover, Sweetspot even goes the extra mile by holding internal contests for staff in order to stoke their creative fires. "One great example is what we're doing right now — we have a contest called 'The Next Sweet Idea.' It's almost like a reality show," Track explains with great enthusiasm. "Basically, we've set aside $15,000 and asked our in-house staff to submit their business ideas. The whole premise is based on the fact that I started Sweetspot with $15,000, so I'm saying 'what are your ideas?' They might have the next sweet idea. They have three months to put together their proposals, then they're going to present them to the senior management team. It's very exciting!

"Whoever's idea we select we're actually going to execute and they also win a prize of $5,000. So, they're getting paid for their ideas. It benefits the company and benefits the individuals because they're learning the fundamentals of building a business and being entrepreneurs. Yet, they have the benefit of having a net, where I didn't. If it doesn't work out and you don't win, you still get your salary." Unlike an infamous business-based reality show, nobody will be hearing the words 'You're fired.' Although, Joanna admits, "it would make it more dramatic."

Aside from finding fun and novel ways to harness and continue to invest in the best employees, Track says the company's overall success and dynamism in the marketplace is relatively simple. "From a purely business point of view, I think we hit the market at the right time. I had a bit of luck in that, because since I started Sweetspot there've been quite a number of people trying to capture this market, but I had the 'first-mover' advantage.

"I think I had a good idea and a good brand, and I thought it through. Other entrepreneurs might come up with an idea but not understand the importance of the brand and being consistent. Whereas, my marketing and brand experience really gave me an edge."

After such rapid growth at the beginning, Joanna Track is now focused on maintaining her already strong brand to ensure its longevity. "I'm of the school of thought that you start small and let it grow organically. And that's part of the reason why we've been successful. Yet, we are calling 2009 the year of stabilization. We're still growing and our revenue is targeted to go up by another 30 percent, but 2008 was an insane year — we doubled our revenue. In January of '08, we had 11 employees and now we have 25. So, it's exciting, but it's very stressful. And, I believe, where you see a lot of companies going bust is they grew too fast. Too far, too fast.

Sweetspot's Track concludes, "I feel like we had to make those big leaps to get to the next level, to have the infrastructure and everything. But now, this year, it's about digging deep. We have the infrastructure, we have the people and we have the technology. Now let's take everything in, and perfect it."

How sweet it is.

Rob May, CEO
of Tricrest

Tricrest
Headquarters

Tricrest Professional Services

After working in top-level management jobs for blue-chip corporations for many years, Rob May was steeling himself to take the plunge and start his own company when he received an offer he couldn't ignore. One of Canada's largest telcos called him up with an invitation to become Vice-President of Operations. "It was a big job, with lots of prestige attached," says May.

He didn't take the job, and the reasons why go a long way towards explaining a crucial difference between life inside the world of mega-corporate culture and the motives that drive the independent entrepreneurial spirit.

Entrepreneurs are, in fact, of a different breed. Even though, like May, they recognize that experience within the corporate world is a necessary step in their career development, they are also aware that working for a major company can be limiting in ways that stifle individual initiative.

Even in his early corporate career, it occurred to May that his entrepreneurial outlook made him stick out like a sore thumb. "I'd be doing things because it was the right thing to do for the organization as a whole, not just because it was the right thing to do for my little piece of the world. Sometimes I received kudos for it, and sometimes I was taken aside and asked, 'Why would you do that?'"

The Telco's offer was tempting enough that May went through the motions of attending interviews, undergoing psychological tests and the whole rigmarole involved in high-level recruitment. The experience only confirmed his resolve to abandon the corporate world and set out on his own.

What May endured is also a warning to young people planning a corporate career of the often-humiliating hoops through which they will be expected to jump.

After his initial interview, May saw that what was being offered was, in fact, everything he wanted to leave behind. "After this excellent interview, I had to get into the psychological testing. This is a daylong thing. You have to answer thousands of multiple-choice questions and it's the same type of questions over and over, just written in different ways to see if you are consistent in your thinking.

"Following that, I got into a discussion with a psychologist they brought in to talk about your management style. Apparently I said the wrong thing right away. I said, 'I'm very results orientated. I've always been good at meeting my numbers. I'm tough on people, but I'm very fair with them.' Well, we must have gone over the word 'tough' for three hours, back and forth. 'What do you mean by tough? Verbal abuse? Physical abuse? Do you get along with other managers?'

"It got to the point where I'd had enough. I said to myself, 'If this is what the job is all about, I want nothing to do with it.' I actually called up the guy that wanted to hire me and I said, 'this environment is not for me. I want to be able to get things done, not manipulate circumstances to look good.' That's part of the problem with the big corporate environments that exists today. They still have that issue internally. So, I'm happy to say that I've been on my own now since 2001."

It was in 2001 that May founded Tricrest Professional Services, a technology services provider. For the first time in his career he was able to manage his affairs the way his entrepreneurial instincts told him was appropriate. "Why wouldn't you think about what's the right thing to do for the business as a whole? You can't just look at your little entity and say, 'Well, this is the whole business.' Yet, that's the way the corporate world thinks. And if it works for them, it works for them. But in a business of this size, you can't do that. There's no place to hide in a small business."

May's challenge now, he says, is recruiting the kind of talent who have corporate experience certainly, but who are not cast in the rigid corporate mould.

"You want to be able to take the best of the corporate culture, with the best of the entrepreneurial world, and combine those two entities into a winning strategy. Corporate is definitely great at training, great at health and safety, great at quality and controls, great at processes. But it's not adaptable; it's not flexible. Corporations don't have speed and agility. If you can take those two models and bring them together you'll have a fascinating organization. And that's been our challenge, to try to do that."

Today, Tricrest provides single-source solutions to fulfil outsourcing initiatives and time-sensitive services. These are turnkey solutions, allowing organizations — including several of the big corporations he once worked for — to meet their business objectives on time and on budget. As a result, Tricrest is emerging as a national leader in cost effective and quality network servicing solutions. The company was named in the 2008 PROFIT 100 ranking of Canada's fastest growing companies.

Despite the company's rising profile, the 47-year-old May remains largely anonymous. Google his name and the Internet search results are scant. He has given few interviews and prefers to keep a low profile.

"My focus is really on servicing our clients. I've never been a big political guy. I'm not a crowds and big-room type person. I never have been. My wife, Cathy, is the exact opposite. She loves that environment. She can talk to anybody at any time about anything. I'm more of a behind-the-scenes kind of guy. I've done my run in operations and services and sales, but I've always been more comfortable in a customer-service type environment where you know there's satisfaction out of helping somebody.

"I did well when I was in sales — never had any issues there. It's just a different environment. And I've always been a proponent, especially with operations people, that you don't know what the world's like until you do go through the sales environment, because it's a different world altogether. I say the same things to my sales people. Sales people are pretty good at beating down on operations people if things go wrong, or they go off the rails or whatever. But they're tough jobs as well and they're thankless jobs in part. So, it's a case of seeing things from both sides of the fence."

In the course of an impressive career, May has certainly seen life from many different perspectives. He first got into the telecom world back in 1977. His father had worked in the industry for years and secured him a summer placement at Canadian National. "I really enjoyed it, I just stuck to it," he says. Next he tried university. "I had the chance to go to Ryerson, but I didn't get into the course that I wanted. I only spent a couple months there and then just said, 'heck with it. I'm going to go out into the work world.' In the final outcome it was probably a good decision. But when he was just 10 years into his career, rising up the ladder from technician to management, he wasn't so sure.

"The lack of a university education or an engineering degree definitely held me back for a number of years," he admits. "The toughest part was getting from managerial level to the director level. I was probably passed over for at least 10 opportunities because I was up against individuals with engineering degrees. So, I preach that same thing to my children — education is more important now than it has ever been. When I started working, you could still go get a job without a college or university education and still have the ability to grow your career. It's not that easy any more, it's really not."

Despite the obstacles, May eventually climbed his way to the top of the ladder. His last corporate job before breaking out on his own was at AT&T Canada as Vice-President of Data Services. Before that, he worked at MetroNet Communications Corp (which merged with AT&T in 1999, in a $7-billion transaction that created Canada's first national, networks-based telecommunications company). "MetroNet was the first CLEC (competitive local exchange carrier). When they came out with competition for local phone service in the late 1990s, MetroNet really took off. I had left AT&T as a director and went to MetroNet as a general manager. I helped them build out to their local 416, 905 and 519 networks. And then we merged with AT&T, so I went back into AT&T as Vice-President of Business Development."

Then, in 2000, May went to a small consulting company to run their telecom position. "I told the guy that I'll give them about a year and see how it goes. At the time, I was thinking about getting into consulting. I did really well for this guy and at the end of the year I made a decision that this was kind of crazy. Why not go out and develop a business plan myself, and go to the banks to see if they would help me out? Luckily enough, they were able to give me a small operating line to get started. And it went from there."

After the first few years, business grew modestly. Through meetings and talks with industry contacts and business associates, he was able to find help on the sales side. It was August 2004. The hiring of Tricrest's first designated sales and business development manager proved to be an important decision in the short history of the company. Frank Palmieri, a graduate of Ryerson University, with a degree in Business Administration, was a 20-year veteran of sales with large OEM's and other technology start-ups. With his background and experience, he was just what Tricrest needed at the time.

Palmieri's appointment would allow Tricrest to aggressively grow, and pursue strategic relationships. As importantly, it would allow May to focus on longer-term planning for the business, while Palmieri focused on customer sales opportunities. The ability to work closer with existing and new clients led to further expansion for Tricrest into Enterprise Networking, which now comprises more than 50 percent of service revenues. The service footprint was also expanded to include all cities in Canada. These moves and decisions make Tricrest unique in the industry to this day.

May and Palmieri have a close and successful working relationship, complementing each other's skills. Together, they fought and won battles to win new business. One of the key strategies to their success has always been to place the customer first. May says that by providing excellent customer service in everything the company has to offer has made it a different player that stands out from its competition.

May's goals for the future include international acquisitions in the United Kingdom and expansion into other markets outside of Canada, including the U.S. and Caribbean. The plans keep the founder and CEO very busy. He wouldn't have it any other way.

"I enjoy working. Cathy and I are very much the same in that respect. Cathy grew up on a farm and understands what hard work is and what it takes to achieve success. She works every bit as hard as I do, supporting both the business and our family life. I wouldn't say we have a lot of down time. We're usually in here, in our Mississauga office, around six a.m. and don't leave till well after six or seven p.m. There is no short cut to success. You must work hard to achieve it, and everyone who is part of the Tricrest team does that.

The company's three main areas of focus are Telecom Services, Professional Services and Enterprise Network Services. Tricrest handles consulting, planning, installation, testing, 24/7 service assurance and post-installation support. Thus, things never really stand still for May and his team.

"We don't develop product, make product, or manufacture product — we provide service. "That's our business," he says. "So it's very, very important that we have a high 'touch level' with our clients. You can't over-communicate with clients when you're providing a service. They want to know what's going on at every minute of the day."

May's company provides turnkey outsourced services for other companies, but it's not always obvious that Tricrest is the player. The company often works behind the scenes. "We 'white label' our services because we're not a big brand name — we're not an IBM, HP, or Bell Canada, or anything like that. But we are the talent in the trucks that actually do the work for these corporations.

"Approximately 85 percent of our staff are technical people. Multi-billion dollar corporations have hundreds of salespeople. It would take me a lifetime to be able to touch the number of clients that they touch on a monthly basis. We try to work among those organizations, especially on the integrator side. Because they touch so many clients, we become their feet on the street. We do the various types of work that are required to be done."

Sometimes, this means that Tricrest's employees are literally changing their shirts two or three times a day. "Our techs go in wearing a shirt from Company ABC in the morning and Company DEF in the afternoon and Company GHI the next morning. Often we're told, 'Don't park in front of the store with the (Tricrest) truck — park at the end of the street.' And then we go in, representing that company," says May.

"We call it 'smart hands,' because really we're out there representing either ourselves, or an integrator, or a carrier." White labelling has another interesting upside. In some cases, Tricrest divisions are working the same big project under several different monikers. "In the retail industry, which is predominantly driven out of the U.S., we do a lot of point of sale (POS) work under our Enterprise banner. Anything with CPE — customer-premises equipment — is considered Enterprise, whether that's POS, structured cable, or a Wi-Fi solution making a network wireless. Over a number of years, we've been able to develop a very good base of U.S. integrators that we support up here in Canada. They tend to segregate their work on the retail side, so they don't typically go with one supplier on a project, they tend to go with three or four." This can mean that the three or four suppliers are actually all Tricrest units. "We'll be quoting on the same project through five or six different companies," says May. "The retailer may be trying to segregate the work between integrators. But it could end up that we have 90 percent of the work. It is without a doubt a unique situation. The retailer's trying to get away from having a single integrator, but they're really not in the end."

On the telecom side of Tricrest's business, the company's techs are principally ensuring that the core infrastructure works. "We could be working in a Bell or Telus central office — that's where you'll find all your Internet gateways, your phone switches, your data switches. We also do 'turn-ups' for the Bells and Teluses of the world" — 'turn-ups' being when a tech is needed at a residential or commercial address to implement the service for the client.

"Tricrest was strictly a telecom infrastructure company for the first three years, and if you know the environment of telecom in North America as a whole, you know it tends to go through peaks and valleys," says May. "We went through the dotcom craze until about 2000/01, and then everything dropped out of the sky. It was tough going in that market until about a year ago (2008). And now it's on a real high again because we've got this new wireless spectrum that was sold by the government last year. There are all these new entrants who want to build networks and who will now be spending billions of dollars to do that.

"The thing we noticed with the telecom infrastructure is that there are probably only seven to 10 key clients you can work with in Canada. You have to think, 'What happens if you mess up on a job and you lose that client?' It can happen easily. In the service industry, you're only as good as your last job. I can do a thousand jobs great in a month, but if I do one job wrong, that person remembers the job that was done wrong, not the other 999 that were done great. That's human nature. The last thing you want to do is let a customer down because of something you did poorly. When there are only 10 clients, if you lose one, you can take a heck of a hit to your bottom line."

It was by taking this situation into account that May first began thinking about moving Tricrest into the Enterprise market. "We said, 'our technicians are out there, they're installing core routers, big network routers, within a central office. Why don't we look at playing the Enterprise game? We could just as easily get that technician to take a small router, go to a customer's location and install it on behalf of an integrator or carrier.' Therefore, we went into Enterprise about four years ago, and now it represents about 50 percent of our revenue."

Moreover, compared to the telecom marketplace, "there are thousands of customers that you can deal with from the Enterprise play. That was really part of our strategy — growing our customer base while growing our revenue stream as well."

The third prong at Tricrest is the Professional division, which is mostly contract-based manpower. "We are not recruiters. We don't recruit people for full-time work. Basically, we'll provide engineers, or project managers, or technical designers — that sort of thing — to the carrier environment. It could be a two-week project or it could be a two-year project.

Strategically, it helps to have employees in these contracted positions where they can act as Tricrest's eyes and ears for new opportunities, says May. "We stay in touch with the individual, as he or she is working in the 'guts' of the organization. They hear lots of things that are going on, so of course we tap their shoulders every couple of weeks to ask 'what's the latest and greatest going on? What do you hear? Who needs what?' Then, we will give the customer a call and say, 'Hey, how's it going? You know we do this, this, and this?' And usually they say, 'you guys do that? Oh, I'm looking for that right now.'"

Recently, Tricrest has begun to offer Security solutions, too. "Again, it's about expanding our service capabilities into other areas. My goal, as we're able to get bigger and bigger, is to move away from having to deal through an integrator and to sell directly to an end customer. I want the ability to be able to provide an annuity type business to them, so that I have them wrapped up — all their security, all their internal networking needs and any local support to that location. The customer just makes a call and we show up and we resolve the problem. You wrap the customer up, so they know that they can depend on you for all their needs."

This strategy is reflected in Tricrest's new slogan, 'One Company, One Call, One Solution.' "We want to make it very, very simple for our clients," says May. "One of the biggest differences we see in our services versus some of our competitors is that we are national — soon to be international — and we provide a full turnkey solution. Turnkey is important, because a lot of clients don't have the time to deal with 10 different people. They want to deal with one company."

Tricrest wants to be that company. So, what's Rob May's secret to being the best, and edging out the competition, as an entrepreneur and as a business? "The biggest thing I do is I constantly talk to people. I constantly preach the need to communicate to our clients. We need to understand their needs and build their trust. We have to ensure that we show up when we say we're going to show up. You know what? Most companies don't do it.

"The analogy I like to use is: you buy some furniture and you have to wait for the delivery truck, which means taking the day off work. How would you feel if the delivery was rescheduled and nobody called to let you know? You'd be annoyed over the whole experience. I tell my team to think about that every time they're dealing with a client. If we're not going to be there on time, they must call that customer, give them the reason why and let them know when they are going to be there.

"You have to communicate. Most people are reasonable. And if you just keep them abreast and they know that you're working on it, they will understand. But, if you don't communicate with them, and you let them down by not doing what you said you would, then it's going to tarnish the reputation of the company, not only with that client but also with their friends."

Instilling this level of trust and respect into Tricrest's ongoing relationships with customers is how May keeps focused on the big picture. As a goal-setter, his current target is taking Tricrest's revenue to half-a-billion dollars.

"If I go back to my original business plan, we're definitely ahead of where I expected to be. But, you never sit on your laurels and you must revisit your goals regularly and readjust as required. In the service industry you can never be too comfortable. Somebody is always looking to win your clients. So, am I happy where I am today? No, I don't think I'm ever really satisfied. I'm always looking for bigger and better things. I'm always resetting my goals. I definitely think we can grow this company and we're on the right path."

Undeniably, May has come a long way since his days as a summer student and a man who began his career without an engineering degree but with a determination to succeed. "I'm a firm believer that the longer you go in your career, your education really doesn't matter once you get to a certain level. It's more about how you do your job, how you use common sense in your dealings. And common sense is so important to everything you do — it's actually more important in an entrepreneurial environment than it is in a big corporate world, where everything is politics. Of course, I can play politics with the best of them, but it doesn't get you to where you want to go.

May tells applicants to Tricrest, the fresh-faced college kids who aspire to be the CEOs of tomorrow: "If you can go into a corporate organization and suck up all the training you can get for the first five or so years, I would do that before I would go into the entrepreneurial environment."

From his experience of all the young people who have sat in his office for job interviews, May has witnessed a trend that "it's tough getting young kids today to come in and just want to learn the business and work. They sit there and say, 'I want the top wage, I want a car allowance, I want, I want, I want.' But, they have no idea on the business side, and what it takes to succeed. Our goal as leaders is to help develop these kids for success and set the appropriate career path to allow that success. Respect comes with hard work and if they learn that they will succeed."

May had to earn his respect and he worked hard for it. Furthermore, he says, "I've got three daughters, aged 22, 20 and 17. And they're all good workers. You have to build that mentality in them — the kids started off paper routes at 13 and we got them debit cards and their own bank accounts, so that they would understand the value of money.

"My eldest daughter, she's in Australia right now; she did her e-commerce diploma at Sheridan for three years and she's over in Brisbane getting her degree in Business Management through a university that's affiliated with Sheridan. She also worked full-time at Tricrest, about 35 hours a week, at the same time as going to Sheridan. All our kids are the same way," says May.

That hard-working mentality is how you get ahead. And it's not rocket science, notes the Tricrest CEO. "Ultimately, our business is not difficult. Treat clients and suppliers as you would want to be treated. It's that simple. Remember that providing service is not difficult — it's how diligent and dedicated you are to ensuring that the service happens the way that the client wants it."

As Rob May knows from his years of experience, working up from the ground floor through the upper echelons of the corporate world to running his own successful company, diligence and dedication are born out of an entrepreneurial spirit, with an ever-watchful eye on the big picture.

"You set one goal, then you achieve it, then you set a new goal, and that's how you make things happen." That's the motto of this dynamic entrepreneur, and he thrives on it.

Ali Mozaffari

WebServe

It can be surprising how dreams really do come true if you work hard enough on them, and refuse to be discouraged by even the most persistent obstacles. Perseverance, indeed, may be among the most valuable personal qualities an entrepreneur can hope to possess.

As a child growing up in his native Iran, Ali Mozaffari suspected the career that beckoned him was going to be almost impossible to achieve in his homeland, given the circumstances then prevailing. It might have been enough to deter someone of a less robust character. But Mozaffari was not to be easily sidetracked. And by dealing head-on with the problems he faced, he believes it made him a stronger person.

Today, Mozaffari is the president and chief executive officer of WebServe Canada, an industry leading, privately held web hosting and Internet solution provider. His hugely successful company, founded in 1999 and based in North Vancouver, B.C., offers high-quality web hosting services for companies of all sizes, across Canada and around the world. His clients include governments, universities and such big corporate names as Nokia Canada, Samsung, Siemens, Mitsubishi, and Holiday Inn Hotels. And his profits have allowed him to diversify into real estate investments, both in Canada and Iran.

The story of how Mozaffari went from a youth experimenting with a primitive Commodore 64 computer in his native Iran to heading what was in 2008 British Columbia's fastest growing company has more ups and downs than a yo-yo. From an early age, he had nurtured a passion for the newly emerging technology. He was fascinated by the potential of the computer and resolved to dedicate his studies to mathematics and computer science.

After attending university in Iran, the question he faced was where to pursue his future? He had grown disillusioned with his prospects in his homeland. He describes his life there in the seventies as "really tough — the culture, the environment, everything is totally different. There was pressure from the government, a lack of resources, difficult working conditions." While the experience made him "really strong," he was eager to explore opportunities abroad. He decided to complete his final year of university in Germany, where he eventually obtained his degree. "By the time I got to Germany, I was ready to accept a different culture with open arms and was looking forward to the change," he says. "I was thirsty for new ideas and new experiences."

So, Mozaffari arrived in Germany with an "open heart and an open mind" to study and begin planning his post-university life. But once his student days were over, he discovered that life in Germany outside the halls of academe was very different. As a foreigner, he felt unwelcome and discriminated against. Nostalgic for home, he remembered an old saying he had learned in Iran: "You don't know what you've got until you've lost it." He supported himself with low-paying evening and late-night shifts as a restaurant server — one of the few jobs available to any foreign student in Germany at the time. Gradually, he became more and more convinced that, if he was not going back to Iran, he would have to seek his fortune further afield.

For some time, he had come to regard Canada as a promising country of great ethnic diversity and tolerance. He thought that Toronto, as its economic capital, would offer him the most opportunities. Having finished his degree, he saved enough money from his restaurant jobs for a flight to Canada. As soon as he could secure a ticket, he bundled up his few possessions and said goodbye to his few friends.

His first night in Toronto was a long one, spent mostly on an airport bench. Restless, unable to sleep, he boarded a bus heading downtown and asked for directions to inexpensive student accommodation. Once he had a roof over his head, he steeled himself to ask for a small loan from an Iranian friend in the city. "I would eat whatever I could, mostly cheap fast food, basically anything that I could afford," he recalls. Once his day-to-day survival needs were taken care of, he began to work on the more substantial goals that would determine his long-term future in Canada.

An early, major task was to learn English, and so the new immigrant turned to government-sponsored language training. ESL (English as a Second Language) schools were free to new immigrants and Mozaffari took full advantage of this and other opportunities. He cites these services, and the positive attitude of the Canadian people towards new immigrants, as major reasons for his immediate love of the country.

"I felt so welcomed. Everyone was making me feel like I belonged, especially after I became [a permanent resident], then got my citizenship. I loved knowing that I was in a country surrounded by people who all appreciate freedom — the freedom to live, and the freedom to be yourself." After six months of English language training, Mozaffari began his first part-time job in the country at an electronics repair shop in downtown Toronto. Here began a learning curve that was to stand him in good stead for the future.

It is entirely probable that, but for the hand of fate, Mozaffari would have remained in Toronto. But, just at this time, his long-time girlfriend from Iran, who had immigrated to Canada, called him from Vancouver. She invited him to visit. Mozaffari made the trip to the West Coast and liked what he saw. When he discovered Vancouver, he says, it felt as though he were in a different country. He fell in love with the city, seeing it as an ideal place to settle down. Acting with typical resolve, he returned briefly to Toronto to pack his gear, sell what he could and flew right back to the coast.

Looking back, he says he came to realize — as many have before and since — that Vancouver is not yet the commercial powerhouse that has emerged in Toronto. He is obliged to agree with those who say he might have been even more successful financially had he stayed in Canada's largest city. Choosing Vancouver, however, enriched his life in other ways and today he says he has no regrets.

Mozaffari's relocation to Vancouver led him to the B.C. Institute of Technology (BCIT). Feeling confident about his knowledge of computer software, he decided to follow up on the experience he had gained from his part-time job in Toronto and continue learning the intricacies of computer hardware.

Once again, he had to be flexible to take into account his new circumstances. He enrolled in his second, full degree program, this time in electronics. And to make ends meet he took a position as a sales assistant in the computer department of an office supply store. It may not have been the ideal position for a future businessman, but it was not an unusual one either. Canadian electronics stores employ many savvy immigrants with a wide knowledge of computers who themselves plan one day to run their own businesses.

Balancing his full-time studies with enough work that he could afford to live was no easy matter, but Mozaffari persevered and soon found his efforts rewarded. Upon graduating from BCIT, he was promoted to department manager. He was looking forward to his new position and he and his girlfriend felt confident enough to make plans for their wedding.

At that very moment, however, a friend from Iran who had moved to Vancouver suggested to Mozaffari that they should start a business of their own. The friend had some financial means and offered to provide a significant amount of capital to get things up and running. He asked for ideas. The time was late 1998 and the dot.com bubble was fully inflated. Share prices and stock markets were seeing their values increasing sharply. Excessive venture capital and high-spirited spending had created an atmosphere of euphoria not seen since the 1980s.

Mozaffari eagerly suggested a business built around providing Internet services for dot.com companies. After talking it over, the two partners decided to go for it. In their first year, they were caught up in the heady atmosphere of the era. Hugely optimistic, they spent nearly $200,000 on marketing and advertising, in addition to recruiting and hiring employees. Mozaffari was at the helm while his friend was essentially a silent, though involved, partner.

In the early days of e-commerce only a niche group of people worldwide were totally familiar with Internet services. Most consumers didn't have home computers or e-mail accounts as they do today and the average business owner did not understand how e-mail worked, or how to code a website, much less how to host and manage one. Mozaffari's company was slightly ahead of its time. It had to wait for the market to catch up, but it lacked the resources to ride out the wait.

Shortly after the dot.com bubble burst in spring 2000, the partners lost everything. His friend and investor pulled out. "Of course it was scary. We had been pouring our money and time into this round the clock," Mozaffari says. "Emotionally, at this point, I was completely drained." Thanks to his gut instincts, the partners had not borrowed any money nor had they taken out any business loans. "We didn't have to declare bankruptcy, but we lost all the cash and simply had to close down."

As he tried to put the pieces of his life back together, Mozaffari went back over every step, pondering how to reposition himself. "I kept telling myself that I had the experience, the education, the will — and, most of all, the love. I believe you have to follow what you love." He was convinced he was in the right business, but recognized that his timing had been bad. However, he was persuaded that the outlook would improve very soon.

The growth of the Internet as a business platform really began in the nineties when a succession of browsers appeared and opened up Internet use to vast numbers of consumers. The Internet subsequently became the medium for providing information to users and potential customers on a global scale. By the late nineties, the capabilities and reach of the Internet created a new form of commerce — online business or e-commerce — powered by ever more capable computers operating at increasing speeds. Goods and services began to be sold between businesses and from businesses to consumers. Almost as quickly, it became clear that public companies, educational institutions and governmental bodies needed a web presence in order to provide information to their many stakeholders.

It was at this time, just a year before the new millennium, that Mozaffari launched a new business aimed at meeting these revolutionary demands. Instead of wallowing in self-pity over his initial failure, he summoned up the resilience and determination of his youth and began his next foray. Though stunned by what had happened, he wasted no time. He didn't have much cash in hand. And there was trouble even meeting the mortgage payments on the home he shared with his wife in West Vancouver. But he did have a $5,000 credit card limit, and his wife offered her credit card, too. Together, they decided their home basement would become the nerve centre for his bold, new entrepreneurial venture.

Mozaffari bought two servers from eBay, the Internet auction site, and sited them in the basement. He resumed the networking he'd been doing previously, and put on a brave face. Outwardly, he radiated confidence. Inwardly, he confesses to having had doubts. But he would tell everyone how good the business was going to be and he began by hosting websites for friends and family. This was at a time when only the most technology-aware companies operated websites. But companies large and small were starting to realize that they would need at least a basic presence on the Internet. Mozaffari set out to make contact with the people and the businesses that were looking for expert guidance to establish a web presence.

Mozaffari was in no doubt that he could tap into this market, initially via friends and family. He was right, though many of his early clients had no clue that the services Mozaffari offered were operated from down in his basement. "I started with one client site, then two. Soon I had three. It felt like I just blinked and suddenly I was hosting 50 sites."

Business grew so quickly that soon he had to officially register his company, in part so that he could start formal advertising. After much deliberation, he came up with the company name WebServe. The domain address webserve.ca was available and Mozaffari secured it. He also registered new phone numbers and — for lack of a business space — had calls forwarded to his home. The phones were ringing off the hook.

"I was getting many more clients and business was roaring. At the time, the main competition was coming from the U.S. It was difficult because they could offer many more features and much more storage space and bandwidth for a lot less money." He admits to also feeling like a kid with a new train set, to the extent that over time he wanted to keep adding more and more trains to his collection. "I was enjoying what I was doing, so my clients kept referring me. Before I knew it I had a couple thousand."

Perhaps more out of circumstance than intent, Mozaffari had discovered a method of marketing that today is taught in schools. Word-of-mouth referrals are often touted as the most advantageous means of marketing. A global Nielsen survey of 26,486 Internet users found that consumer recommendations were seen as the most credible form of advertising among 78 percent of the study's respondents.

According to other studies, recommendations from family and friends carry more weight than anything else in influencing a consumer's choice. The importance and impact of viral marketing becomes all the more critical without significant advertising or marketing funds — as was the case with Mozaffari. Instead, he developed an intimate working relationship with clients early on, placing his trust in referrals from them to attract new business.

Soon, however, Mozaffari, like many other entrepreneurs, began to experience both the blessing and burden of being a one-man show.

His growing clientele appreciated the personal nature of his business that may be lacking in a large corporation. He was answering every call 24/7. He alone knew every inch of his workspace. He installed every circuit board, ethernet connection and power supply. He could solve any problem that might come up. But the personal touch was taking its toll. With a dozen servers whirring away in his basement, making enough noise that his pregnant wife couldn't sleep, and with the phone ringing constantly, Mozaffari decided it was time to secure an office and hire some help.

Until then, he had been responsible for all his own accounting, marketing and sales, as well as managing the programming and system administration. Mozaffari rented some office space and moved the servers to a data centre, hiring someone to help with the phone and technical support. "By now I was adding one or two servers per month, right up to when I decided to buy the current WebServe offices. We had about 10,000 clients when we moved in here."

When that move happened, to its current location in North Vancouver, Mozaffari immediately hired 10 more people. He also thought beyond his base city. He began looking to India for outsourcing phone inquiries, and chose the United States and the Middle East as places to open sales offices. Having an international presence is not a choice, but an imperative, for a growing company wanting to explore new markets, new ways to service clients and novel approaches to running a business.

Competition knows no borders. For WebServe, the Middle East made good sense, particularly considering Mozaffari's Iranian roots. The United States was a logical choice, not merely for its proximity to Canada, but also due to the size of the customer base. "I'd say 70 or 80 per cent of our clients are Canadian, with the rest international, mainly from America and the Middle East," says Mozaffari. "Our branch in Tehran has been going for four years now."

Awards and accolades have been coming WebServe's way almost

since its inception. In 2002, the company received a gold medal from The Golden Web Awards, an international program honouring creativity, integrity and excellence. In 2003, the company was in the Top 15 award from TopHosts, the next year it was in the Top10, and the year after that the Top5. In 2005, it was ranked as B.C.'s fifth fastest growing company as listed by Business in Vancouver magazine. In 2006 it took the No.1 Top Web Hosting Company award from TopHosts. The same year, WebServe was adjudged B.C.'s fastest growing company, according to Business in Vancouver magazine.

Today, the company's services are offered on an optical fibre network that spans over 50,000km in Canada and the United States and provides seamless connectivity through 60 North American cities including New York, Toronto, Chicago, Denver, Dallas, Los Angeles and Vancouver. This is one of the largest North American networks, and one of the most advanced. The network is based on Dense Wave Division Multiplexing (DWDM) and intelligent optical switching technology. When compared to older networks that essentially still employ wires, the DWDM structure provides for faster and greater flexibility, and an optical signal that can be amplified as required. This means it can accommodate scale, technological advancements and service upgrades.

The company's rapid growth slowed during the economic downturn of 2008/09 and Mozaffari concedes that the business climate has been challenging. WebServe's sales dropped by 40 percent in 2008, forcing Mozaffari to adapt once more. His approach was to centre his attention on the company's infrastructure and its client base. "We all focused on existing clients, tried to service their every need, and brought down prices. I've been making the company stronger by re-injecting the money it makes, investing in our staff and getting better equipment and supplies and managing the process as efficiently as possible."

A new website for his company will soon be developed, along with new products, features and pricing. Going green is on the horizon, too, with plans for a new, energy-efficient data centre. Mozaffari believes that these advances will reflect his original choice to build a life in Vancouver, famous for its healthy lifestyles and natural beauty.

WebServe's greatest asset remains its loyal customer base of more than 30,000 clients. Mozaffari does his utmost to see that they receive secure, reliable and value-rich hosting. With his history of adapting to change, Mozaffari is confident about the years ahead. He puts great faith in his ability to be flexible. "The experience gained moving from one place to another so many times is huge," he says. "Knowing different people, different languages and different cultures — that gives you energy and confidence."

WebServe's mission statement makes its goals clear. It is: "To provide our clients, both personal and business, with top-quality web hosting at affordable prices. Top-quality support is seen by us as a vital part of our company. That is why we have invested heavily in this department to be able to offer a great service.

"We are a company providing high-quality, cost effective Internet services to both private and corporate clients throughout the world. We continue to experience growth since our infancy in web design and development, marketing, web site promotion and domain registration services. Our clients benefit from the most advanced, feature-rich, web-based control panel in the industry, combined with first class technical support. Customer service is a key element in the satisfaction of our clients, as we continue to go well beyond the expected when it comes to meeting the needs of our customers. First, in having a knowledgeable and well trained staff, second in ensuring that they are easily accessible when needed."

Mozaffari's company has made money in every quarter since its founding in 1999. He explains: "Unlike other hi-tech players, and at a time when many telecom Internet service providers are closing, WebServe is expanding. We are growing because we are small, focused, and able to provide reliable services that are increasingly important to small and medium businesses today."

Profitability depends upon WebServe's ability to deliver the quality service it promises: "We operate with some simple concepts in mind. First and foremost, we take care of the customer. We make sure customers' needs are met, instead of expecting them to conform to what we supply. Second, we produce the best product we can innovate with the assistance of our impressive in-house development team. We operate at ultimate efficiency, and are able to offer a feature set beyond any other system you will find on the market."

WebServe boasts that its remarkable reliability record — 99.9 percent — and "superb" technical support translate into a world-class environment for any company's web needs. And satisfied clients of the company are generous in their praise of the services it offers, as examples from its website show: Writes Alex Taylor of Shoregard Alarms Ltd.: "I recently set up a hosting account with WebServe for a client of mine; I was immediately impressed by the prices. No set-up fee, plus one of the lowest rates I've seen on the 'net. I thought it might be too good to be true until I began to upload the site to your server. I was used to other web hosts I work with having sluggish servers, so I was blown away by the amazing speed of yours. It was like I was working on a local hard drive. I'm very impressed so far, and I will definitely be sticking with WebServe for a long time to come."

Gordon Helwig of Moody Cat Studios writes: "Just like to say that the support service here is outstanding! I have never had such an easy time dealing with people in terms of support — and the fact that I will never see them in person and yet they do such a fabulous job makes it even more incredible. The online, live chatting with support staff is the greatest thing since sliced bread. I've been with companies that took five hours or more to e-mail me back with support. Hats off to this outstanding support team."

As the business has grown, so has its field of operations. Over the years, Mozaffari has been ploughing back profits into land, property and real estate, both in Vancouver and Iran. He has seen those investments grow considerably and they have been a source of security for the company. He says proudly: "Once the business started growing, I started trying to wisely spend the money that the company generates. This has proven worthwhile during these difficult times."

Looking back at his journey — leaving his homeland of Iran in his late teens, enduring a tough year in Germany, moving to Toronto, then relocating to Vancouver, starting a business that failed, then starting another that is succeeding — and starting a family — Mozaffari sees the humour in it. "It makes me laugh to think about the things that I've done in my life to get here. But, everything has helped make me the businessman I am now. Dealing with all sorts of employers and employees and learning to be flexible and adapt in different circumstances has all led to this point."

He sums up his philosophy this way: "If I didn't love this business, if I wasn't really passionate about my work, I wouldn't have survived. When you start at anything, you must strive to be the best at it — it doesn't matter what it is."

CORPORATE CONTACTS

Annex Consulting Group Inc.
555 Burrard Street
Suite 900
Vancouver, BC
V7X 1M8
1.604.443.5036
www.annexgroup.com

Curve Communications Corp.
1020 Mainland Street
Suite 1020
Vancouver, BC
V6B 2T5
1.604.684.3170
www.curvecommunications.com

Digital Fortress Corp.
931 Commissioners Road East
Suite 200
London, ON
N5Z 3H9
1.519.432.3222
www.digitalfortress.ca

ExitCertified Corp.
220 Laurier Avenue
Suite 1000
Ottawa, ON
K1P 5Z9
1.613.232.3948
www.exitcertified.ca

Extreme Brandz
2187 Dunwin Drive
Mississauga, ON
L5L 1X2
1.905.820.7887
www.extremebrandz.com

Fusion Learning Inc.

272 Richmond Street East
Suite 200
Toronto, ON
M5A 1P4
1.416.424.2999
www.fusionlearninginc.com

The Futura Corporation

700 West Georgia Street
29th Floor
Vancouver, BC
V7Y 1A1
1.604.608.6600
www.futuracorporation.com

Globalive Communications Corp.

48 Yonge Street
Suite 1200
Toronto, ON
M5E 1G6
1.877.455.8606
www.globalive.com

Holeys

2440 Viking Way
Richmond, BC
V6V 1N2
1.604.248.3663
www.holeys.com

International Orthotic Labs

6777 Fairmount Drive SE
Calgary, AB
T2H 0X6
1.403.236.8540
www.orthotic.ca

Knightsbridge

2 Bloor Street West
30th Floor
Toronto, ON
M4W 1A8
1.416.923.5555
www.knightsbridge.ca

League Assets Corp.

2187 Oak Bay Avenue
Suite 217
Victoria, BC
V8R 1G1
www.league.ca

M & R Environmental

4623 Byrne Road
Burnaby, BC
V5J 3H6
1.604.876.0506
www.wepayforwasteoil.com

MetroBridge Networks

1030 West Georgia Street
Suite 918
Vancouver, BC
V6E 2Y3
1.888.628.1240
www.metrobridge.com

Mezzanine Consulting

266 King Street West
Suite 403
Toronto, ON
M5V 1H8
1.888.413.3911
www.mezzanineconsulting.com

Pacific R.I.M. Services

30435 Progressive Way
Unit #1
Abbotsford, BC
V2T 6Z1
1.604.504.0988
www.pacificrimservices.ca

Pareto

2225 Sheppard Avenue East
Suite 1700
Toronto, ON
M2J 5C2
1.416.790.2350
www.pareto.ca

Sweetspot

60 Bloor Street West
Suite 1005
Toronto, ON
M4W 3B8
1.416.922.7772
www.sweetspot.ca

Tricrest Profession Services

5200 Dixie Road
Unit #27
Mississauga, ON
L4W 1E4
1.866.877.9192
www.tricrest.ca

WebServe

1000 Roosevelt Crescent
Suite 235
North Vancouver, BC
V7P 1M3
1.888.443.4678
www.webserve.ca